Oracle®7 For Dummies®

D FOR Dummies
COMPUTER
BOOK SERIES
FROM IDG

KU-053-323

Cheat Sheet

SQL*Plus Commands

Basic query

```
select column , column , ...
from table
where clause
group by clause
order by clause
```

Query with join

```
select alias1.column , alias2.column , ...
from table alias1, table alias2, ...
where alias1.column = alias2.column
and clause
group by clause
order by clause
```

Create a table

```
create table tablename
(column datatype(precision[,scale]) [null/not null] [primary key],
 column datatype(precision[,scale]) [null/not null] [primary key],
column datatype(precision[,scale]) [null/not null])
[tablespace tablespacename]
```

Datatypes for Oracle 7

Datatype	Parameters	Description
VARCHAR2(n)	n=1 to 2,000	Text string with variable length. Most commonly used datatype. For regular text.
NUMBER(p,s)	p=1 to 38, s=-84 to 127 or FLOAT	Number. *p = precision* (total number of digits); *s = scale* (number of digits to the right of the decimal place).
LONG	none	Text string with variable length. Maximum length is 2 gigabytes. Seldom used.
DATE	none	For dates and times. Valid date range from January 1, 4712 BC to December 31, 4712 AD.
RAW(n)	n=1 to 255	Raw binary data of variable length. For files like MS Word documents.
LONGRAW	none	Raw binary data of variable length. For graphics.
CHAR(n)	n=1 to 255	Text string with fixed length. For short codes, like state abbreviations.

...For Dummies: #1 Computer Book Series for Beginners

COMPUTER
BOOK SERIES
FROM IDG

Oracle®7 For Dummies®

Cheat Sheet

PO7 Navigator's Main Window

Object window
Object Contents window

Control menu button · Title bar · Main menu bar · Toolbar · Window controls

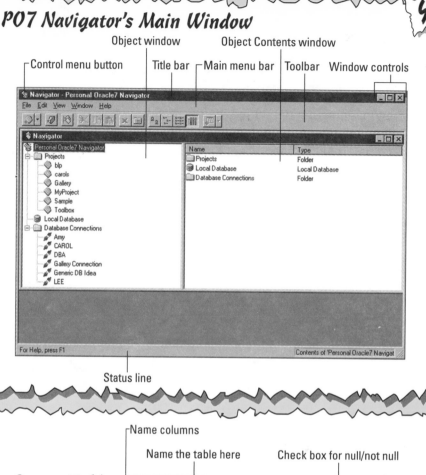

Status line

The Create Table Dialog Box in PO7 Navigator:

Name columns

Name the table here
Check box for null/not null

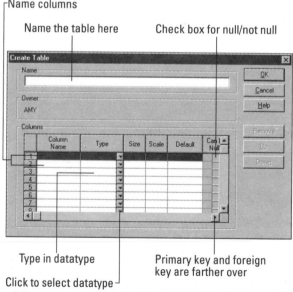

Type in datatype

Click to select datatype

Primary key and foreign
key are farther over

...For Dummies: #1 Computer Book Series for Beginners

 ®

References for the Rest of Us!®

COMPUTER BOOK SERIES FROM IDG

Are you intimidated and confused by computers? Do you find that traditional manuals are overloaded with technical details you'll never use? Do your friends and family always call you to fix simple problems on their PCs? Then the *...For Dummies®* computer book series from IDG Books Worldwide is for you.

...For Dummies books are written for those frustrated computer users who know they aren't really dumb but find that PC hardware, software, and indeed the unique vocabulary of computing make them feel helpless. *...For Dummies* books use a lighthearted approach, a down-to-earth style, and even cartoons and humorous icons to diffuse computer novices' fears and build their confidence. Lighthearted but not lightweight, these books are a perfect survival guide for anyone forced to use a computer.

> *"I like my copy so much I told friends; now they bought copies."*
>
> **Irene C., Orwell, Ohio**

> *"Quick, concise, nontechnical, and humorous."*
>
> **Jay A., Elburn, Illinois**

> *"Thanks, I needed this book. Now I can sleep at night."*
>
> **Robin F., British Columbia, Canada**

Already, hundreds of thousands of satisfied readers agree. They have made *...For Dummies* books the #1 introductory level computer book series and have written asking for more. So, if you're looking for the most fun and easy way to learn about computers, look to *...For Dummies* books to give you a helping hand.

IDG BOOKS WORLDWIDE™

ORACLE7™ FOR DUMMIES®

by Carol McCullough

Foreword by International Oracle Users Group — Americas

IDG Books Worldwide, Inc.
An International Data Group Company

Foster City, CA ♦ Chicago, IL ♦ Indianapolis, IN ♦ Southlake, TX

Oracle7™ For Dummies

Published by
IDG Books Worldwide, Inc.
An International Data Group Company
919 E. Hillsdale Blvd.
Suite 400
Foster City, CA 94404
http://www.idgbooks.com (IDG Books Worldwide Web site)
http://www.dummies.com (Dummies Press Web site)

Library of Congress Catalog Card No.: 96-80230

ISBN: 0-7645-0083-X

Printed in the United States of America

10 9 8 7 6 5 4 3 2 1

1DD/SR/QS/ZX/IN

Distributed in the United States by IDG Books Worldwide, Inc.

Distributed by Macmillan Canada for Canada; by Transworld Publishers Limited in the United Kingdom and Europe; by WoodsLane Pty. Ltd. for Australia; by WoodsLane Enterprises Ltd. for New Zealand; by Longman Singapore Publishers Ltd. for Singapore, Malaysia, Thailand, and Indonesia; by Simron Pty. Ltd. for South Africa; by Toppan Company Ltd. for Japan; by Distribuidora Cuspide for Argentina; by Livraria Cultura for Brazil; by Ediciencia S.A. for Ecuador; by Addison-Wesley Publishing Company for Korea; by Ediciones ZETA S.C.R. Ltda. for Peru; by WS Computer Publishing Company, Inc., for the Philippines; by Unalis Corporation for Taiwan; by Contemporanea de Ediciones for Venezuela. Authorized Sales Agent: Anthony Rudkin Associates for the Middle East and North Africa.

For general information on IDG Books Worldwide's books in the U.S., please call our Consumer Customer Service department at 800-762-2974. For reseller information, including discounts and premium sales, please call our Reseller Customer Service department at 800-434-3422.

For information on where to purchase IDG Books Worldwide's books outside the U.S., please contact our International Sales department at 415-655-3023 or fax 415-655-3299.

For information on foreign language translations, please contact our Foreign & Subsidiary Rights department at 415-655-3021 or fax 415-655-3281.

For sales inquiries and special prices for bulk quantities, please contact our Sales department at 415-655-3200 or write to the address above.

For information on using IDG Books Worldwide's books in the classroom or for ordering examination copies, please contact our Educational Sales department at 800-434-2086 or fax 817-251-8174.

For press review copies, author interviews, or other publicity information, please contact our Public Relations department at 415-655-3000 or fax 415-655-3299.

For authorization to photocopy items for corporate, personal, or educational use, please contact Copyright Clearance Center, 222 Rosewood Drive, Danvers, MA 01923, or fax 508-750-4470.

 is a trademark under exclusive license to IDG Books Worldwide, Inc., from International Data Group, Inc.

About the Author

Carol McCullough has a busy life. She was married after her first year of college to her high school sweetheart. She quit school and began working full time as a draftsman (one of two women in a 50-man shop), drawing floor plans for houses. After five years, she went back to college to get her degree. When she started back to school, she had a two-year-old son and a new-born son. She graduated with honors in two and a half years. She received a B.A. degree in Computer Systems Analysis and Design from the University of Wisconsin — Madison.

Carol began right from the start focusing on system design and database systems. She signed on with a telephone billing company in Madison and became its resident expert in Oracle programming and tuning. She designed a series of courses for the 70+ programming staff (which included many consultants as well as employees) to help them design better database applications. Later, as an independent consultant, she developed several large Oracle database systems for the State of Wisconsin. Her specialty became "the project that can't be done," which she'd tackle with enthusiasm. Many of her friends and co-workers kidded her, "You should write a book!" Well . . . here it is.

She has since divorced, remarried (gaining two stepdaughters), and had a third son, now seven years old. She is living in beautiful Maui, Hawaii, a far cry from the frigid winters of the Midwest. She works as the Database Administrator for the Pacific Disaster Center, a federally funded project for aiding in disaster mitigation and recovery for Hawaii and neighboring island countries. Her office has a view of the ocean where she can watch the humpback whales frolic in the water (on lunch breaks, of course!)

This is her second book for IDG Books Worldwide, Inc. The first one, co-authored with Joseph Sinclair, is titled *Creating Cool Web Databases*. It tells all about how to incorporate a database into the World Wide Web using many different non-programmer's software packages and tricks and techniques.

Carol's own personal foray into the World Wide Web has met with some acclaim as well. Surf over to Maui (parental guidance advised) and see it at

http://www.maui.net/~mcculc/resource.htm

ABOUT IDG BOOKS WORLDWIDE

Welcome to the world of IDG Books Worldwide.

IDG Books Worldwide, Inc., is a subsidiary of International Data Group, the world's largest publisher of computer-related information and the leading global provider of information services on information technology. IDG was founded more than 25 years ago and now employs more than 8,500 people worldwide. IDG publishes more than 275 computer publications in over 75 countries (see listing below). More than 60 million people read one or more IDG publications each month.

Launched in 1990, IDG Books Worldwide is today the #1 publisher of best-selling computer books in the United States. We are proud to have received eight awards from the Computer Press Association in recognition of editorial excellence and three from *Computer Currents'* First Annual Readers' Choice Awards. Our best-selling *...For Dummies®* series has more than 30 million copies in print with translations in 30 languages. IDG Books Worldwide, through a joint venture with IDG's Hi-Tech Beijing, became the first U.S. publisher to publish a computer book in the People's Republic of China. In record time, IDG Books Worldwide has become the first choice for millions of readers around the world who want to learn how to better manage their businesses.

Our mission is simple: Every one of our books is designed to bring extra value and skill-building instructions to the reader. Our books are written by experts who understand and care about our readers. The knowledge base of our editorial staff comes from years of experience in publishing, education, and journalism — experience we use to produce books for the '90s. In short, we care about books, so we attract the best people. We devote special attention to details such as audience, interior design, use of icons, and illustrations. And because we use an efficient process of authoring, editing, and desktop publishing our books electronically, we can spend more time ensuring superior content and spend less time on the technicalities of making books.

You can count on our commitment to deliver high-quality books at competitive prices on topics you want to read about. At IDG Books Worldwide, we continue in the IDG tradition of delivering quality for more than 25 years. You'll find no better book on a subject than one from IDG Books Worldwide.

John J. Kilcullen

John Kilcullen
CEO
IDG Books Worldwide, Inc.

Eighth Annual Computer Press Awards ≥1992

Ninth Annual Computer Press Awards ≥1993

Tenth Annual Computer Press Awards ≥1994

Eleventh Annual Computer Press Awards ≥1995

Dedication

To Pat, who married me on a sunset beach on Maui on January 2, 1997, after 10 years of unwedded bliss.

To Blue and Jesse, who put up with hearing "Mom's still writing!" for what seemed like ages last winter.

To Mom and Dad and my stepdaughters, Deja and Chrystal, for being patient and supportive, even though they were on vacation.

To Dustin, my oldest, for being a great son.

My heartfelt thanks and love.

Author's Acknowledgments

This has been quite a ride! I've gone through a lot of changes in the middle of writing this book. While writing it, I moved to a new house, bought a new car, got married, started a new full-time job, and cut my hair. I wrote this book on a dare — just kidding! I have wanted to write this book for a long time and feel very fortunate to have had the opportunity to make it real.

When I thought of a writer, I saw some solitary thinker, off alone in a dark den stewing in creative juices. I soon discovered, when I became a writer, that a book is a team effort. While I do spend some time alone clicking away at my computer, a host of other folks do a heap of work to make it all stick together and get onto the bookshelves. I'd like to thank all those people at IDG Books who were on my team for the whole game (sound effects — huge crowd cheering): Rev Mengle, Project Editor; Jill Brummett, Copy Editor; Eric Rudie, Technical Editor; Gareth Hancock, Acquisitions Editor; Darlene Wong, Acquisitions Assistant; and many others. *We* did it!

Finally, thanks to my new husband and my partner of many years, Pat, who supported me as if his life depended on it. He is my ghost editor, saving me from my own terrible spelling, and adding some great one-liners here and there. I'm not kidding!

Publisher's Acknowledgments

We're proud of this book; please send us your comments about it by using the Reader Response Card at the back of the book or by e-mailing us at feedback/dummies@idgbooks.com. Some of the people who helped bring this book to market include the following:

Acquisitions, Development, and Editorial

Project Editor: Rev Mengle

Acquisitions Editor: Gareth Hancock

Product Development Director:
Mary Bednarek

Media Development Manager: Joyce Pepple

Associate Permissions Editor:
Heather H. Dismore

Copy Editor: Jill Brummett

Technical Editor: Eric Rudie

Editorial Manager: Seta K. Frantz

Editorial Assistants: Chris H. Collins,
Michael D. Sullivan

Production

Project Coordinator: Regina Snyder

Layout and Graphics: Brett Black,
Cameron Booker, Linda M. Boyer,
Elizabeth Cárdenas-Nelson,
Dominique DeFelice, Maridee V. Ennis,
Angela F. Hunckler, Todd Klemme,
Ruth Loiacano, Jane Martin, Anna Rohrer,
Theresa Sánchez-Baker, Brent Savage,
Kate Snell, Michael A. Sullivan

Proofreaders: Michael Hall, Rachel Garvey,
Nancy Price, Dwight Ramsey,
Robert Springer, Carrie Voorhis,
Karen York

Indexer: Sherry Massey

Special Help

Stephanie Koutek, Proof Editor;
Suzanne Packer, Lead Copy Editor;
Robert Wallace, Project Editor; Kevin Spencer,
Associate Technical Editor; Access Technology

General and Administrative

IDG Books Worldwide, Inc.: John Kilcullen, CEO; Steven Berkowitz, President and Publisher

IDG Books Technology Publishing: Brenda McLaughlin, Senior Vice President and
Group Publisher

Dummies Technology Press and Dummies Editorial: Diane Graves Steele, Vice President and
Associate Publisher; Judith A. Taylor, Brand Manager; Kristin A. Cocks, Editorial Director

Dummies Trade Press: Kathleen A. Welton, Vice President and Publisher; Stacy S. Collins,
Brand Manager

IDG Books Production for Dummies Press: Beth Jenkins, Production Director; Cindy L. Phipps,
Supervisor of Project Coordination, Production Proofreading and Indexing; Kathie S. Schutte,
Supervisor of Page Layout; Shelley Lea, Supervisor of Graphics and Design; Debbie J. Gates,
Production Systems Specialist; Tony Augsburger, Supervisor of Reprints and Bluelines;
Leslie Popplewell, Media Archive Coordinator

Dummies Packaging and Book Design: Patti Sandez, Packaging Assistant; Kavish+Kavish,
Cover Design

◆

The publisher would like to give special thanks to Patrick J. McGovern,
without whom this book would not have been possible.

◆

Contents at a Glance

Cartoons at a Glance

By Rich Tennant • Fax: 508-546-7747 • E-mail: the5wave@tiac.net

page 63

page 7

page 113

page 259

page 193

page 325

Table of Contents

Foreword

• •

Oracle databases are complex. However, *Oracle7 For Dummies* helps users understand these complex database issues by breaking them down and talking about them in simple terms. From Oracle database basics to tuning tips and techniques, this book is an Oracle user's resource for answering current questions and questions users haven't even thought of yet.

The Oracle7 software runs on most hardware platforms from PC desktops all the way up to large mainframes. Because *Oracle7 For Dummies* focuses on the database engine, this book is applicable to all readers regardless of the platform upon which Oracle operates.

Pick up the nuances of the Oracle7 environment and how Oracle7 keeps track of your tables. Read about tables and tablespaces and how to design them. See how foreign keys work and how to add them to your tables. Understand how to create and assign security roles to users. Discover Oracle's internal structure and the Oracle7 user. Find out the best strategies for using roles, synonyms, views, and table grants. Get a complete list of the naming standards that Oracle uses for columns, tables, indexes, and more. Discover *security options,* methods of safeguarding your data, and the nuts and bolts of SQL*Plus and Personal Oracle7 Navigator.

This book shows you (with lots of examples) how to use uncommon features, such as the EXISTS clause and the WHENEVER clause for SQL*Plus. Make the most of SQL*Plus by harnessing its report-generating powers. Figure out how easily queries can be built and controlled, flaws corrected, and data shared with others. Four entire chapters are dedicated to turbocharging and tuning your database tables and SQL*Plus code.

The "Part of Tens" section is also extremely valuable to Oracle users. In this section, author Carol McCullough gives users 10 hot tips on 5 challenging topics, including tuning tips and handy SQL scripts. These chapters alone save Oracle users tremendous frustration and countless hours.

The book includes a CD-ROM with a full-featured, 60-day trial copy of Personal Oracle7 on it.

The International Oracle Users Group-Americas (IOUG-A) is an independent, not-for-profit organization of users of Oracle products and services. IOUG-A is dedicated to educating the Oracle users community and communicating users' needs to the Oracle Corporation. The IOUG-A is always looking for resources for Oracle users, and *Oracle7 For Dummies* is one such resource.

This book is truly helpful to Oracle users; it cuts the learning curve way down because it's written in simple terms that make even the most complex database issues easy to understand. Understanding these complex issues is important for users to get the most from Oracle database products.

The International Oracle Users Group-Americas

For more information about the International Oracle Users Group-Americas (IOUG-A), its member benefits, its publication Select Magazine *and its conference, visit the IOUG-A Web site,* www.ioug.org, *or call 312-245-1579.*

Introduction

• •

Or-a-cle (noun) 1: a person (as a priestess of ancient Greece) through whom a deity is believed to speak. 2: an authoritative or wise expression or answer.

That definition pretty much says it all, doesn't it? You've got Oracle7. You've got the database to beat all databases. You've got the cream of the crop, the tip of the top, the best of the best, the oracle from which all wisdom and answers flow. And if you only had your own Greek priestess to consult you'd have no problem figuring out how to use the pesky thing!

Besides being one of the best relational database packages around, Oracle7 is one of the most complex. Oracle7 does some very fancy things — it's the easy things that are sometimes tricky.

Fear not, for you have come to the right place. This book is the Oracle's oracle, written by the high priestess of database knowledge. Well, all right, I'm just a normal human, but I have lots of experience as a database programmer with Oracle7. I had to learn the hard way — on the job, bribing nerds with doughnuts, even (shudder!) reading manuals. You can learn from my experience by reading this book, which easily guides you along the path to Oracle enlightenment with more fun than you're supposed to have at work.

This book focuses on Oracle Version 7.0 or higher. The vast majority of the subject matter applies to all platforms, from Mac and PC to Unix and mainframes. Where appropriate, I demonstrate how to use the Personal Oracle7 Navigator, Oracle's desktop tool. As of Oracle7.3, the Personal Oracle7 Navigator is renamed Oracle Navigator, but I refer to it as the Personal Oracle7 Navigator (PO7 Navigator, for short) in this book. The figures in this book were taken using Personal Oracle7.2, so if you have Version 7.3, your screens may differ somewhat. Nearly all the step-by-step instructions for the Personal Oracle7 Navigator work with both the old and new version; I note differences.

Why This Book Makes Sense

Oracle now puts its entire software documentation — the manuals — on a CD-ROM. Putting the documentation on CD saves a lot of trees but doesn't help you much, because the CD version is cross-referenced about as well as the old paperback volumes. If you know what your answer is before you start looking, the answer is really easy to find. If you don't know the answer, it can take days to discover.

This book gives you answers fast. Use it to get results quickly and easily. Hide it under your Oracle manuals and then dazzle your friends with your incredible know-how!

Some Basic Assumptions

To keep the book focused on database matters, I make some assumptions about your innate (or learned) talents. You

- ✔ Own or have access to Oracle7 on any platform
- ✔ Use tables others created, and sometimes create tables yourself
- ✔ Use and create queries, reports, and sometimes enter data
- ✔ Are comfortable using a mouse and Windows (not a requirement)

Quickie Overview of This Book

So that you can find what you want to know more about quickly and easily, I've broken this book up into parts. Here's a quick look at what's inside:

Part I: Road Map

Here you find important concepts and definitions used throughout the book. Chapter 1 is an introduction to Oracle7. There's a quick discussion of tasks that a database can (and cannot) be used to accomplish. The part has an in-depth look at SQL*Plus, a utility that uses the SQL programming language to let you get at your data and includes powerful reporting tools like summarizing, grouping, and so forth. Use it now and use it well.

Part II: Getting Started

An important part of using Oracle7 is knowing the way that a relational database fits together all the pieces of data that it stores. Even if you never design a table of your own, knowing a little of the basics helps you make better use of the database. Look here to find out how to read a diagram. You know, those strange looking drawings with boxes and lines that look like a cross between a floor plan and a crossword puzzle.

Part II takes a look backstage at the props Oracle uses to keep track of you and all the things that you and others have created. You find a bit of technical stuff here, but it's carefully contained with the proper hexes and spells, so don't worry.

Part III: Putting Oracle 7 to Work

This section launches right into the heart of using Oracle7. Here's where you see how to create a table or two. After you get some tables, you might be upset if they get lost or get changed by some ham-handed programmer (possibly even someone who looks suspiciously like yourself). That's where the sections on security, backups, and sharing data come in really handy.

Finally, with tables in place, it's time to see if you can actually use the data in some way. Contrary to the opinion of many techno-systems analysts, data is actually intended for some purpose other than calculating disk storage space.

Part IV: Tuning Up and Turbocharging

After you've given SQL*Plus a whirl, you're ready to find out why it took three days to execute a three-line SQL command. Part IV looks at what's slowing you down, how to speed everything up, and what to do when you hit a speed bump, or a wall, or other obstacles that slow you down.

Part V: The Part of Tens

The wonderful part of tens. Does this remind you of grade school, where you had to count ten sticks, wrap a rubber band around them, and then repeat ten times to make a hundred? Only me, huh? The part of tens covers the same ground as the previous four parts but with emphasis on quick, really useful tips that could save you hours of research. Dazzle your toddler, the neighbor's dog, maybe even your boss with your cunning.

Appendix A: Resources Guide

Lists. Lots of lists.

Appendix B: About the CD

If you haven't noticed yet, a CD-ROM is attached to the inside of the back cover of this book. On it, you'll find all sorts of helpful stuff, from SQL scripts to a trial version of Personal Oracle7. This appendix gives you a brief overview of the CD's contents and how to install them.

Glossary

Terms defined. Not an index. Please refer to the index for an index.

Of Mice and Sven (Mouse Moves and Special Text)

For the most part, you won't need to do any special mouse functions, because this book is mouse independent and covers Oracle on a lot of different platforms. Once in a while, I illustrate how to use the Oracle7 tool for Windows, the Personal Oracle Navigator. In these cases, your mouse does the walking. For clarity, here's the way I define mouse activities:

- **Click** — select an object with the mouse by pointing at it and clicking one time with the left mouse button.
- **Double-click** — point at an object and click with the left mouse button two times.
- **Right-click** — point and click with the right mouse button.

Now what does Sven have to do with it? Nothing really. He's just a friendly fellow who wants to say everything clearly. He's here to tell you that when you see the kind of printing on the next line, it means one of two things:

```
I am something you type into the computer.
```

or (where indicated)

```
I am what your computer says back to you.
```

Here's what words channeled from the little voice in my head look like:

You are so funny I could die.

Just kidding on that last one.

In the sections that talk about the Personal Oracle7 Navigator, sometimes I tell you to use a menu command, like File⇨Open. You can do this by moving your mouse pointer up to the File menu, clicking it, and then choosing the Open command.

On a final note, Oracle7 is not case sensitive, so you may see table, row, or column names in uppercase or lowercase throughout this book.

Reading the icons

All of the ...*For Dummies* books use icons to help you pick out the important details without reading the fine print. Here are the ones you find sprinkled like confetti all around the pages of this book.

As you may have guessed, this icon marks some technical details to be avoided, or indulged in, depending on your moods. I have taken great pains to make the sections marked with this icon no more than the size of the average palm so that the entire section can be conveniently covered up.

This icon signifies hard-won advice, from time-saving tricks to shortcuts.

Reserved for important and critical details, this icon is your cue to read carefully. Missing the stuff next to this icon can mean missing an important step and creating a query that never dies or some such freak of nature.

Watch out here. You may have to walk through a minefield to get to your goal. This icon shows you the safest route to take.

This icon alerts you to new terms and their definitions. Plain English gets you a long way in this book, but occasionally I fall back on a commonly used technical term. When I do, I mark it with this icon and put the word in italics.

Lots and lots of examples are in this book. This icon shows where the discussion ends and the action begins.

SQL code, the raw bare facts, appears wherever clear and concise syntax must be followed for good results. I use a different font for SQL code, and add this symbol to help set it apart.

The Personal Oracle7 Navigator has some really handy tools. Watch for this icon to see concrete examples of the Navigator in action.

I use this icon to tell you about related software that I've included on the CD-ROM that comes with this book.

Ready or not, here you come. You are now primed and ready to dive right into the wonderful world of Oracle7. Get out your little tinfoil hat (to ward off evil thoughts and cosmic rays), grab your mouse and this book, and take the plunge!

Bells and whistles that Oracle7 doesn't have

Perhaps you bought Oracle7 from the Oracle Store on the Internet. Perhaps you work with Oracle on the job. Whatever way you came to work with Oracle, I'd like to clear something up right now: You have at your command a truly versatile and complex database engine, but Oracle7 does *not* have all the niceties that software buyers take for granted in this age of "plug and play" technology.

Oracle7 by itself is not like Microsoft Access or Paradox, programs that include everything in one box, ready and easy to use. Oracle7 is very plain in appearance. And the basic Oracle7 database product does not include any tools for creating data entry forms. It does not include any report-writing tool except SQL*Plus, and SQL*Plus — while powerful as a tool for database management — does not measure up very well as a reporting tool.

But don't be fooled. Behind the plain facade of Oracle7 is a relational database engine far more powerful than most other database tools on the market. Unquestionably, Oracle7 has more computing power and can handle more complex applications than any desktop relational database. You have paid for raw power. You don't get the nice, fun bells and whistles unless you pay more.

This book covers how to use the basic Oracle7 relational database engine via SQL*Plus and the Personal Oracle7 Navigator. You learn how to tap the Oracle7 power at the source — and that knowledge enables you to better utilize the additional software tools that support Oracle7.

Do I cover those tools? You bet. Chapter 23 covers ten tools, some sold by Oracle and some by other vendors, which give you a more user-friendly interface with Oracle7.

Part I
Road Map

The 5th Wave By Rich Tennant

"THIS IS YOUR GROUPWARE?! THIS IS WHAT YOU'RE RUNNING?! WELL HECK — I THINK THIS COULD BE YOUR PROBLEM!"

In this part...

*B*efore launching full tilt into the brave new world of Oracle7, Part I paves the way with bits of knowledge.

The motto of Part I is "forewarned is forearmed!" I figure it's better to have some idea what's in the refrigerator before you start making a birthday cake. Otherwise, you're running to the store in the middle of it all for a teaspoon of vanilla. With that in mind, Part I gives you a nice tour of all the tools that come as standard equipment with Oracle7.

Another very important part of getting to know your database is learning the common terms used when working with a relational database. Database words stem from ordinary words, the kind you use around the house every day.

Chapter 1
A Quick Tour of Oracle7

. . . .

In This Chapter

▶ Discovering what you've gotten into

▶ Starting Oracle7

▶ Looking over your tools

▶ Checking out other Oracle7 software

▶ Glancing at SQL*Plus

▶ Shutting down Oracle7

. . . .

Well, you lucky duck! Your world is about to expand into the great unknown territory called Oracle7. Actually, the territory is not really unknown, because some of us have ventured there and returned with a map. I suppose you would have preferred Chinese take-out or donuts. Sorry, Charlie.

This chapter is your guide map. You look at what Oracle7 is all about and what components are included, and then rev it up and give it a test drive.

Oracle 7: The Program That Runs It All

Once upon a time, back in the '70s, there was a man named Larry Ellison who built a great big software program called Oracle. The Oracle program lived in a giant mainframe, and when it fired up its boilers and started huffing and puffing, it expanded to the size of a house. Only the biggest mainframes had room for Oracle.

Then one day, a neighbor of Larry's saw what the big Oracle program could do and told Larry, "Hey! I want one too, but my mainframe cannot handle that really big program. If you make me a smaller one, I'll pay you big bucks."

Larry took the challenge and, in less than a year, created another Oracle program to fit into the smaller mainframe. He delivered it to his neighbor, who exclaimed, "It's a miracle!"

This inspired Larry to think that other small-computer owners would want the Oracle program. So Larry went to all corners of the earth, found the best engineers, and gathered them together in the Promised Land of California to help him create Oracle for all sizes and shapes of computers.

Today, the Oracle engine is all that Larry dreamed it could be, and more. With Oracle7, you're sitting on a database powerhouse.

Oracle 7's core package

Figure 1-1 shows the Oracle7 database engine and the core utilities that are standard equipment with Oracle7 *regardless of your operating system or hardware*. These core utilities and the database itself behave the same on all platforms. The differences are on the inside, where Oracle7 takes advantage of each computer's unique features for storage, reading, writing, and so on. The core utilities are:

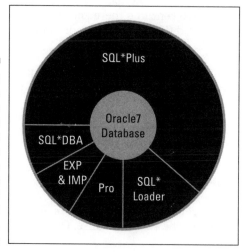

Figure 1-1:
Oracle's
powerhouse
database
with its
core
utilities is
portable to
dozens of
kinds of
computers.

✔ **SQL*Plus:** This tool allows you to create tables or queries, add rows, modify data, even perform duties typically reserved for database administrators (DBAs), such as creating new users. To use SQL*Plus, you must learn SQL, the Standard Query Language. You can use this on nearly any relational database. The Oracle7 version is called SQL*Plus because Oracle has embellished the usual SQL suite of commands. These embellishments allow you to customize reports, edit and save files, define variables, and do other cool stuff.

I describe SQL*Plus throughout the book. You see SQL examples that you can run in SQL*Plus in most of the chapters. SQL*Plus gets the big part of that outer circle in Figure 1-1 because it is a primary resource for working with the database.

✔ **EXP** and **IMP:** You can export (EXP) data from or import (IMP) data to any Oracle7 database. For example, you can use EXP on a PC to copy into a file data and tables you have created; move this file to a UNIX computer, a Power Mac, an IBM mainframe, or any other platform where there's an Oracle7 database; and then use IMP to place the information into that database.

✔ **SQL*DBA:** This utility has been expanded since it was implemented in the mid-'80s, but now it is not as useful a tool as its name would indicate. Having worked with both SQL*DBA and SQL*Plus, I find that SQL*DBA adds very little value. To quote Oracle's own documentation: "You can use SQL*DBA or not use it." I don't. In this book, I use SQL*Plus to show you how to perform DBA tasks. (By the way, SQL*DBA has been replaced in Oracle Versions 7.3 and up with the Enterprise Manager tool.)

✔ **SQL*Loader:** This utility used to be only one way to get data into an Oracle7 database from a different brand of database. The procedure is very basic: SQL*Loader reads a standard text file that contains the data from a table and loads that data into an Oracle7 table. You set up a file for SQL*Loader telling it all the details of what you want it to do.

Today, other alternatives take advantage of the modern trend toward common communications. SQL*Loader is still an option, but more up-to-date methods, such as using new software that connects databases directly, are often a good alternative. For example, you can get a connection between Microsoft's SQLServer and Oracle7 for free from the Oracle Web site.

✔ **Pre-compilers**: There are a bunch of these, actually, one for each different programming language. There's one for COBOL, Ada, C, C+, Pascal, and Fortran. The mix varies on different platforms (hardware/operating systems). I don't cover these at all in this book. You need to learn a programming language to use them.

Personal Oracle7's extras

You almost certainly have Personal Oracle7 (PO7) if you have installed Oracle7 on your Windows 3.1, Windows 95, Power Mac, or Windows NT computer. (In some instances, you may be working on a networked PC that does not have Personal Oracle7 but has a connection into Oracle7 on another computer.)

When you install Personal Oracle7 (PO7), you get all the tools I mentioned in the preceding section, and — as icing on the cake — a bunch of nice utilities that either replace or augment the basic tool set. Figure 1-2 shows the configuration of tools you get with Personal Oracle7.

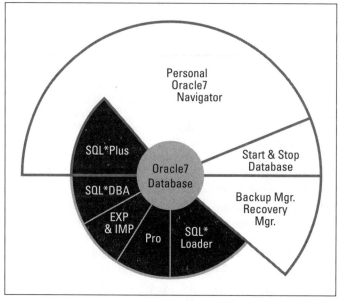

Figure 1-2:
The Personal Oracle7 family offers a few more tools around the same Oracle7 database.

The extra tools you get with Personal Oracle7 include:

- **Personal Oracle7 Navigator:** This guide to PO7 is a gem of a program! You get a whole bunch of features with PO7 Navigator that take advantage of Windows. Inside PO7 Navigator are:

    - **Visual Database Map:** This allows you to see your database a lot like your File Manager (or Explorer) layout, using icons for tables, users, and other parts of the database.

    - **Table Wizard:** This tool knows all about the Oracle7 program. The job of the wizard is to create tables, walking you through the process so that you don't get bogged down in SQL*Plus.

    - **Dialog boxes:** These are like miniature wizards or sorcerer's apprentices. Dialog boxes guide you through creating a table, creating an index, creating a new user, and many other tasks by giving you multiple- choice selections. Dialog boxes are great for fast results. They require that you know a little more than when you work directly with a wizard, but an apprentice is never quite as smart as the master. I've found them helpful, even to an experienced Oracle7 priestess like myself.

- **SQL*Plus For Windows:** This is an addition to SQL*Plus that Navigator adds to make SQL*Plus easier to use, more like you'd expect from a Windows tool.

✔ **Backup Manager** and **Recovery Manager:** These two utilities work to save your database to a disk or tape. This acts as a backup in case of a hardware failure. From this, you can restore the original copy of the database to your hard drive. I show you how they work in Chapter 14.

✔ **Start Database** and **Stop Database:** These two tools start and stop the database. PO7 Navigator also handles both of these functions. If you want to start up or stop the database itself without using PO7 Navigator, use these tools.

Starting Up Oracle7

The procedures for starting up Oracle7 depend on what kind of computer you have. With PCs or Macs, you use desktop selections to start up. If you are working with a mainframe or on a network where Oracle7 is not installed on your desktop, your startup usually involves issuing startup commands directly to the operating system.

Starting up on a PC or a Mac

If you have installed Personal Oracle7 on your PC or Power Mac, you can do almost everything using Personal Oracle7 Navigator. This includes starting and stopping Oracle7, creating tables, and generally getting around easily within Oracle7. The steps to start up Oracle7 are very simple with Personal Oracle7 Navigator.

To start in Windows 95, follow these steps:

1. **Click the Start menu on the taskbar in the lower-left corner of the screen.**

2. **Select Programs⇨Personal Oracle7 for Windows 95⇨Personal Oracle7 Navigator, as shown in Figure 1-3.**

If you have a Mac, simply double-click the Oracle7 Navigator icon on the Mac desktop to start up the PO7 Navigator.

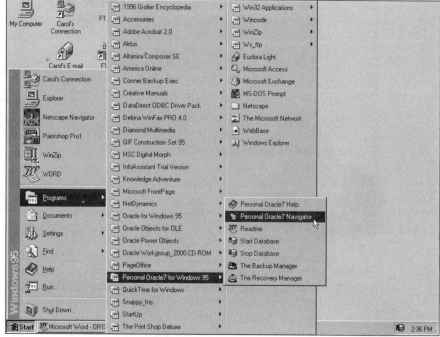

Figure 1-3:
Windows 95
lets you
select the
Navigator
from a maze
of other
programs.

When you fire up Oracle7, the first thing that pops up on your screen is the Personal Oracle7 Navigator, shown in Figure 1-4. Notice how neatly the PO7 Navigator arranges the files, icons, and buttons you use to work with Oracle7. This is certainly much neater than my husband's arrangement of tools, documents, and other assorted items on his workbench.

Starting the PO7 Navigator versus starting the database

I have a nit-picky point to discuss here. When you start PO7 Navigator, you are not actually starting the central database engine itself. You can start the database in either of these two ways:

✔ Select Start Database from the same group of programs where you chose PO7 Navigator.

✔ Let PO7 Navigator start the database automatically the first time you do anything that requires database access.

I prefer the second method, but either works perfectly well.

Control menu button   Object Contents window   Window controls

Object window   Title bar   Main menu bar   Toolbar

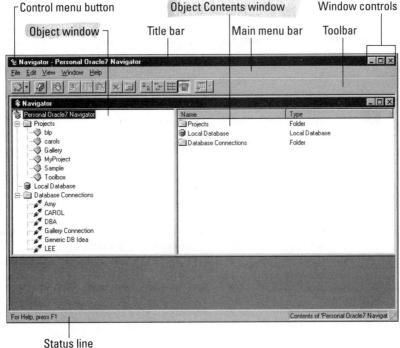

Figure 1-4:
Personal
Oracle7
Navigator
sets sail in
Windows.

Status line

Learning about the parts of PO7 Navigator that I've highlighted in Figure 1-4 helps you get around like a pro. Think of the figure as a VCR manual. No, actually, it's a whole lot simpler than that. Just don't try to set the clock.

The PO7 Navigator window has two important groups of elements: the Object and Object Contents windows, and everything else.

The Object windows

The Object and Object Contents windows give you a visual representation of all of the files you can access in Oracle7. *Objects* are any one of several kinds of things in a database or in PO7 itself, such as projects, tables, users, views, and connections.

The cool thing about PO7 Navigator is that it uses a lot of the basics you learned about getting around in the Windows 95 Explorer. Here are some examples:

- ✔ The left half of the screen shows a hierarchy of *objects* available for you to look at. The right half of the screen shows the contents of whatever you select (via a mouse click) on the left side.

- ✔ You can click on the plus or minus signs next to the icons in the left half to expand or contract the contents.

✓ Right-click on an object to get a little menu that tells what you can do with the object.

✓ Double-click on objects to execute them or to expand them, depending on what they are.

- Double-clicking on a database connection takes you to a list of all the objects owned by the user ID defined in the connection. It also connects you to the database (surprise!), logging in with the user ID and password for the connection.

- Double-clicking a table folder opens and shows all the tables inside.

- Double-clicking a table opens and starts up a window displaying the table's contents.

✓ Click and drag an item from the right window into the left side and the item is copied. For instance, you can copy a table from one user to another this way. Not everything can be copied, so the click-and-drag method does not always work. You see a little circle with a line through it (the universal sign for "No way, dude") if you try to move something totally illegal.

✓ Highlight something and then use the Edit menu to cut and paste.

✓ If you get lost, click the Help button, which offers context-sensitive instructions.

By the way, if you have Windows 95 and are not familiar with it, check out *Windows 95 For Dummies* by Andy Rathbone (IDG Books Worldwide, Inc.) for a good start.

The other Navigator elements

The Object window and the Object Contents window are far from the only elements in the PO7 Navigator. Look for these additional goodies:

✓ **Control menu button:** This barely noticeable button looks like a table being put into a martini shaker. You can click this to see a menu of standard controls, such as Exit, Move, and so on. Most of these are unneeded once you know how to use your mouse and the Windows Control Buttons. Olives are optional at this point, and please! Go easy on the vermouth.

✓ **Windows control buttons:** These are standard Windows 95 window controls for moving the window to the bottom taskbar, filling the whole screen, and closing the window. Close the window; I feel a draft.

✓ **Title bar:** If you are not sure where you are, the Title bar tells you. If you are still not sure, I suggest you go easier on the martinis. Also, if you click here and drag, you move the whole window. I wish I could do that with the window over my sink. It's too close to the refrigerator.

✔ **Main menu bar:** Here you find the usual collection of menus, such as File, Edit, and Help. A click on any of them shows the selections available.

✔ **Toolbar:** This bar shows little buttons of tools you have available. Most of them you use only occasionally. Nearly all of them are available either with a right-click of the mouse or by clicking on a menu bar. The buttons are (from left to right)

- **New Project/New Connection:** This lets you toggle between two selections according to which one you did last. The little arrow button next to it lets you pick either one.

- **Open project:** Surprise! — this opens a project.

- **Show Navigator main window:** Takes you to the main window from other parts of the Navigator.

- **Cut:** Cuts something from a project.

- **Copy:** Copies something, like a table or user.

- **Paste:** Pastes whatever you copied or cut.

- **Delete:** Deletes a table or some other object from the database or from a project.

- **Properties:** Views the properties of the highlighted object.

- **Large icons:** Shows things with big icons on the right side of the Navigator.

- **Small icons:** Like large icons, only smaller so you get more of them to fit in your window.

- **List:** Small icons arranged in a list instead of across the window.

- **Details:** Like the List tool but with additional information, such as the Type or Owner for each item.

- **New database object:** This one changes depending on what you last created. The little arrow button next to it lets you select an action, such as New Table, New View, and so on.

Starting up on a network or mainframe

I know there are a lot of you who are using Oracle7 on a mainframe or on a network. Oracle7 should be up and running as part of the initial startup routine for the computer. I hate to say it, but check your installation guide for instructions on how to do this if it's your responsibility. Ask your database administrator (DBA) how to start Oracle7, or ask the DBA to start Oracle7 for you. Ask nicely. The DBA is your friend!

The usual way of starting up Oracle7 on a mainframe is to start up SQL*DBA or Enterprise Manager and issue the startup command.

SQL*Plus: The Messenger Priestess of Oracle7

So how do you communicate with Oracle7? With a utility called SQL*Plus, which has been a part of the Oracle7 program from the very start. SQL*Plus allows you to create tables, put parameters on the data that goes into the tables, manipulate the data in the tables, write reports, and administer the database. Think of SQL*Plus as the high priestess who channels questions from the masses to Oracle7 and faithfully returns answers from Oracle7.

Unlike a number of Windows-based programs out today, SQL*Plus still works in ancient ways. No point-and-click mousing around with SQL*Plus; only command-line input is involved.

You can do many things in *both* Personal Oracle7 Navigator and SQL*Plus. In a lot of chapters, I show you the steps for a task in both tools, so you use the one that you have. If you have both, I recommend using Personal Oracle7 rather than SQL*Plus in all but a few instances. In these cases, I include only the SQL*Plus instructions.

Starting and stopping SQL*Plus on a PC or a Mac

You reach SQL*Plus through PO7 Navigator. Start up the Navigator as shown in the section above. Then follow these steps:

1. **Click the Toolbox icon in the left window.**

   In Oracle7.3, click the plus (+) sign next to the Projects icon to reveal the Toolbox icon, and then click on the Toolbox icon.

   This opens the Toolbox project. Navigator shows the contents of the Toolbox in the right window.

2. **Double-click the SQL*Plus icon in the right window.**

   The icon has a yellow plus sign (see Figure 1-5).

3. **Fill in your user name and password in the security screen that pops up, shown in Figure 1-6.**

   If you don't have your very own, you can use Oracle7's sample user name (SCOTT) and password (TIGER). The password shows up as asterisks (*) when you type.

   Now some status screens may pop up telling you that Oracle7 is starting up the database. This occurs if you have not done any work on the database yet.

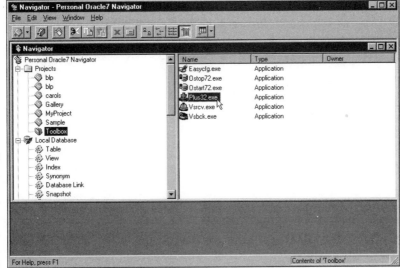

Figure 1-5:
Choose
your
weapon
from the
Toolbox.

Figure 1-6:
Know your
secret
password
to enter the
Oracle7
clubhouse.

4. Click OK to go past the status screens (if they appear) and get to a SQL*Plus window.

Figure 1-7 shows the SQL*Plus window that you can use to type in your commands. It also points out the extra features you get by having Navigator run SQL*Plus for you.

The SQL*Plus window is the body of the window where you type in and run SQL*Plus commands and see feedback from Oracle7. Even though you're in a window, SQL*Plus is still an old-fashioned, line-by-line kind of utility. Go ahead and click anywhere in the window; then type in this little one-line query:

```
select table_name from user_tables;
```

Press Enter to run the query. You see that SQL*Plus lists the results of the query right below the command, as shown in Figure 1-8.

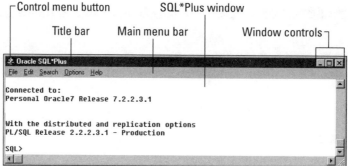

Control menu button   SQL*Plus window

Title bar   Main menu bar   Window controls

Figure 1-7:
The
SQL*Plus
window has
typical
Windows
features.

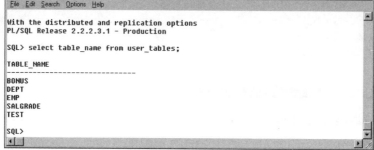

Figure 1-8:
When you
type,
SQL*Plus
listens —
and
responds.

To stop SQL*Plus, just close the window by clicking on the Close box (the
one with the *X* in the upper-right corner). You return to the main PO7
Navigator window.

Starting and stopping SQL*Plus on a mainframe or a network

To start SQL*Plus on a mainframe or network, go to your operating system
command line and type:

```
SQLPLUS username/password
```

Replace username with your Oracle7 user name. Replace password with
your actual password. If you are not a person according to Oracle7, you can
impersonate the guy who has all the sample tables in Oracle7. Type in
SCOTT as the user name and TIGER as the password. You get a few status
messages and then your prompt changes to this one:

```
SQL>
```

This prompt means you are now in SQL*Plus and are ready to go! Now, you can create queries, tables, and generally have fun to your heart's content. You can do one right now! Type in this line and press Enter to run it:

```
select table_name from user_tables;
```

The results are listed on your screen and look just like the results shown in Figure 1-8 above, except it does not have the window around it. When you're done, you leave SQL*Plus by typing:

```
EXIT;
```

Then you press the Enter key. You return to your operating system and the prompt returns to its normal state.

Many of the chapters in this book contain examples of SQL code that you can type into SQL*Plus and run (notice the SQL icon next to the code). Chapters 9 through 14 have sample SQL code for you. Chapter 3 is dedicated exclusively to SQL*Plus. Chapter 22 includes ten very useful SQL *scripts,* or lines of code that work together to create a small program, that you can use.

Getting to know Oracle7 — and Scott and Tiger

Every Oracle database comes with demonstration tables that you may want to get familiar with. And if you do, you'll quickly notice references to Scott or Scott/Tiger. Perhaps you have already noticed these in the Oracle7 documentation.

So who are Scott and Tiger? I heard that Scott is a real human, or was at one time. Now he's a legend whose name is engraved in every Oracle database around the world, and whose name you can use as an acceptable user name. And Scott's cat, Tiger, is a legend of his own, now immortalized as Scott's password.

In the Oracle7 demonstration tables, Scott is one of only two highly paid analysts in a small company that is set on selling something. The head honcho's name is King. This company has four departments in four cities across America. All the salesmen get commissions, although one poor guy gets a zero commission. Nobody has ever earned a bonus. You can find out more about the people who work for Scott by typing these SQL commands into SQL*Plus:

```
select * from emp;
select * from dept;
select * from bonus;
select * from salgrade;
```

You can see that the boss lives in New York; the analysts, who all get paid more than their manager, live in Dallas; and the salesmen live in Chicago. Apparently a puppet office in Boston exists — probably as a shady tax write-off. No doubt Tiger's behind it all!

Getting Help: Let Your Mouse Do the Walking

Oracle7's tools always have a ton of documentation dragging along with them. The documentation actually holds a lot of valuable information and is indexed and cross-referenced ad nauseam. Your mouse may get dizzy running the maze of trails through backtracks, side streets, riddles, and *CMI* — Completely Meaningless Information.

Here are several ways to find the Oracle7 documentation:

- ✔ Click the Help button that is located in almost every Oracle7 window.
- ✔ Type `HELP` when in SQL*Plus and hit the Enter key. This works only if the online help option was installed with SQL*Plus. If you get an error message, ask your DBA to install the help utility for SQL*Plus.
- ✔ Select one of the Help icons in Oracle7's program groups.

The Index tab on the Help screens takes you to the window shown in Figure 1-9. The Index tab seems to be the fastest path to answers, and it works best if you know the special Oracle7 term connected with your problem. For instance, when you want to learn about how to make a new table, typing in *create* or *table* gets you there fastest. Typing in *make* gets you nowhere.

Figure 1-9:
The Help index is the fastest path to true enlightenment and instant gratification.

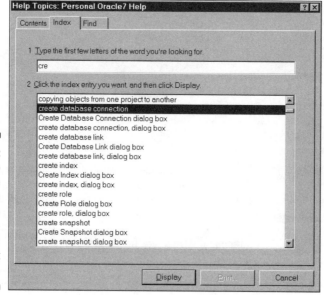

For those of you who like a totally comprehensive index, a wizard can be summoned to rescue you. On the Help screen, click on the Find tab. The wizard appears, giving you some choices and then creating the index that beats all indexes. Once the wizard's magic is worked, the index remains for you to use anytime you go back to the Help window.

In Oracle7.3, the documentation about SQL and SQL*Plus was not included inside Oracle Navigator. Here's how you find the documentation:

1. **Run the Acrobat Reader 2.0 by pressing Start⇨Programs⇨Adobe Acrobat 2.0⇨Acrobat Reader 2.0.**

   This brings you to a window where you select the directory and documentation.

2. **Go to the directory where you installed Oracle7 (for example, C:\orawin95) and select the subdirectory named doc, and then open the file named doclib73.pdf.**

   This file contains the table of contents of all the documents in the directory.

3. **Select Oracle 7 RDBMS, which brings up a list of chapters.**

4. **Select the chapter called Oracle7 Server SQL Reference, which contains all the SQL commands, their syntax, and lots of good documentation.**

If you need additional help resources, Appendix A offers a bunch of them. As a last resort, call the Oracle Corporation at 415-506-1500 and scream "HEEELLLP!!"

Shutting Down Oracle7

Now that you've had a short flyby tour, here's how to shut down the database.

Shutting down Oracle7 on a PC or a Mac

This is a two-tiered operation.

1. **First, close PO7 Navigator by clicking the Close box (the *X*) in the upper-right corner of the main window.**

   Look at your task bar. You see a small icon in the right corner that looks like a stack of three blue disks. This symbol tells you that the database is still running.

2. **Shut down the database by clicking the Start button on the bottom task bar, going to the Personal Oracle7 program selections, and choosing Stop Database.**

   Oracle7 sends you some status messages in a pop-up window and then shuts down the database. When it's done, Oracle7 tells you so (as shown in Figure 1-10).

3. **Click OK to acknowledge Oracle7's message and shut down the program.**

Figure 1-10:
Oracle7
says
goodnight.

Shutting down Oracle 7 on a mainframe or a network

Do not shut down Oracle7 without permission from your DBA every time. On mainframes, processes that require the database can be running — processes that you may not know about. (Some processes are scheduled to run after business hours so that they don't affect normal operations.)

Check with your DBA, if you have one. If you don't have one, you have to check the manuals that came with Oracle7 to find out the specific command to shut down Oracle7. The most common shut down method is going into SQL*DBA or Enterprise Manager and issuing the shutdown command.

Oftentimes, you set up the computer so that it starts up Oracle7 automatically at the beginning of the day and shuts down Oracle7 at bedtime. Sometimes, Oracle7 never goes to bed. Oracle7 actually is designed to run 24 hours a day if you need it that way.

Chapter 2

Data Whaaaaat? A Database Primer

S o you just installed Oracle7, you have the shiny new box sitting on your office shelf for your colleagues to envy, and you're ready to do some heavy-duty computing with databases. Good for you. That's great. But first, wouldn't it be nice if you knew something about databases?

This section focuses on databases, tables, rows, columns, and how they all join together to form one big happy family. For the most part, databases are designed to make your life easier. I offer lots of cute examples and scenarios in this chapter, just to show you how practical databases really are.

If, after reading this chapter, your head is spinning like that girl's in *The Exorcist,* please do not fret. Database development is as easy as, well, rocket science. After sifting through this book, you can create relational databases in your sleep. Next stop: the very pricey sleep disorder clinic. Better take a sleeping pill.

Dataspeak: Definitions for the Techno-Impaired

Shakespeare wrote "A rose by any other name would smell as sweet" — but when you order one by phone in today's world, you probably should call it a rose. Similarly, you probably should understand some common database terms, including

- Databases
- Users and roles
- Tables
- Columns and rows
- Relationships

The following sections are an expanded look at each of these terms and how they relate to Oracle7 users.

Databases

Database — this general term has many meanings, depending on the context. For the world of *Oracle7 For Dummies,* this term refers to the Oracle7 software, all the tables, and all data inside the tables.

The tools surrounding the Oracle7 database, such as SQL*Plus or PO7 Navigator, are not a part of the database in the definition. This convention is also used in all Oracle7 documentation.

A *relational database* is a collection of tables connected together in a series of relationships so that they reflect a small part of the real world.

Databases can store information better than most other methods, for many reasons:

- Databases keep similar pieces of information, like names and addresses, in one place so that you can use them in many places.
- Databases categorize, sort, filter, and pool items in multiple ways without duplicating the data.

You can harness databases to manage and reorganize your information. For example, say you have two address books, one for clients and one for friends. Helen started out as just a client but has become your friend. Would you copy her address into the friends address book? Would you leave Helen's address in the clients book and remember to look for her there? Would you give up and make a new book with both clients and friends in it? Would Helen really put up with all these address-book shenanigans? I think not!

If you had both address books in tables in Oracle7, the program could combine the tables for you, as illustrated in Figure 2-1. Push a button and Oracle7 would open with your friends' addresses, including Helen's, in alphabetical order. Close the file, push another button, and Oracle7 opens with your clients' addresses, including Helen's, in alphabetical order. Best of all, Oracle7 does not duplicate entries. You only have to enter Helen's address once, although it seems as if you have recorded it twice. How practical of you! Soon you will need to start paying yourself twice.

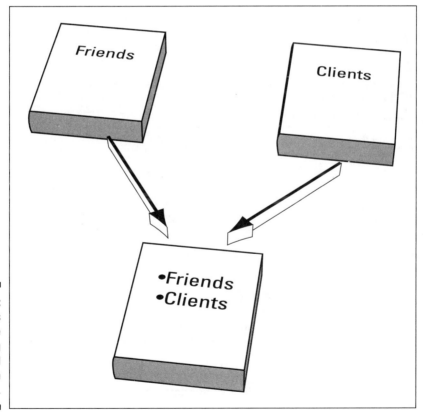

Figure 2-1:
Databases make managing unrelated information easier.

Can a database darn my socks?

Who darns socks anymore? Your grandma probably did, and she could not rely on her database to help, either. Actually, for that matter, who actually uses the word "darn" anymore? This table shows database can-do and can't-do tasks:

Task	Can Do	Can't Do
Balance the checkbook	X	
Summarize by year, or other criteria	X	
Configure your printer		X
Store and retrieve pictures, audio, and video	X	
Track sales calls	X	
Help you draw artistic pictures		X
Find your lost cat		X
Search for information embedded in text	X	
Decide the selling price for stock		X
Interact with the Internet	X	
Raid your refrigerator		X
Validate dates, numbers	X	
Sort your laundry	X	

This list of tasks just barely scratches the surface. Databases are growing in popularity because they can do so much, both at home and in the workplace. Someday, Oracle officials will name their newest version C-3PO. It will talk to you sarcastically and do the dishes.

Users and roles

A *user* is a unique login name in Oracle7. Before any data goes into your database, there must be users to *own* the data. All users have these characteristics:

- A unique name that is 1 to 30 characters long.

- A password, which does not have to be unique, that is 1 to 30 characters long.

- At least one *role* assignment. Roles determine the capabilities and privileges a user has inside the database. The database administrator (DBA) can add and remove roles. Privileges can be assigned directly to each user, but the easiest way to manage privileges is by assigning them to roles. (Users and roles are discussed in Chapter 8.)

Figure 2-2 illustrates the contents of all Oracle7 databases. The right side of the diagram shows you the *physical* system. The physical system puts all the data into multiple files on the hard drive of your computer. Aside from occasionally adding a new file, the physical system runs almost totally behind the scenes. Oracle7 decides where to physically place the data. The only control you have is to map your physical files to logical *tablespaces.* Then you can tell Oracle7 what tables go into which tablespaces. You cannot tell Oracle7 which physical file to write your CAR table data into, for example (unless you map exactly one physical file to the tablespace where CAR resides). Chapter 9 goes into more detail about tablespaces. The DBA role (explained below) does have some control over the physical system, however.

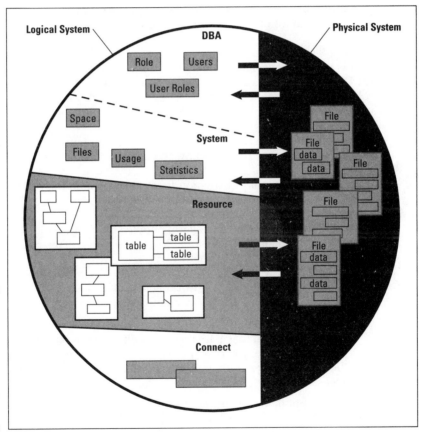

Figure 2-2:
Oracle7
database
components
fall into
logical and
physical
halves.

The left side of the diagram shows how Oracle7 *logically* (conceptually) divides the database up by roles. The diagram defines the logical system by the following roles:

✔ DBA: The most important job of the DBA (or *database administrator*) is to assign roles to users. The DBA role also adds and removes users. Further, the DBA role controls the physical side of the database by adding new files and telling Oracle7 what can go into the files.

✔ SYSTEM: This is a special section of the DBA role, an area inside the database where Oracle7 does a lot of behind-the-scenes work, such as controlling how data is written into the physical files. The tables in the SYSTEM area show where everything else in the whole database gets stored.

✔ RESOURCE: This role allows users to create their own set of tables and relate them together into a unit (*schema*). A user that creates a table is the *owner* of the table.

✔ CONNECT: This role allows users to gain access to the database. The users cannot create any tables of their own.

Chapter 9 shows you how to see what roles your Oracle7 user has. Every user is minimally assigned the CONNECT role when added to the database by the DBA. If the user is going to create tables, the DBA assigns the RESOURCE role as a second role to that user. The DBA can delegate his or her own privileges to another user by assigning the DBA role to a user.

Roles also determine a user's ability to look at or change another user's tables. Read Chapter 10 to see how to use roles in this way.

An Oracle7 user usually corresponds to one person in the real world. That person has his or her own user name and password.

Sometimes, for convenience, several people share an Oracle7 user between them. All of them know the user name and password. This can have legitimate uses, such as in these situations:

✔ A team of programmers is working on one project. One Oracle7 user owns all the tables and other elements.

✔ A large and constantly changing group of people must be given limited access to the database. It is too difficult to administer all the changes. For convenience, you distribute a single user name and password to all these people. Generally you only do this for a user with restricted access to prevent inadvertent damage to data.

✔ A large public or government bureau needs to find more effective ways to waste money on training everyone and their brother how to log into Oracle7 so next year's budget will be larger.

Tables

A table holds information inside a database. Oracle7 stores the information in an orderly fashion using rows and columns. It is easy to sort, filter, add, average, find, combine, and otherwise manipulate. Every bit of information that goes into the relational database must also go into a table. Even Oracle7 itself keeps track of its own information in tables (see Chapter 8).

Tables are real-life objects and database objects. Table 2-1 shows the similarities and differences between the table in your dining room and the one in your computer.

Table 2-1	The Table versus the Table
Furniture Table	*Database Table*
built of wood	created out of thin air
holds coffee cups	holds the description and price of a coffee cup
holds many different objects	holds information about only one kind of object
runs out of space	runs out of space
has four legs	has at least one column
usually one exists per room	usually many exist per database
gets scratched	gets fragmented

Chapter 9 goes into nauseating detail on how to build a better database table. Oracle7 itself stores information about your tables and your data in its own *system tables,* which are tables of tables. Refer to Chapter 7 to read more about tables of columns.

Every table has a name. Try to keep table names to singular nouns or noun phrases. Descriptive table names are helpful. A table named CAR probably has something to do with automobiles, or perhaps toy cars, or possibly train cars, or maybe even cable cars. A table named X1000 probably requires a comment explaining its contents. Without a comment attached, you may be reduced to asking someone for help, which could definitely interfere with your ultra-cool image at the office.

How to name any database object in Oracle7

When you name a table, a column, an index, or any other database object, I have a few rules, exceptions, and suggestions for you. This table gives you a rundown.

Rules and suggestions for naming anything in Oracle7

Rule	Exception	Suggestion
Names must be no greater than thirty characters long. A character is a letter or a single-digit number.		
Names must only contain these characters: A-Z, 0-9, $, #, @, and _.	You can use other characters, such as -, +, and blanks if you always enclose the name in quotation marks.	Apparently, someone has bought the publishing rights to these characters. Use A-Z, 0-9, and _ only. For clarity, use _ (underscore) to separate words or acronyms in the name.
Oracle7 does not differentiate uppercase and lowercase names.	Names created in quotation marks and always enclosed in quotation marks evaluate uppercase and lowercase differently.	Never use quotation marks when defining a name, and always use uppercase.
You cannot have two objects with the same name.	This rule only applies to narrow circumstances. Columns in the same table cannot have the same name. Columns in *different tables* can have the same name.	Use the same name for the same information unless this rule prevents you by not allowing you to create the item. Even tables with *different owners* can have the same name.
Name cannot be a reserved word. The list of reserved words keeps growing. Some of the more common ones you might be tempted to use include: comment, access, date,default, definition, and resource		Do not include table names in the column names. Make up a standard and stick to it for column names. For example, "always put_ID on the end of primary keys," or "always add _DATE on the end of date columns." Name the foreign key exactly the same name as the primary key it refers to.

Using these naming conventions simplifies reading a diagram, especially the relationship portions.

Tables always have columns and rows, which you learn more about in the very next section. Tables also have a size. Here are the main reasons for defining the size of a table:

- ✔ **To reserve room in the database for the table (*initial space*).** The database can store the table's data in one place, which makes the data more efficient to service. This is similar to when you go to a restaurant with a big group. If you call ahead and reserve space, the waiter seats you together and can take your orders and deliver your food more efficiently. If you are scattered all over the restaurant, the waiter works harder, and you have less fun (watching the wait staff try to total multiple checks in a table configuration like this is especially fun). Keep your tables happy and reserve the right amount of space for them.

- ✔ **To prevent a table from taking over the entire database (*maximum space*).** You may encounter a situation in which you are unable to predict how much information the table will store. All you know is that you want it to stop growing when it eats up all the available database space. (This is known in some circles as the Rush Limbaugh Syndrome.) Fortunately, there is a cure for it: the incremental space parameter. This is not one of them dashboard buttons on the Enterprise. ("More power, Scotty!" "I'm givin' 'er all she's got, Cap'n! Any more and she's going to blow!")

- ✔ **To control growth in a way that keeps the table from becoming scattered in the database (*incremental space*).** Some tables contain a lot of data in one row. Tables containing video or graphics have rows much larger than the average bear. Larger tables benefit from having large chunks of space. Getting back to our restaurant example: Suppose your group grows in 50-person increments because members are arriving on buses. The wait staff would be wise to seat the group in one of the restaurant's larger areas, rather than seating the group at random tables throughout the restaurant. If you use this method, be sure to add an automatic 15 percent gratuity.

See Chapter 9 for details on how to calculate space needs and include them in your table definition.

Tables also have a *primary key* (a column or group of columns that uniquely identifies each row in the table), one or more indexes (see Chapter 17), and relationships (see Chapter 5). This is not to be confused with *one too many*. That topic is dealt with in a future book called *Avoiding Excessive Drinking For Dummies*.

Columns and rows

Columns are the vertical parts of tables. *Rows,* on the other hand, are the horizontal parts of tables.

Are there other differences between the two? Absolutely. Columns and rows have different purposes in a table. A row holds different kinds of information about one item. For example, the row for my Maui cruiser in Figure 2-3 tells you the car is a Buick Century, has four doors, and was made in 1982.

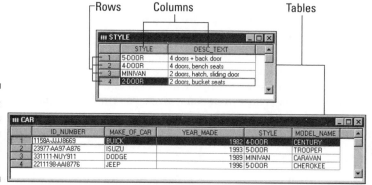

Figure 2-3:
Two tables
with
labeled
parts.

A column holds the same kind of information about many items. For example, one column in the CAR table in Figure 2-3 tells you about the YEAR_MADE of all the vehicles in the table.

Columns determine all the information that you allow in a table. These items can be cars, animals, people, sales figures, or whatever you choose — but if you don't have a column for the item, *you can't enter it into your table.* For example, you use the CAR table to gather only certain information about cars: the ID_NUMBER, MAKE_OF_CAR, YEAR_MADE, STYLE, and MODEL_NAME. Cars also have owners, color, options, tires, mileage, selling prices, and so on. You cannot place all this other information into the CAR table until you add an appropriate column for each one. As it stands in Figure 2-3, you only know five distinct kinds of information about the cars in the table.

When you first create a table, the columns exist, but not the rows. Columns are like ground rules, which must be in place before the game starts. Of course, like some games, the rules (that is, the set of columns) can be refined, added, modified, or even removed later. See Chapter 17 for commentary on how to change your table's columns.

Each *column* holds one piece of information. You define a column by giving it a name and some guidelines about what it contains. Here are the components of a column:

- **Datatype:** This component describes the general class of data. High-class data own Cadillacs. Actually, the most popular classes break down like this:

  - VARCHAR2: This class has a funny name that stands for variable character string, version 2. VARCHAR2 is used most often for any kind of text data, like names, addresses, favorite colors, or eye colors.

  - NUMBER: Obviously, this class holds numbers.

  - DATE: Oracle7 keeps dates in a special format so date math is performed faster. Some databases get flustered on a date, but not Oracle7.

- **Length:** This component is needed for VARCHAR2 and NUMBER datatypes. If you leave length out, Oracle7 plugs in a very big default length. Putting in a reasonable length prevents you from getting an enormous essay in the FAVORITE_COLOR column.

- **Null/not null:** Nulls are okay in any column except the *primary key* column, which by definition cannot be null. You add the *not null* parameter to primary key columns. Chapter 3 has more about the null value. Chapter 9 has a helpful section called "Nulls or not nulls."

My advice is to allow nulls except in primary key columns. A common mistake is to go overboard when setting up a table by adding the not null parameter to any column you predict to be required data. This process gets hairy when you want to add test data and you have to make up a value for every column you defined as not null in every row of test data you create. If later on you decide that the column truly is required, you can add the not null parameter into that column with a simple SQL command. Chapter 9 goes into more detail defining columns.

Chapters 3 and 4 show you how to make changes to data in your table using SQL*Plus or PO7 Navigator. See Chapter 17 for complete instructions for adding or removing columns to and from your tables.

Relationships

A database *relationship* is how two tables fit together. When two tables kiss, they're in a relationship. Even if they don't kiss, any connection between tables is a relationship in database lingo.

Looking back at the CAR and STYLE tables in the previous section, Figure 2-4 highlights their relationship. The CAR and STYLE tables have the STYLE column in common. The relationship between them looks like this:

> ✔ A car in the CAR table can have one style, which exists in the STYLE table.
>
> ✔ A style in the STYLE table can be selected for none, one, or many cars in the CAR table.

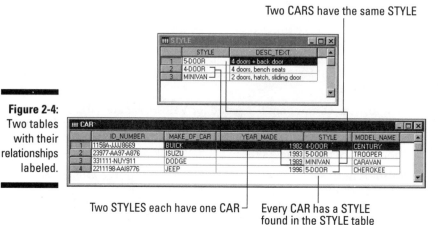

Two CARS have the same STYLE

Figure 2-4:
Two tables
with their
relationships
labeled.

Two STYLES each have one CAR — Every CAR has a STYLE
found in the STYLE table

The key to the power of a database is the *integrity* of its relationships. When you say a person has integrity, you imply that you trust him or her — that person does not say one thing and do another. Integrity in table relationships means that *once you define the relationship, every row in both tables fits into the relationship*. For example, in the CAR and STYLE example, integrity means that no cars in the CAR table have a style that is not found in the STYLE table.

The lines between tables in a diagram define relationships. Chapter 6 shows you how to accurately convey a wealth of information about the table relationships with a few lines and words on your diagrams.

The mechanics of connecting or relating tables to one another requires careful study. A good way to approach relationships, shown in Chapter 5, makes your database powerful, efficient, and streamlined.

Databases, users, roles, tables, rows, columns, and relationships are not the only terms common to database development. Many more terms exist in this book and — if you're really brave — in the Oracle7 manuals. Look in the Glossary at the back of this book for more definitions. I signal you with the Vocabulary icon wherever I have a good definition in the book.

The Kinds of Database Things You Can Do with Oracle 7

This section shows three scenarios that help you get a feel for what databases do in real life. I hope you enjoy these examples. Let your imagination run wild and think about what you want your database to do for you.

Keeping track of a fish bowl (the easy example)

Why are aquarium fish so nervous when their world is quiet, rocking them in an endless cradle of gentle bubbles and waves? Well, I guess I would be nervous, too, if 12-foot eyeballs kept popping up in my picture window.

I have a small aquarium with one little gold guppy named Wesley, who was born on January 1, 1996. The aquarium once contained four guppies, but Wesley ate the other three. Your mission, if you choose to accept it, is to design a set of tables that accurately depicts the world of my aquarium.

When you create sets of tables that relate together and all the database things that go with these tables, you create a *schema*.

Continuing with the aquarium, here are the facts you have to work with:

- ✔ I have one aquarium that holds one gallon of water, if my 7-year old doesn't get to it.
- ✔ I feed Wesley once a day, whether he asks for it or not.
- ✔ I change the water once every 14 days, even if I can still see Wesley.
- ✔ Three fish died. Their headstones read:
  - Fish Two (black & tan female guppy), born 1/1/96, died 3/15/96
  - Fish Three (red & white male guppy), born 1/1/96, died 4/8/96
  - Fish Four (transparent guppy), born 3/1/96, died on an unknown date, under very suspicious circumstances, while I was out of town

You can easily track all of this information in a simple two-table schema, as shown in Figure 2-5. I discuss the kind of diagram shown in this figure in more detail in Chapter 6.

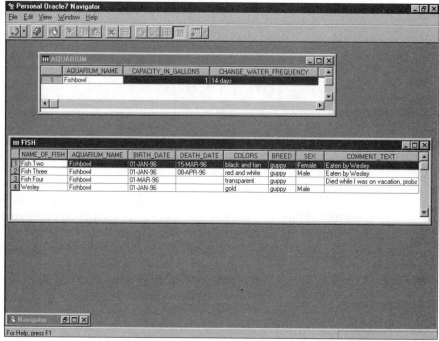

Figure 2-5:
The aquatic world in the author's kitchen, accurately reflected in database tables.

Running a pet shop (the medium example)

I buy fish food at the pet shop around the corner from my house. The owner stocked the pet shop with bird cages, dog collars, flea powder, and a few hundred other items — including birds, rabbits, and even a monkey. Here are sundry activities the shopkeeper handles with her database:

✔ Logging every item, purchase price, selling price, and number in stock

✔ Tallying tax on every sale

✔ Adjusting in-stock numbers on all inventory as sales occur

✔ Creating monthly accounting statements

✔ Creating annual tax reports

✔ Tracking names and addresses of customers

✔ Printing customized letters for advertising to customers

✔ Printing mailing labels

Now, keeping tabs on the pet shop is a great use for Oracle7! You get to use the power of the relational model so that your data can be stored once and used in a variety of ways.

For your information, if you were to try implementing the pet-shop system using only the Oracle7 database and the tools that are part of the basic package, you would have to do some advanced programming, or you'd have to get some additional tools. The portions that you cannot do easily with your Oracle7 database are:

✔ Automatically adjusting inventory

This requires programming a *database trigger,* which is beyond the scope of this book.

✔ Tallying tax on every sale

You would require a database trigger or an additional tool such as Oracle Forms to calculate tax at the time of the sale.

No part of your Oracle7 basic package allows you to design online data entry screens. Even Personal Oracle7 has no capabilities for data entry screens beyond the default spreadsheet-like tables it presents for editing data. These are crude compared to desktop spreadsheets — the default tables don't even let you sort the data. See Chapter 23 for a list of additional tools that you might want to invest in. See also Appendix A for a list of resources available on the World Wide Web.

Tracking endangered species globally (the hard example)

Tracking endangered species globally is a worthy cause, for sure. If I were creating a database design for the effort, here are the features I would

include:

✔ Information-gathering from around the world using the Internet

✔ Massive text archiving of news articles about both positive and negative activities

✔ Full text search capabilities

✔ Pictures of cute little animals to adopt by sending monthly payments

✔ Letters from cute little animals to their sponsors

- ✔ A Save the Guppies program, with a multibillion-dollar government grant award

- ✔ Engraved identification tags for all card-carrying members of endangered species

- ✔ A clearinghouse of resources available to people and organizations, cross-referenced by needs, skills, locations, and funding

- ✔ Graphic maps showing populations of animals, color-coded by level of danger of extinction

- ✔ Internet search capabilities linked to graphic maps of areas with zoom in, zoom out capabilities from global to local maps

- ✔ Maps that allow you to click on an area and go to a screen with all the data about the animals, resources, organizations, and any other items related to the area that you select on the map

- ✔ Automatic coffee dispensers in every cubicle at state offices

Read Chapters 5 and 6 before diving in and designing your own relational database. Those chapters have invaluable insights on how to put your world into the relational database format. Remember, the best design for your situation might not be the obvious choice.

As you learn more about databases, you will discover that you can fit many pieces of information into the database world. Just remember to let the databases, like art, imitate life. When you start expecting life to imitate your database, it's time to come up for air. You could turn into one of those nerds who write database books.

Chapter 3
SQL*Plus Nuts and Bolts

● ●

● ●

*Y*ou are going to wear out the book flipping to this chapter so often. In this chapter, I cover information that spans about 300 pages of Oracle7 documentation, so you may want to get your coffee pot going, put on your reading glasses, and break out the little tinfoil hat.

This entire chapter is about SQL*Plus. I include lots of examples to review and try out. Be brave. Enjoy yourself. Master the possibilities. If this chapter bores you to tears, consider buying a fancy report writer that connects to Oracle7. SQL*Plus can do a lot, though it is not the best reporting tool on the market. But I have worked with it for years and have survived. If SQL*Plus seems to be malfunctioning, try thinking of the malfunction as a feature, not a bug.

First, I cover some background information about SQL*Plus. Then I show you how to get some great results using this powerful but very basic tool.

How SQL*Plus and SQL Fit Together

What is the difference between SQL and SQL*Plus? Some people theorize that Oracle's marketing department was being cute with the name SQL*Plus. ("Well, guys, it sounds better than plain old SQL!") In reality, a difference definitely exists!

SQL (pronounced sequel) is the standard database query language that all relational databases use to manipulate data. SQL*Plus is a *programming environment* in Oracle7 where you can use SQL.

SQL*Plus is surprisingly easy to use. In fact, learning your way around SQL*Plus is a lot easier than understanding SQL itself.

When you work in SQL*Plus, figuring out where the SQL ends and the SQL*Plus begins is difficult. This is also a bone of contention within the Oracle7 documentation, which is divided between SQL language books and SQL*Plus references, making it difficult to find the answers when you're unclear whether to look under SQL or SQL*Plus. Follow these guidelines to figure out where to look:

SQL Language consists of the following commands:

- Data Definition Language (*DDL*) commands: These create, change, or remove database objects such as users, tables, indexes, columns, views, and so on. Examples of DDL commands are:
  - CREATE TABLE
  - ALTER TABLE
  - GRANT
  - DROP INDEX
- Data Manipulation Language (*DML*) commands: These commands work directly with the data in tables, adding, changing, and deleting data. They also pull data out of the tables. Examples of DML commands are:
  - INSERT
  - UPDATE
  - DELETE
  - SELECT

SQL*Plus consists of all the commands that do these tasks:

- Edit, save, retrieve, and run files of SQL commands.
- Perform report generating tasks, such as:
  - Summarizing.
  - Calculating.
  - Using titles, headers, and footers.
  - Using column titles.
  - Using page breaks.
  - Printing reports or saving results to files.
- Work directly with the Oracle7 procedural programming language, PL/SQL, *without* compiling programs.

✔ Send and receive variable information to and from an end user.

✔ Display the column definitions for any table, view, or synonym in the database.

✔ Copy data between two databases.

Examples of SQL*Plus commands are

✔ COLUMN

✔ TTITLE

✔ BREAK

✔ SET

✔ EDIT

Now that you have a better idea how the two fit together, proceed in SQL*Plus as if there is no distinction between them. You know which reference book to look in (*this* book, of course), and you know which parts you can and cannot use outside of SQL*Plus. For example, you cannot set a title in PO7 Navigator because it is a SQL*Plus command.

SQL*Plus is so old. "How old is it?" you ask. It's so old that you had to crank it by hand to get it started. Then you had to drive it through 20 feet of snow just to get to the terminal, and it was uphill both ways! This is why SQL*Plus to this day uses text command line mode and no mouse. The Personal Oracle7 Navigator puts SQL*Plus in a window. This way, at least you can start and stop, or do a little cut and paste here and there. Even in Navigator, SQL*Plus is still a one-line-at-a-time kind of animal.

Fixing Mistakes, or Where's the Brake?!

When Oracle7 makes a change permanent, it calls this a *commit,* or committing the change. After Oracle7 has committed something, you cannot undo it. Before the commit occurs, you can undo the command with the *rollback* command.

When you use these commands, here's what you tell Oracle7 to do:

✔ COMMIT — save all changes since the last commit was done to the database as permanent.

✔ ROLLBACK — remove all changes since the last commit was done.

The interesting thing about this comes when you look at things in SQL*Plus. Your data looks changed to you, but just like in life, until you commit the changes, all other users (if any) see the old version.

Perhaps I'm jumping the gun, but I think that you should know what you are up against. You'll experiment with a database in the near future, creating and destroying tables just to see what happens. Using SQL*Plus gives you great power, especially when working on the desktop model where you are by default the database administrator (or DBA, for short). Inevitably, you will make mistakes. Most will be minor, but when you make the kind of mistake that makes you gulp down the lump in your throat while murmuring, "Uh-oh," here's a safety net: rollback.

How to use ROLLBACK

If you have made certain kinds of mistakes, like washing your trousers with a peanut butter sandwich in your pocket, you are in need of a kind of help this book cannot provide. If you have made a big mistake, like deleting all your data instead of one row from a database, *do not exit the database.* Exiting generally commits all changes. To reverse the changes, type

```
rollback;
```

Sometimes your SQL*Plus session saves every change you make and you have no chance to rollback. To find out if this is the case for you, type this command into SQL*Plus:

```
show autocommit
```

Oracle7 replies with the status of the autocommit setting. Table 3-1 explains what's going on.

Table 3-1	Show Autocommit Settings
Response from Oracle7	*What Response Means*
AUTOCOMMIT OFF	This lets you use rollback. Commits occur only when you tell it with the COMMIT command, or when you EXIT.
AUTOCOMMIT ON	You cannot rollback with this. All commands are committed immediately upon execution.
AUTOCOMMIT IMMEDIATE	Same as AUTOCOMMIT ON.

The rollback buffer and the commit

Oracle7 has a special holding spot, the roll-back *segment,* where it keeps track of all the changes you make while you run SQL*Plus. The rollback segment is not a janitorial tool, but it does have a shorthand method of tracking all your changes. The changes do not actually occur in the database tables until you tell Oracle7 to commit them, so anyone who looks at the tables while you are changing them sees the unchanged tables. After you commit your changes, users see the changes the next time they look at the tables.

Commands that can't be undone, even with rollback

Regardless of the autocommit setting, some commands have an automatic commit built in. This means that, if you have made some changes that you did not commit yet and you execute one of these commands, those changes get committed automatically. These DML commands change the structure of the database rather than the contents of the tables. Here's a partial list:

- ALTER: You can alter a table, index, or tablespace — plus a few other things.
- CREATE: You create tables, indexes, tablespaces, database links, synonyms, views, and so on.
- DROP: Just about anything you create, you can also drop.
- RENAME: This command changes the name of a table, view, or index.

How to Ask a Question in SQL

In SQL, you ask a question when you write a query. The example queries in this book all begin with SELECT, which is your clue that they're queries. Your best weapon when you look at your data is a good knowledge of the *schema* (your set of tables) and how the schema relate to one another. You may want to read the stuff about diagrams in Chapter 6 and the stuff about keys in Chapter 5 before you go further in this chapter.

Very simply put, anything that goes into tables in the database can come out through using a query. With queries you can also do interesting things, like calculate average sales, find the highest-paid employee, sort by employees' middle initials, and so on.

Here's the magic formula for constructing queries: *Know what you want and where it is.* Knowing the proper syntax (format) of SQL queries also helps. One of the goals of this chapter is to give you a good working knowledge of how to construct some basic SQL*Plus queries for getting data out of a table.

The basic SQL query

A SQL query has five main parts, or clauses:

- ✔ SELECT: Put the list of columns you want to see here. List all the columns, even if they are from several tables. Separate them with commas.

- ✔ FROM: Put the table name here. If you have more than one table, list them all here, separated with commas.

- ✔ WHERE (optional): Put comparisons, limits, and connections between tables here. List them with either AND or OR between each set. When left out, all rows are chosen.

- ✔ GROUP BY (optional): Tell how you want data summarized here. This is only needed for a query that summarizes data. See Chapter 12 for examples of this clause.

- ✔ ORDER BY (optional): List columns to use for sorting here. When left out, rows are returned in no specific order.

A few other clauses can go into a query, but the preceding clauses are the primary ones.

Here's how the five parts all fit together into a single SQL query:

```
select column , column , ...
from table
where clause
group by clause
order by clause
```

Sampling some queries

Pretend that you are an art dealer with ten artists around the country. You want a list of all your artists, showing their first name, their city of residence, and their creative specialty. The query looks like this:

```
select FIRST_NAME, CITY, SPECIALTY
from ARTIST;
```

Three columns are chosen from one table. The results may look like this:

```
FIRST_NAME CITY                SPECIALTY
---------------------------------------------------------------
Lina       Lone Rock           OTHER
Nikki      Makawao             ACRYLIC
Lorri      Madison             WATERCOLOR
Robert     Salt Lake City      MIXED MEDIA
Thomas     Madison             OIL
Stephen    Makawao             MIXED ON PAPER
Ken        Marin County        DIGITAL
Sherry     San Francisco       WATERCOLOR
Terence                        DIGITAL
Sharron    San Francisco       DIGITAL

10 rows selected.
```

You want the list in alphabetical order, so you add an ORDER BY clause like this:

```
select FIRST_NAME, CITY, SPECIALTY
from ARTIST
order by FIRST_NAME;
```

You then sort the results in ascending alphabetical order by first name:

```
FIRST_NAME CITY                SPECIALTY
---------------------------------------------------------------
Ken        Marin County        DIGITAL
Lina       Lone Rock           OTHER
Lorri      Madison             WATERCOLOR
Nikki      Makawao             ACRYLIC
Robert     Salt Lake City      MIXED MEDIA
Sharron    San Francisco       DIGITAL
Sherry     San Francisco       WATERCOLOR
Stephen    Makawao             MIXED ON PAPER
Terence                        DIGITAL
Thomas     Madison             OIL
```

Suppose you want only the artists who paint with watercolor. Add the WHERE clause to narrow down your selection. The WHERE clause comes between the FROM clause and the ORDER BY clause. When using a word or phrase in the WHERE clause, you enclose it in single quotes. Any entry other than a number must be in single quotes. Otherwise, Oracle7 assumes that the entry is a column name.

```
select FIRST_NAME, CITY, SPECIALTY
from ARTIST
where SPECIALTY = 'WATERCOLOR'
order by FIRST_NAME;
```

Oracle7 looks for rows that have WATERCOLOR in the SPECIALTY column and then sorts the rows in proper order.

```
FIRST_NAME   CITY              SPECIALTY
------------------------------------------------------------
Lorri        Madison           WATERCOLOR
Sherry       San Francisco     WATERCOLOR
```

Some tips to help you write good queries

These tips may help you write good queries. Some of these tips are guidelines, or hints for "good form." Others are simply possibilities — options you have available that you may not be aware of.

✔ List columns in the sequence they appear in your report. The SELECT clause is your only chance to specify which column comes first, second, and so on.

✔ Use the asterisk to select all the columns in a table to save yourself some typing time when you need all the columns (in the sequence they appear in your table) in your query.

```
SELECT * from ARTIST;
```

✔ List columns in the order you sort them. This is not a requirement, but it is logical — like listing people's names in the phone book with their last name first to facilitate quick visual searching.

```
select COUNTRY, CITY, STREET ...
order by COUNTRY, CITY, STREET
```

✔ Add words or phrases in your select statement if you need them to make your report clearer. For instance:

```
select 'My name is', NAME
from ARTIST;
```

✔ Sort by multiple columns if you need to do so. List the columns in the ORDER BY clause. For example:

```
... ORDER BY COUNTRY, CITY, STREET
```

✔ Oracle7 is sensitive to uppercase and lowercase in the words or phrases you place inside single quotes.

```
... where SPECIALTY = 'Watercolor'
```

The preceding phrase is not the same as the following one.

```
... where SPECIALTY = 'WATERCOLOR'
```

✔ Oracle7 does not differentiate between uppercase and lowercase for column names, table names, and the SELECT statement clauses.

```
SELECT CITY FROM ARTIST
```

The query above is identical to the one below.

```
select city from artist
```

In fact, you can mix and match, which I do all the time, and Oracle7 sees it as the same as the other two above!

```
select CITY from ARTIST
```

✔ Oracle7 does not care how you arrange your query as far as blank spaces and line breaks are concerned.

```
select CITY, SPECIALTY from ARTIST order by CITY
```

The preceding query, to Oracle7, is identical to the following one.

```
select CITY, SPECIALTY
from ARTIST
order by CITY
```

This tip is purely for aesthetics: My personal preference is to start each clause (SELECT, FROM, WHERE, and ORDER BY) on a new line.

Using an Editor While Running SQL*Plus

I call my editor to beg for a deadline extension. You can call an editor to save files, edit files, and start up files from within SQL*Plus. The following are the editing commands.

✔ EDIT — opens up a temporary file and starts up the local text editor for the current SQL query.

✔ SAVE *filename* — saves the current SQL query in a file. You replace *filename* with the actual filename, and if you want, include the path and suffix.

✔ GET `filename` — retrieves a SQL query from the file you name. The file must be one SQL statement make; for example, a select statement, or an update statement.

✔ START `filename` — retrieves a file and runs it in the current SQL*Plus session. The file can include both SQL commands and formatting commands, like TTITLE, COLUMN, and SPOOL.

✔ LIST — lists your current SQL command.

Pulling Data Out without Breaking Anything

"Don't touch that! I said don't! You broke it! Are you happy?!" Do these phrases sound familiar? If so, you may have a nagging hesitation about constructing a new query.

Don't worry. Data is *never* changed when you run a query — *never*. You may slow the entire company to a halt and black out the lights on a city block, but the data is okay.

I lie awake nights worrying that you might break your fingers if you spend a lot of time typing in long, involved queries. When this insomnia occurs, I just slip on my handy (you guessed it) little tinfoil hat to filter out evil thoughts. In an effort to save your fingers, I want to share with you the secret of the alias. An *alias* is an alternate name for a table or a column in a query. Using aliases in the FROM clause of a query saves typing.

An alias is defined by placing it immediately after the table name and is separated from the table name by a space. In the following partial query, A is the alias for the ARTIST table.

```
select A.FIRST_NAME, B.ARTWORK_TITLE
FROM ARTIST A, ARTWORK B
where A.ARTIST_ID = B.ARTIST_ID
```

Combining Tables — The Meat and Potatoes of SQL*Plus

When a query combines data from two different tables, it is called a *join,* or *joining tables.* The key to joining tables is — the *key!* Know your tables, their keys, and how they connect together. I've created examples for you, beginning with simple ones and moving on to more complex ones.

Basic join query structure

The basic structure of a join is the same as that for any other query. The primary difference is that you list columns from several tables in the SELECT clause and you list several tables in the WHERE clause and tell SQL*Plus how they fit together in the WHERE clause. Here's the basic layout:

```
select alias1.column , alias2.column , ...
from table alias1, table alias2, ...
where alias1.column = alias2.column
and where clause
group by clause
order by clause
```

A table *alias* (indicated in the query above as alias1 and alias2) assigns each table in the FROM clause a shorthand nickname. Use the alias (followed by a period) as an identifier to show which table is the source of each column in the other parts of the query (the SELECT, WHERE, GROUP BY, and ORDER BY clauses). While a table alias is not technically required, I find it important for creating clear and easy-to-follow join queries.

The next section shows several examples of join queries in action. As a general rule of thumb, the more tables you add to a query, the more complex the WHERE clause becomes.

Build your query gradually by starting off with one table in the query and getting it to run. Next, add one more table and get it working with two tables. Build on to the query, always stopping to test your results to make sure that your query still works. This way, if you do run into problems, figuring out what part of the query caused the problem — most likely, where you made your most recent change — is much easier. This simple technique saves hours of guesswork over constructing an entire query and then trying to figure out which part does not work.

Examples of join queries

Now for the fun part! Imagine that you are a mermaid. You have categorized and catalogued your fantastic collection of rare seaweeds in your Oracle7 tables. You have two tables, one called TYPE_OF_SEAWEED for the kind of seaweed, and one called SEAWEED_SAMPLE for each unique specimen in your collection. Figure 3-1 shows the two tables, their relationship, and sample data.

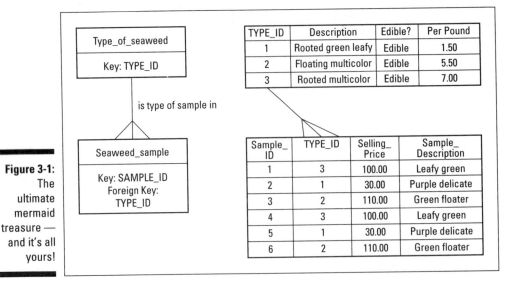

Figure 3-1:
The
ultimate
mermaid
treasure —
and it's all
yours!

You want a simple report that lists the seaweed samples and shows whether or not they are edible. Here's the SQL code:

```
select SS.SAMPLE_ID, SS.SELLING_PRICE,
SS.SAMPLE_DESCRIPTION, TS.EDIBLE
from SEAWEED_SAMPLE SS, TYPE_OF_SEAWEED TS
where TS.TYPE_ID = SS.TYPE_ID
order by SS.SAMPLE_ID;
```

Here are the results:

```
SAMPLE_ID    SELLING_PRICE    SAMPLE_DESCRIPTION    EDIBLE
---------    -------------    ------------------    ----------
1            100              Leafy green           INEDIBLE
2            30               Purple delicate       EDIBLE
3            110              Green floater         EDIBLE
4            100              Leafy green           INEDIBLE
5            30               Purple delicate       EDIBLE
6            110              Green floater         EDIBLE
```

Your seaweed is in big demand because of the tidal wave that wiped out all the seaweed farms in the area. You begin selling your seaweed collection. You want to keep track of those who buy from you, in case you want to send them a flyer next year, so you add a table called CLIENT into your database. Now you have three tables, as shown in Figure 3-2. You add a new column into the SEAWEED_SAMPLE table, which is a foreign key to the CLIENT table. (If you don't know what a foreign key is, look it up in Chapter 5.)

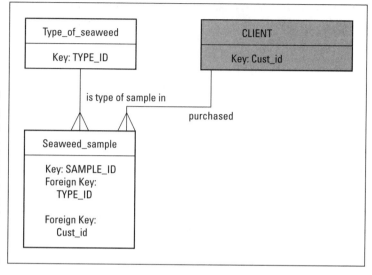

Figure 3-2:
The
entrepre-
neurial
mermaid
now tracks
clients who
buy her
seaweed
samples.

This query combines all three tables:

```
select SAMPLE_ID, TS.EDIBLE, C.NAME
from SEAWEED_SAMPLE SS, TYPE_OF_SEAWEED TS, client c
where TS.TYPE_ID = SS.TYPE_ID
and SS.CUST_ID = C.CUST_ID;
```

The results look something like this:

```
SAMPLE_ID EDIBLE       NAME
------------------------------------------------------------------
        1 INEDIBLE     Jane
        4 INEDIBLE     Jane
        3 EDIBLE       Joe
        6 EDIBLE       Joe
        2 EDIBLE       Harry
        5 EDIBLE       Amy
```

The results show a list of the samples, which types of seaweed are edible, which are inedible, and which of your little mermaid friends bought the sample. You are such an enterprising mermaid!

Now you have gone through several exercises where you have seen how to use SQL*Plus commands to get a basic report out of the database.

See Chapter 12 for more examples and lots more extras to make your reports look great. Chapter 4 shows you how to use SQL*Plus (and PO7 Navigator) to make changes to the data stored in an Oracle7 table.

Chapter 4

Using the Personal Oracle7 Navigator

In This Chapter

▶ Starting the PO7 Navigator
▶ Reading about the basics
▶ Viewing table contents
▶ Changing current rows
▶ Adding new rows
▶ Changing table structure
▶ Confronting commitment issues
▶ Finding out what *voilà!* really means
▶ Deleting unwanted rows

The Personal Oracle7 Navigator (PO7 Navigator) offers great service, helping you create tables, view all items in the database, add rows, and change data in tables. The graphical icon style lets you review the entire database quickly. This chapter reviews how to insert, update, and delete rows from your database using PO7 Navigator.

You can find out about creating tables using PO7 Navigator in Chapter 9 and creating indexes using PO7 Navigator in Chapter 16. The PO7 Navigator is covered in many other chapters, too. You can check the index to find the location of specific PO7 Navigator topics.

PO7 Navigator is a great tool for creating tables, indexes, even new users. You can make changes to the data inside your tables, too. If you have PO7 Navigator, you can choose for yourself whether to use SQL*Plus or PO7 Navigator for these tasks. However, some tasks can be done in only one or the other of these two tools. Tasks that are unique to PO7 Navigator are

✔ Creating projects that contain groups of tables, users, programs or applications that you create

✔ Creating and maintaining database connections

Tasks that can be done in SQL*Plus but not in PO7 Navigator include

✔ Making reports

✔ Looking at your data online in sorted order

✔ Updating, inserting, or deleting many rows of data at once

Note: The Personal Oracle7 Navigator was renamed the Oracle Navigator for Oracle7.3. However, I refer to the item as the Personal Oracle7 Navigator (or PO7 Navigator, for short) throughout this book. Most of my instructions work for both versions. And if you have Oracle7.3, your screens may look a little different than those in this book.

Starting PO7 Navigator

Start up the PO7 Navigator and then set up a database connection. I cover both of these procedures in other chapters. Because it's a simple procedure, I describe how to start the PO7 Navigator here. Read "Creating a Database Session for Yourself" in Chapter 8 to find out how to create a database connection. After a database connection is established, you can experiment with the PO7 Navigator features that I discuss in this chapter.

All you have to do is start PO7 Navigator from the program icons.

1. **If you are using Windows 95, select Start⇨Programs.**

2. **Choose Personal Oracle7 for Windows 95.**

3. **Select Personal Oracle7 Navigator as shown in Figure 4-1.**

Starting PO7 Navigator varies from platform to platform. After you are inside PO7 Navigator, the steps for using it are the same, even though the *window* (the area where PO7 is placed) may look a little different.

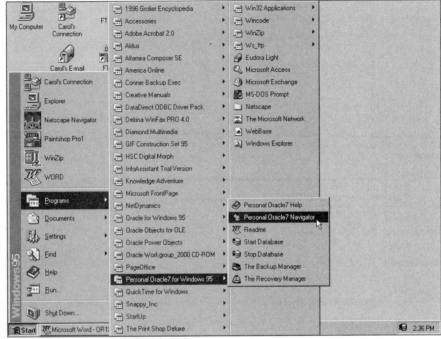

Figure 4-1:
In Windows
95 you
select the
PO7
Navigator
from a maze
of other
programs.

Viewing Your Tables

You may want to look at what your co-workers have created in Oracle7. Or perhaps you've just installed Oracle7 on your desktop and want to poke around to see what's there for you to use in the demonstration tables.

Viewing the contents of a table is just a mouse click away. Here are the steps:

1. **Start Personal Oracle7 Navigator.**

2. **Double-click the database connection for the owner of the table.**

3. **Double-click the table icon to see a list of the tables.**

Figure 4-2 shows an example of a list of tables.

Click on the Name column heading to arrange the tables in alphabetical order.

4. **Double-click the table you wish to view.**

Voilà! The table rows appear in a spreadsheet-style window. Use the mouse or the Tab key to move around within this window (see Figure 4-3).

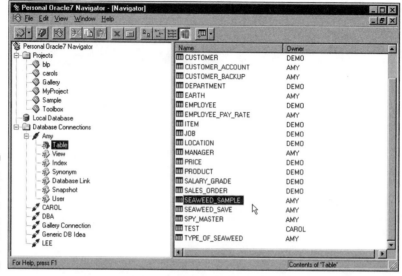

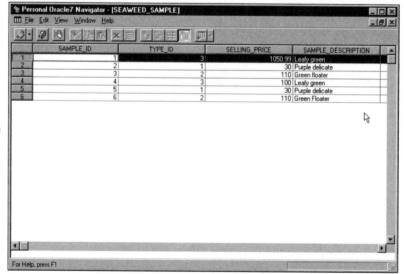

Updating Your Data the Mouse Way

After you have created your own tables (or are in good graces with the people who have their own tables), you will undoubtedly find times when you need to change some data in those tables.

The initial steps to update data are the same as looking at the tables:

1. **Start Personal Oracle7 Navigator.**

2. **Double-click the database connection for the owner of the table.**

3. **Double-click the table icon to see a list of the tables.**

   Figure 4-2 shows an example of a list of tables.

4. **Double-click the table you wish to view.**

   The table's rows appear in a spreadsheet-style window. Use your mouse or the Tab key to move around within this window (refer to Figure 4-3). You can update the data in any column and row that you see in the window.

5. **Make the appropriate click on the box where you want to make a change and type.**

   • Double-click to place the mouse inside the existing text. Now you can add to the data or modify it.

   • Single-click to highlight the whole entry so that anything you type replaces the entry. For example, you might click on the box for Jane's Address (first row, third column in Figure 4-4) and type **400 West Main Street** (Jane's address).

Figure 4-4:
Save your
changes
with a right-
click of the
mouse.

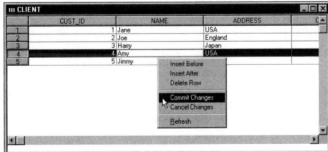

6. **After you are done, save your changes.**

   Oracle7 gives you two options:

   • Right-click and select Commit Changes (see Figure 4-4). This method leaves you in the same spreadsheet-style window. Your mouse must be outside the current row (the row with the high-lighted columns) when you right-click. Otherwise, you get the text-editing sub-menu.

   • Exit the window (click the *X* in the upper-right corner). Oracle7 asks you if you want to save your changes (see Figure 4-5). Click Yes to save your changes.

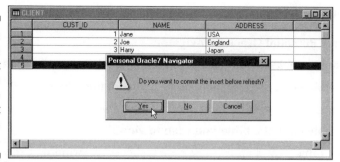

Moving into Inserts

A table with no data is like a teacup with no tea! Adding new rows to a table is called *inserting* rows in SQL parlance. Here's how to insert new rows in good ol' PO7 Navigator:

1. **Start PO7 Navigator.**

2. **Double-click the database connection for the owner of the table.**

3. **Double-click the table icon to see a list of the tables.**

4. **Double-click the table you wish to view.**

   The table rows appear in the now-familiar spreadsheet-style window.

5. **Click any row.**

6. **Right-click and select Insert Before or Insert After from the pop-up menu that appears.**

   Either one of these opens up a new row in your table and puts the cursor into a column. Insert Before places the new row above the row that your mouse is near, and Insert After places the new row after the row that your mouse is near.

7. **Type in the value for the column, as shown in Figure 4-6.**

   • Use the Tab key to move from one column to the next.

   • Use the Shift+Tab keys to move back a column.

8. **Press the Enter key after you're finished editing.**

9. **Save the new row the same way you save updates — by using either of these two methods:**

   • Right-click and select Commit Insert (see Figure 4-7).

   • Exit the spreadsheet by clicking on the *X* in the upper-right corner (in Windows 95) and then telling Oracle7 to save your changes when it asks (refer to Figure 4-5).

Figure 4-6:
Type data
into the
boxes to
add a new
row.

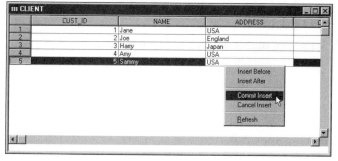

Figure 4-7:
Commit
inserts by
selecting
Commit
Insert.

Deleting a Row

After inserting and updating rows, you may find that you have a row that you no longer want in your table. Removing, or deleting, a row is just a few mouse clicks away. Go to the spreadsheet view of the table. Do this by following these steps:

1. **Start PO7 Navigator.**

2. **Double-click the database connection for the owner of the table.**

3. **Double-click the table icon to see a list of the tables.**

4. **Double-click the table you wish to view.**

    You guessed! That spreadsheet-style window appears. Now to delete a row.

5. **Move the mouse to the row you want to delete.**

    Use the scroll bars on the right side of the window to find the row.

6. **Click a row to select it.**

7. **Right-click and select Delete Row from the pop-up menu that appears, as shown in Figure 4-8.**

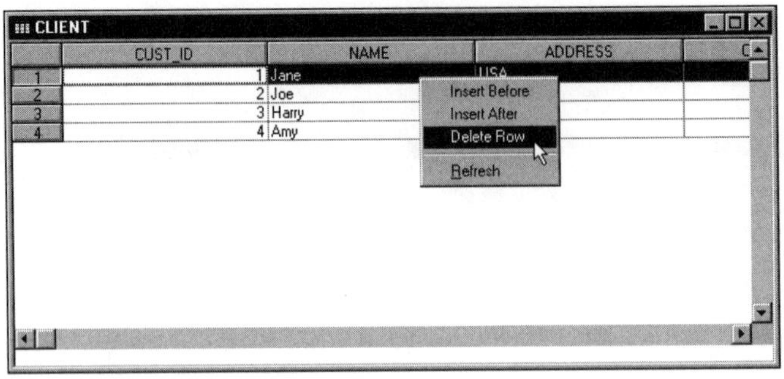

Figure 4-8:
Delete a
row by
selecting
Delete Row.

PO7 Navigator asks you again if you really, really, really want to commit
this and delete the row.

8. Click the Yes button and you are home free.

Part II
Getting Started

The 5th Wave · By Rich Tennant

"I TOLD HIM WE WERE LOOKING FOR SOFTWARE THAT WOULD GIVE US GREATER PRODUCTIVITY, SO HE SOLD ME A SPREADSHEET THAT CAME WITH THESE SIGNS."

In this part...

Databases don't grow on trees. They are carefully (or carelessly) grown from an idea hatched in the mind of some crazed genius, namely you. Perhaps you don't actually do the creating. This means you are at the mercy of the whims of some other crazed genius. This section is your mini-lesson on database design and the inner workings of Oracle7. It helps you answer these burning questions:

- ✔ If I put data into these tables, should I buy another hard drive?

- ✔ Who am I and what is my role in the world?

- ✔ What the heck did Joe Programmer/Analyst do six months ago?

Once you've discovered that there is some method to the madness, I'll show you step by step how to create a new Oracle7 user. Enough theory, now get down to business and do something.

Chapter 5

The Relational Model and You

*T*his chapter gives you the information and the self-esteem needed to create really terrific tables and join them together into a relational database. While you are playing matchmaker and creating relationships between these tables, keep in mind how you're really going to use this stuff once you're on your own.

Redundant Relational Database Redundancy

Imagine you are at your doctor's office with a sprained wrist. The reception-ist gives you a clipboard holding a long yellow form. You dutifully but sloppily begin to fill it out using your left hand because your right wrist is sprained. You fill in your name, last name first, and address. Then, you fill it in again in the next section of the form. By the time you reach the third section in which you read "Patient's name and address," your right wrist is throbbing and your left hand is cramped. You leap up and yell, "I hate repeating myself! I hate repeating myself! I hate repeating myself!" The receptionist calmly replies, "Perhaps you would like to file a complaint. Please fill in your name and address on this form in triplicate."

Most likely, the database that stores the information on that yellow form is not a relational database. Relational databases are famous for saving time, space, and wrists by minimizing repeated data. Data lives in one table and has a key. Other tables retrieve that data with the key. Here's how relational databases minimize repeated data:

At the doctor's office, the database requires your name and address for three reasons, even though in 90% of the cases the name and address are identical:

- ✔ The name and address of the patient
- ✔ The name and address of the person paying the bill
- ✔ The name and address of the person with insurance for the patient

The old style of collecting this data would require you to fill in the name and address three times. The computer operator would then key the data into three separate data files (see Figure 5-1).

The modern, relational database style works like this:

The form looks the same, except a check box appears next to the second and third parts where your name and address is requested. You just put a check into the check box if your entry would be the same as the name and address you just filled in. Figure 5-2 depicts the relationship.

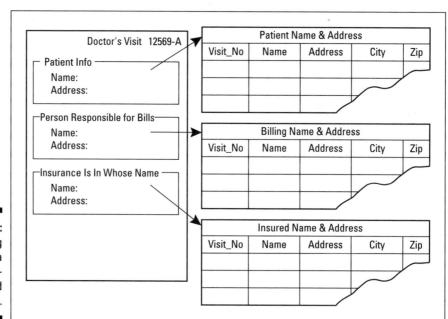

Figure 5-1:
Collecting data the old-fashioned way.

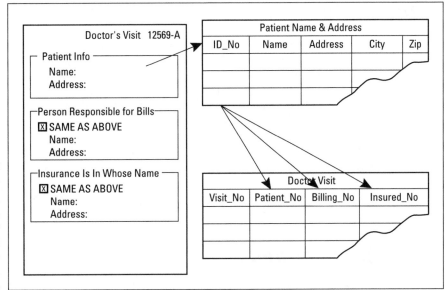

Figure 5-2:
Modern,
streamlined,
fancy
relational
database
stuff.

The database has one table for both name and address. The operator keys it in once, and the database assigns a *key* — a column or set of columns that identifies rows in a table. Another table tracks the doctor visit and contains a column for the key of the row with the patient's name and address. Another column gets the key for the billing name and address. A third column has the key for the insured name and address. Relational databases have many advantages:

- ✔ The name and address are only written once by the patient.

- ✔ The name and address are only entered once into the database.

- ✔ Any time the same patient returns, the same name and address can be used without any repeated typing.

- ✔ Changes to the name and address are entered once and affect all three tables automatically.

- ✔ If the names and addresses are different for the patient, billing party, or insured person, the database handles the differences without making special exceptions. Very simply, the second address is a new row in the Patient Name & Address table, and this new ID goes into the appropriate column in the Doctor Visit table.

Keys Rule

When you think of a key, you probably picture your house key, or perhaps the key to your Jaguar. Without that key, you can admire your Jaguar like all the other poor schmucks on your block, but you cannot drive it. If you lose your key, you have to get a new one made. You may even have to change the locks so that you have a totally new key and the old key no longer works. Database keys have similar attributes:

- ✔ Keys are very important in locating a particular row within a table.

- ✔ Keys get you quickly and directly inside a table.

- ✔ If you lose the key to a table, you must replace it. Losing the key to a table is unlikely, although possible.

Types of keys

Three kinds of keys are used in relational databases:

- ✔ **Primary key:** This is the kingpin of all keys. The primary key may be one column or a set of columns. In all cases, the primary key contains a value that is *unique* across all the rows in that table. If you know the primary key value, you can single out one row in a table, regardless of how many rows the table contains. A primary key for tables is like a Social Security number for U.S. citizens. A single column that contains an ID number is the best kind of primary key for fast retrieval of data.

- ✔ **Foreign key:** A key that resides in one table but is the key to a different table is called a foreign key. The primary key of the connected table is kept in the foreign key column in the other table. Perfectly clear, right? See the "Importing foreign keys" section in this chapter for more details.

- ✔ **Alternate key:** The primary key identifies each row in a table. Sometimes you have a second way to identify a unique row. This second way is called an alternate key and is a column or set of columns just like the primary key.

Importing foreign keys

A foreign key lives in a table for only one reason: The foreign key connects the table to another table. Like a foreign country's diplomat, a foreign key represents its entire country; that is, its entire table. By plugging a foreign key into a table, you make a link to all the information stored in the other table. Strategic and careful use of foreign keys requires logic and common sense, and sometimes experimentation. Be sure to declare all contraband when you pass through Customs. Search and detention can be unpleasant.

Imagine that you're a baker and you make ten kinds of bread. Each one has a price and many different ingredients. Your database administrator (every baker has one) designed two tables for you, one for the bread and one for the ingredients. Each of these tables has a primary key. The BREAD table has a key called BREAD_NO and the INGREDIENT table's primary key is INGREDIENT_NO. To calculate the cost of a loaf of bread, you ask your database administrator to create a third table, the RECIPE table, where you have your head baker enter the ingredients and the amount of each ingredient for the bread. The three tables are diagrammed in Figure 5-3. The diagram shown in the figure is a classic type of diagram used when designing relational databases. It's called an Entity Relationship Diagram, or ERD.

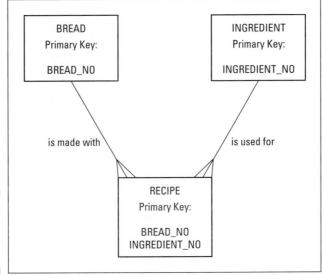

Figure 5-3:
Bakers
knead more
dough.

After dusting off the keyboard and the computer screen, you discover that your head baker has left some data you can use in the tables. Figure 5-4 shows you the three tables in Oracle7.

Now you're probably wondering how to calculate the profit (selling price minus cost) of each kind of bread. By reading each table's foreign key connections, you can determine that Nutty Banana Bread costs $3.54 to make. You're selling it for $3.25, so it must be your "loss leader." Go ahead. Break out your calculator. Do the math. I'll show you the calculation for the first ingredient in Nutty Banana Bread. Follow along with me by looking at Figure 5-4.

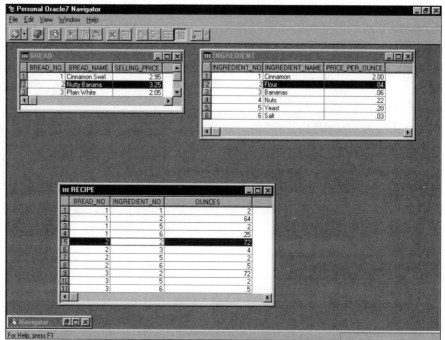

Figure 5-4:
Three great
tables show
their wares.

- ✔ Nutty Banana Bread has a primary key of 2.

- ✔ Look at the RECIPE table; the fifth through the eighth rows have 2 in the foreign key in the BREAD_NO column.

- ✔ Reading across the fifth row, there is a 2 in the foreign key column called INGREDIENT_NO.

- ✔ Going to the INGREDIENT table, you see that Flour has a primary key of 2, and reading across that row, you find the cost of flour is $.04 per ounce.

- ✔ Multiplying the cost, $.04, by the amount, 72 ounces, gives you the cost of the first ingredient: $2.88.

For more foreign key goodies, see Chapter 21.

Giving the foreign key columns the same names as the corresponding primary key columns, as illustrated in the baker example above, clearly defines the relationships. In fact, many software tools generate SQL match tables by looking for identical column names. This is known as the "My other brother Darryl" convention, and you probably want to adhere to it. Appendix A has some tools that can help, such as Oracle Designer/2000.

Shuffling Columns: A Judgment Call

Here's a puzzle: You want to enter both local and long-distance phone numbers into your address book database. Your left brain says, "Logic dictates that each part of the phone number should be a separate column!" Your right brain, being holistic by nature, says, "No! The whole phone number should be in one column." Then, your third eye says, in a booming and authoritative voice, "Better yet, put everything except the extension numbers in one column." Figure 5-5 shows your choices laid out in a perfectly clear diagram.

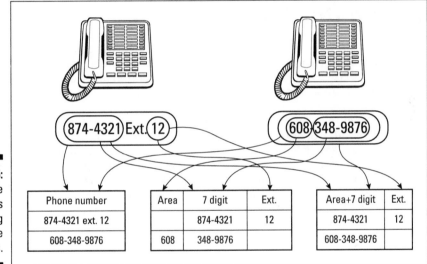

Figure 5-5:
The choices for entering phone numbers.

Phone number
874-4321 ext. 12
608-348-9876

Area	7 digit	Ext.
	874-4321	12
608	348-9876	

Area+7 digit	Ext.
874-4321	12
608-348-9876	

Actually, all three answers are correct. Use your common sense to help you determine which choice makes the most sense for you. Break things up into more than one column when:

- ✔ Pieces derive meaning by themselves.

- ✔ You need to separate a part of the data from the rest.

- ✔ You need to search on a part of the data in a query.

    Imagine the part number for the left-handed watches you assemble is split into three parts. The first two digits show the location of the manufacturer's plant. The next two describe the part, and the final four digits are a serial number. Chapter 19 has more about these kinds of columns when they're used in the primary key.

Combine things into one column when:

- ✔ You nearly always use the two parts together, such as the first three digits and the last four digits of a phone number, or the three parts of a social security number.
- ✔ A repeated column exists.

See the next two sections in this chapter for more about columns.

The Key, the Whole Key, and Nothing but the Key

The heading of this section is the database designer's battle cry. The heading is also a cute summary of the most common style of relational databases, the so-called, much maligned, often imitated, never duplicated *third normal form*.

The gurus who dreamt up relational database theory were very strange. Their idea of normal does not fit in with the average guy's dream date. They have many definitions of normal, starting with the first normal form, and ending somewhere around the 49th normal form. Even the nerds in the software development department gave up after the third one. So, that's how you get third normal form. They never even touched my personal definition of normal, which is 98.6 degrees Fahrenheit.

Here's a breakdown of the third normal form, the normalization rules for primary keys:

1. **The key:** This means that every column in a table and all of the data in that column must relate to the key of the table.

2. **The whole key:** Each column and its data must apply to the entire key, not just part of it.

3. **Nothing but the key:** Every column and its data must relate to the key and not to any other columns in the table.

Here are some real-life database examples.

"Old MacDonald had a farm. E-I-E-I-O. And on that farm he had some cows, E-I-E-I-O."

The table you see in Figure 5-6 breaks rule number one. The FARM_ADDRESS and OWNER columns do not directly relate to the BAD_COW primary key, COW_ID_NO. You can move FARM_ADDRESS and OWNER to a table called FARM as in Figure 5-7. This solves the problem that you run into when you have a change of address or owner for one of the farms in the FARM table. If you leave the address in this BAD_COW table, you have lots of rows to change. If you keep it in a separate table, FARM, you have only one row to change.

Figure 5-6:
The
BAD_COW
violates
Normalization
Rule #1: the
key.

COW_ID_NO	GALLONS_OF_MILK	FARM_ADDRESS	WEIGHT	OWNER
1	1000	RR1 Platteville, WI	1500	Granny Smith
2	1200	RR1 Platteville WI	1450	Granny Smith
3	1345	RR1 Platteville WI	1240	Granny Smith
4	1100	PO Box 120 Asheville, NC	1300	George Taylor
5	1230	PO Box 120 Asheville, NC	1050	George Taylor

(BAD_COW window)

"Peas porridge hot, peas porridge cold, peas porridge in the pot, nine days old."

The table in Figure 5-8 violates rule number two: the whole key. In this case, the key is two columns, FIRST_NAME and FOOD. The TEMPERATURE and FOOD_AGE columns relate to both columns in the key, but the PERSON_AGE column relates only to the first column in the key. Figure 5-9 shows how to correct this. PERSON_AGE moves to a table called PERSON where FIRST_NAME is the primary key. This prevents you having to repeat data in the FOOD_PREFERENCE that really belongs in the PERSON table. If a person's age changes, you only need to change it in the PERSON table. Otherwise, you chase around in the FOOD_PREFERENCE table to update it there, too.

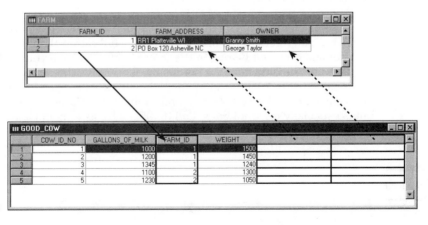

Figure 5-7:
The
GOOD_COW
and FARM
tables
comply with
Normalization
Rule #1: the
key.

Figure 5-8:
FOOD_
PREFERENCE
is out of
alignment
with
Normalization
Rule #2: the
whole key.

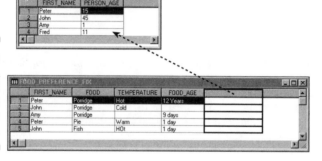

	FIRST_NAME	FOOD	TEMPERATURE	FOOD_AGE	PERSON_AGE
1	Peter	Porridge	Hot	12 Years	15
2	John	Porridge	Cold		45
3	Amy	Porridge		9 days	1
4	Peter	Pie	Warm	1 day	15
5	John	Fish	HOt	1 day	45

Figure 5-8:
FOOD_
PREFERENCE
is out of
alignment
with
Normalization
Rule #2: the
whole key.

PERSON

	FIRST_NAME	PERSON_AGE
1	Peter	15
2	John	45
3	Amy	1
4	Fred	11

Figure 5-9:
FOOD_
PREFERENCE
now has no
out-of-place
columns.

FOOD_PREFERENCE_FIX

	FIRST_NAME	FOOD	TEMPERATURE	FOOD_AGE	
1	Peter	Porridge	Hot	12 Years	
2	John	Porridge	Cold		
3	Amy	Porridge		9 days	
4	Peter	Pie	Warm	1 day	
5	John	Fish	HOt	1 day	

"Baa-baa, black sheep, have you any wool?"

"Yes, sir, yes, sir, three bags full. One for my Master and one for my Dame, and one for the little lad who lives down the lane."

The table in Figure 5-10 violates the third rule: nothing but the key. The OWNER column refers to the sheep's bags of wool rather than to the sheep. This column does not belong in the SHEEP table. Because you put it in the wrong table, the data inside is confusing. It contains three owners. Common sense says that a column called OWNER in a table called SHEEP has the owner of the sheep in it. To fix it, create a new table that relates to the SHEEP table but is especially for wool bags. Call it WOOL_BAG, as I did in Figure 5-11, which shows a diagram of the two tables.

Figure 5-10:
The black
sheep of
the family
breaks
Normalization
Rule #3

SHEEP

	SHEEP_NAME	WOOL_COLOR	NUMBER_OF_BAGS	OWNER_OF_BAGS
1	BAA-BAA	BLACK	3	Master, Dame, Little Lad

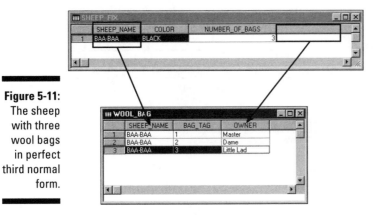

Figure 5-11:
The sheep
with three
wool bags
in perfect
third normal
form.

One to Many: The Bread and Butter of Relational Databases

The concept is delightfully simple. Don't repeat the same column inside one row. Move it to a new table. Or else.

You're tracking all the recycled materials collected in your community by two recycling companies. You create a table (Figure 5-12) which has columns like Material_1, Material_2, and Material_3.

Figure 5-12:
Recyclers
recycle
recycled
materials.

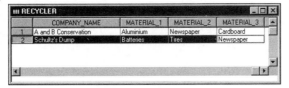

You may already see a problem brewing. What if A&B Conservation starts recycling glass? You have to make big changes whenever the data changes. Maybe you can get extra pay for working overtime.

A better way to handle this problem is with a single column for all the recycled material. This column moves into a separate table so that each new material gets a new row. Figure 5-13 shows the two tables that evolve from this revolutionary change.

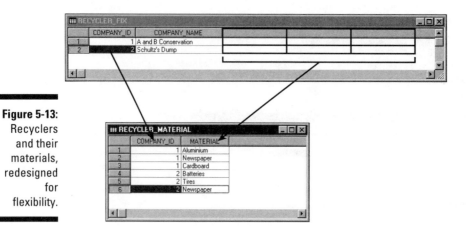

Figure 5-13:
Recyclers
and their
materials,
redesigned
for
flexibility.

This setup makes adding an endless list of recycled materials to either company's repertoire possible. Now you have lots of rows instead of many columns. You have moved repetitive columns out of one table and into their own table so that you have a constant, rather than an increasing, number of columns, and an ever-increasing number of rows. This setup works much better because you are not required to make any changes to your table's design as new information is added. It's very flexible. It's the backbone of every relational database. Maybe you can get extra pay for saving on overtime. If you are working as a civil servant, just ignore my last suggestion and continue what you were doing. Just kidding!

Chapter 6

Diagramming Your World

. . . .

. . . .

*U*sing a pencil and paper may seem like a step backward in this paperless world. Sometimes, however, they're the perfect tools for the job. I would love to see you sit down and diagram your tables so that you understand how they all fit together, and so that you can clearly communicate your understanding. You can diagram tables even if they already exist in a database, which will help you later on when you are creating complex queries. You can refer to your diagram and get a clear picture of how to connect your tables together in the query. Chapter 15 goes over queries.

This chapter gives you the basics on tree diagrams, the easiest and clearest method of depicting a database *schema* (set of related tables). You don't have to be an artist to create nice tree diagrams. The tree diagram is also called the *Entity Relationship Diagram* (ERD). It's an industry standard for the design of relational databases.

Confidentially, I am not all that attached to pencil and paper. You can use your Microsoft Paintbrush program (or any similar kind of drawing software) to create diagrams easily. If you want to get fancier and faster, you can get diagramming software like ERWin or Oracle Designer/2000. Any way you slice it, a diagram is the best way to describe your schema to others (and yourself) quickly.

If you do use pencil and paper, you may want to buy a template that has cutouts of different-sized squares. Use the template to trace your boxes and use the edge of it to draw your lines. You can find a selection of these templates at most art stores or drafting supply stores.

Getting Something Down on Paper

The first step is always the hardest one. For starters, I suggest you put a rough draft of your relational database tables (your schema) down on paper. Once you do that, you can tweak, erase, add, cut, paste, twiddle, and twaddle all day long. Getting a start lets you know where you are. After all, you need to know where you are before you can get where you're going. Figure 6-1 shows a typical first-cut diagram. Only a few boxes and lines exist at this point.

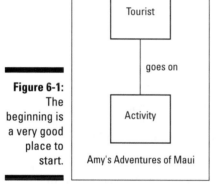

Figure 6-1:
The beginning is a very good place to start.

Here are the simple basics for creating a database on paper:

- **A box with a label:** Symbolizes one piece or a set of pieces of information that you want to keep track of using a database. You may want to use a noun or noun phrase to label the box. This is called an *entity* in the diagram. The entity later (usually) becomes a table in your database.

- **A line with a label connecting two boxes:** Signifies a relationship between the two boxes. You may want to use a verb or verb phrase to describe the relationship.

As depicted in Figure 6-1, Amy's Adventures of Maui is a small business that books tourists for fun activities around the island, such as snorkeling, whale watching, and sunburning. Amy wants to keep track of all the fun activities, the dates she plans to schedule them, the tourists already booked, and the tourists who are potential customers. At first glance, the two main categories Amy wants to track are the tourists and the activities. A tourist goes on an activity, so the line representing the relationship between the two boxes could be labeled *goes on*.

Try not to worry about getting every detail down at first, and just allow the diagramming process to evolve. Typically, the database design cycle (Figure 6-2) starts with too few details, the "Duh!" phase, moves to the over-complicated phase, the "Sucker Doesn't Work!" phase, and then adjusts back to the simple but complete "Aaaaaaah!" phase.

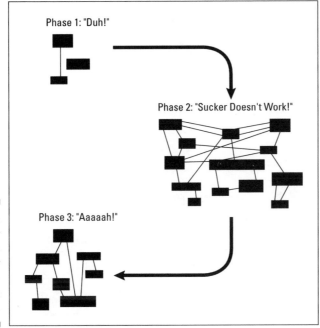

Figure 6-2:
The highly technical names for database design phases.

Figure 6-3 shows a possible second step in the evolution of Amy's database design. This diagram has two more boxes and more complex relationships.

A lot of tech weenies like to think that a relational database is a three-dimensional matrix that resembles a cube, or a space-age Lego block construction, like in Figure 6-4. (Some of these same tech-weenies are the ones that wear aluminum-foil hats to filter out cosmic rays and confuse the spy satellites.) You don't need to be an architect to design databases. You don't need a degree in advanced geometry to understand relational diagrams. All you need is common sense and some pixie dust.

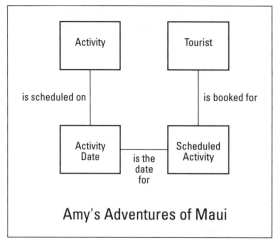

Figure 6-3:
The
database
design
cycle works
best when
you allow
yourself to
be flexible.

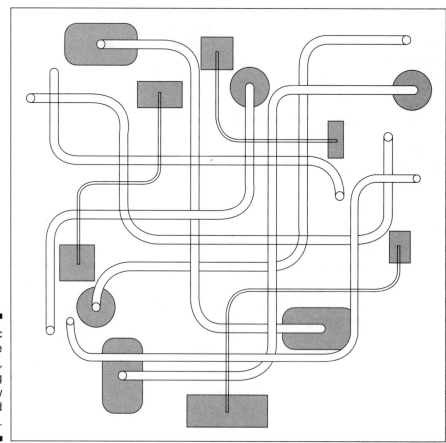

Figure 6-4:
Database
diagrams,
according
to highly
paid
consultants.

As you set out to create a great relational database design, watch out for some of these common pitfalls:

✔ **Primary keys whose contents change.**

These are *primary keys* (see the nearby sidebar text box for definition) that contain columns with "real" data in them, instead of a simple identifying number. See Chapter 19 for more explanation. Designers tend to want the relational model to use the same identifiers that they already use, even if it is an intelligent key. To avoid the pitfalls of an intelligent key, keep the old key as a regular column and create a new column to act as a nonintelligent key.

✔ **Repeating columns in a table.**

As I state in the section above about keys, repeating columns violate the third normal form, discussed in Chapter 5. Repeating columns appear in odd places, so be on the lookout for them.

For example, imagine you are filling out a job application (now I'm not suggesting anything here). You see the question "Job Skills (check all that apply)" followed by a list of skills. If you translate this to a diagram, you may draw a box called Application. You add the columns to it, and it seems obvious that each of the skills becomes a column. Right?

Not so. Job Skill is the column, which has many values (items in the list). The Job Skill column should be placed in its own box labeled Application Job Skill, with a one-to-many relationship between the Application and the Application Job Skill.

✔ **Incorrect relationships.**

The most common error is identifying a relationship as one-to-many when it's actually many-to-many. To avoid this pitfall, be sure to ask yourself (or the person using your creations) these questions:

• Does one row in Table A ever connect to more than one row in Table B?

Primary key and foreign key definitions

A *primary key* is the column or group of columns that uniquely identifies any row in a table. Every row in a table has a value in the primary key that is different from every other row in that table.

A *foreign key* is a copy of a primary key from one table placed into a second table. It is a reference point that ties all the data from the original table into the second table without copying any data except the primary key.

- Does one row in Table A always connect to exactly zero or exactly one row in Table B?

- Can one row in Table A ever connect to more than one row in Table B?

These three questions ask nearly the same thing, but each is deliberately phrased slightly differently to ferret out the hidden relationships.

It helps to phrase the questions according to table names and relationship names. Using the two tables, Tourist and Scheduled Activity, in Figure 6-3 as examples, the three questions above look like this:

- Is one Tourist ever booked for more than one Scheduled Activity?

- Is one Tourist always booked for exactly zero or exactly one Scheduled Activity?

- Can one Tourist ever be booked for more than one Scheduled Activity?

Use diligence and careful thought while designing your database, just like you used when designing your tax return last spring.

Tree Diagram: Easy Once You Know the Lingo

The relational database diagram I recommend is called the *tree diagram,* because it consists of boxes connected together with lines, and, when you're done, it resembles an upside-down tree with branches going downward. The few basic components in the diagram are shown in Figure 6-5. They are:

- ✔ **Table:** This is drawn as a box. Usually the table name appears in the middle. In more detailed diagrams, you may include the primary key, column names, or a sentence or two describing the table.

- ✔ **Relationship:** A relationship is a line drawn between two tables. A short phrase written next to the line describes the relationship. There are several variations on the line, which are used for the different kinds of relationships you can describe. The two most common ones are shown in Figure 6-5.

  - One-to-One Relationship: A simple line between two tables.

  - One-to-Many Relationship: A line with branches on one end (called crow's feet because they resemble chicken feet.)

Use these simple components like tinker toys to assemble your database diagram.

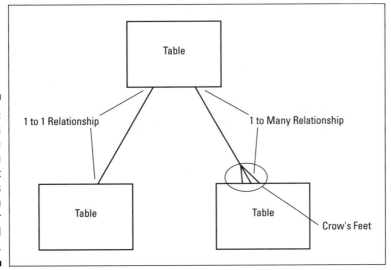

Figure 6-5:
I call this
a tree
diagram
because it
resembles
a tree with
branches or
roots and
square fruit.

The table

Figure 6-6 shows a few variations on the box, which identifies a table in your diagram.

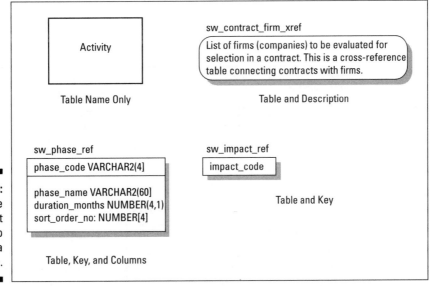

Figure 6-6:
The
different
ways to
diagram a
table.

In strict database parlance, I sometimes use the term *entity* in place of *table*. The entity is what a table is before it actually exists in the databases. Sometimes entities get broken down into several tables, or get combined into one table. Tables always correspond to an actual table in your database. Very little difference exists between a table and an entity. Both symbolize some object or concept from the real world that you wish to keep track of in your database. I diagrammed both with a box and a label. When done psychically, this is called channeling. For practical purposes, I'll use the term table rather than entity throughout the book.

The relationship

Two tables can have three kinds of relationships with each other. Relationships, while they are about tables, are determined by looking at a row inside one table and seeing how it relates to any of the rows in the other table. Here are the three relationship categories:

- ✔ **One to one:** Monogamous, not to be confused with monotonous. Monotonous is a result of the universal law that only boring people get bored. Like an old married couple, one row in Table A is connected to one and only one row in Table B. Either place the primary key (see the earlier sidebar text box or Chapter 5 for an explanation) of Table A into Table B, or place the primary key of Table B into Table A to show the relationship (refer to Figure 6-7). When you copy the primary key of one table into another table, it is called a foreign key.

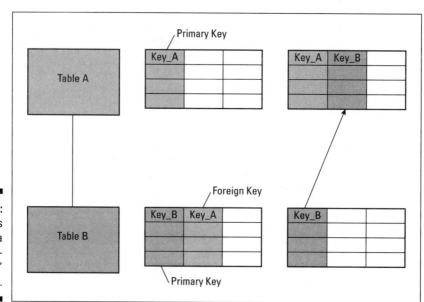

Figure 6-7: Two ways to resolve a "one-to-one" relationship.

✔ **One to many:** Flower to petals. Not a recommended cure for monotony. A flower (row in table A) has many little petals (rows in Table B). Each petal (row in Table B) grows on only one flower (row in Table A). Always place the primary key of Table A into Table B to show the relationship (refer to Figure 6-8).

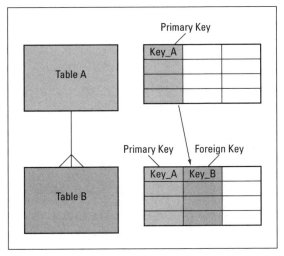

Figure 6-8:
The ever-popular "one-to-many" relationship gets drawn in.

✔ **Many to many:** Free for all. A permanent cure for monogamy. Like an amusement park, one cotton candy-covered kid (row in Table A) goes on lots of rides (rows in Table B). Likewise, one ride (row in Table B) has lots of kids (rows in Table A) riding it. Create a new table and place the primary key of Table A and the primary key of Table B in this intersection table to show the relationship (refer to Figure 6-9).

When you define a many-to-many relationship, you have to break it apart into the appropriate number of one-to-many relationships before actually creating the tables.

You are an entomologist for a day. Your job seems easy enough: Identify the butterflies that land on flowers in a one-acre field, and then identify the flowers. This example is a classic many-to-many relationship between the butterflies and the flowers. Each butterfly lands on many flowers. Each flower gets visited by many butterflies. Figure 6-10 shows the many-to-many table diagram of BUTTERFLY and FLOWER.

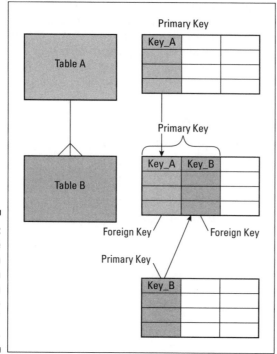

Figure 6-9:
A new table
is born
when
there's a
"many-to-
many"
relationship.

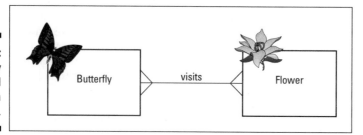

Figure 6-10:
The many
loves and
lives of a
butterfly.

Once you begin to create your tables, you must restructure all many-to-many relationships into pairs of one-to-many relationships — a mathematician's nightmare. Despite the seemingly odd approach, the solution is simple: Create a table that holds both primary keys. Lo and behold, your work is done! Figure 6-11 tells the whole juicy story in lurid detail.

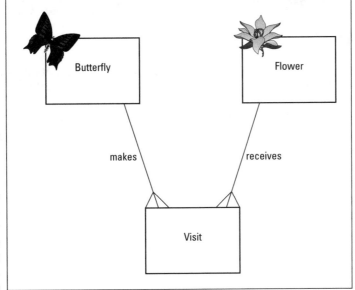

Figure 6-11: Metamorphosis of the butterfly and the flower produces the Visit table.

Arranging the tables and relationships

The fine art of diagramming can be fun and entertaining, but it's meant more for communicating than entertaining. Here are a few simple guidelines to keep in mind when diagramming:

- ✔ Always draw crow's feet, the many ends of the relationship, on the lower or right side. Or, as we tech-weenies always say, "Dead crows fly east!" And please note: These crow's feet are not a sign of aging. Rather, they create a consistent hierarchy of tables.

- ✔ Minimize the number of times that relationship lines go across one another. If you must make two relationship lines cross, make them as close to right angles as possible to make the overlap obvious.

- ✔ Keep the whole diagram on one page, even if you must use a four-foot-long sheet of paper.

- ✔ Be consistent in your use of dashed lines, crow's feet, line width, text size, and upper and lower case. Consistency does not equal monotony in database terms. See the last section in this chapter to find out what dashed lines are for.

- ✔ Be consistent in your choice of phrases on the relationship lines. Always use present tense, assuming a singular subject. For instance, don't use *receives* and *has outlet in*.

- ✔ Avoid using *has* by itself as a relationship phrase. The term is overused and is not a clear description of the relationship.

Sample Chart: Probably Invented by an Accountant

The sample chart, probably invented by an insane accountant, is tedious, boring, thorough, and useful. The best time to use the chart is before you have built any tables. The chart is a tool to help you design the table. Figure 6-12 shows a typical sample chart.

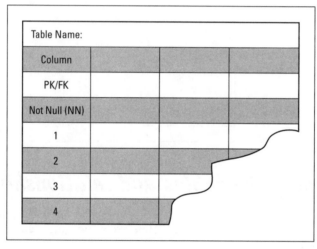

Figure 6-12: Share the sample chart with your friends.

The main idea of the chart is to map out your table and then fill it in with examples of the information that goes in the table. The closer to real data you can get, the better. The chart is a great tool, because if you make a mistake on what kind of data the table should contain, you can clear up the problem right away.

You probably want to review your sample chart with the person or persons who will use the table. If this is your own private table, then go in the bathroom and show it to yourself in the mirror.

Special Effects to Make You Look Clever

Here's a hint: Get some software that draws diagrams! Using a cool diagramming tool saves trees, regardless of whether or not you're creating a tree diagram, because you don't wear out three pencils getting the diagram right in the first place. I like the ERWin software by Logic Works, Inc., (`http://www.logicworks.com/`). Many tools exist, so you may want to go exploring on the Web. I suggest leaving a trail of virtual bread crumbs lest you get lost. Oracle Designer/2000 also does a good job and also produces table creation scripts for you. And, if you haven't seen Oracle Designer/2000, the Oracle Website is `http://www.oracle.com`.

A relationship between tables in which there are no connections at all is valid and can fall into any of the three categories above. You use dashed lines to symbolize this type of relationship in your diagram.

You bought one of those handy dandy add-ons for your database so you can look up ZIP codes and validate them when you add people to your mailing list table. While your mailing list is pretty good, you have not covered every single ZIP code found in the USA, so you have not linked some of the rows in the `ZIPCODE` table you bought to any rows in the `MAILING_ADDRESS` table. Nonetheless, each row in the `MAILING_ADRESS` table is indeed connected to exactly one row in the `ZIPCODE` table.

Figure 6-13 shows a dashed line going from the midpoint of the relationship line to the `MAILING_ADDRESS` table. This dashed line signifies that one `ZIPCODE` is for zero, one, or many `MAILING_ADDRESS`es.

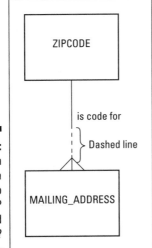

Figure 6-13: How much zip could a ZIP code zip if a ZIP code could zip code?

Chapter 7

Getting Familiar with Oracle7 Structure

• •

In This Chapter

▶ Admiring data dictionary views from afar

▶ Getting to know Oracle7

▶ Using data dictionary views for your own advancement

▶ Using SQL code to peek at data dictionary views

▶ Using the PO7 Navigator to peek at data dictionary views

• •

*W*hat users are in the Oracle7 database and what have they created? How does Oracle7 know which tables a user can see and which a user cannot touch? Where is the off switch?

The answers to all these questions — except the last — can be found in the data dictionary views. *Data dictionary views* are actually views based on underlying tables called the system tables. *System tables* gather information about tables, rows, view, columns, security, users, and even about the files allocated to store the Oracle7 database itself. System tables keep track of all the users and what each one can and cannot do. This chapter tells you how to access that information by looking at the data dictionary views.

Oracle7 depends on the data dictionary views and the underlying system tables, so don't mess with them. Look at the data dictionary views all you want, but do not alter these views or the system tables in any way. Unless you are given special permission from the database administrator (DBA), you are not able to make changes to either the data dictionary views or the system tables; but if you have your own desktop version of Oracle7, you're the DBA. You can, if a demon possesses you, add rows or alter the structure of these views or tables, but you just have to restrain yourself.

Data Dictionary Views You Can Really Use

The following little table of views shows you the best-kept secrets in the Oracle7 database, including what resides in data dictionary views. The views make it easy for you to interpret the internal workings of Oracle7.

Table 7-1	The Ultimate Table of Views	
View	*Who Needs It*	*What the View Shows You*
ALL_CATALOG	DBA, Table Owner, User	Every table, view, and synonym you can look at. You may or may not be allowed to update these. Helps you determine what resources the database has.
ALL_TAB_COMMENTS	Anyone	Comments, which usually contain a short description of the table's contents. You may occasionally find useful puns or one-liners here.
ALL_TAB_GRANTS	DBA, Table Owner	Lists the privileges you currently have on any table in the database. Includes grants to PUBLIC (Oracle's special user that is shared by all Oracle users; see the Tip after this table for more about PUBLIC). See Chapter 11 about using PUBLIC with table privileges (grants).
ALL_TAB_GRANTS_RECD	DBA, Table Owner	The privileges you received from others for any table; includes grants to PUBLIC.
ALL_USERS	Anyone	The names and creation dates of all other users in the database.
DBA_FREE_SPACE	DBA	The remaining free space in each tablespace.
PRODUCT_COMPONENT_VERSION	Anyone	Shows all installed products, like SQL*Plus and PL/SQL, and their complete version numbers, which is useful if you're reporting errors to Oracle.
USER_CATALOG	Anyone	All tables, views, and synonyms you can see, even if you did not create them.

View	Who Needs It	What the View Shows You
USER_INDEXES	Table Owner	All the indexes you create. See Chapter 22 for SQL code that uses this table.
USER_TABLES	Table Owner	Your tables and statistics about each one. See Chapter 22 for SQL code that uses this table.
USER_TAB_COLUMNS	Table Owner	All the columns you create. See Chapter 22 for SQL code that uses this table in a cool report.
USER_TAB_GRANTS_MADE	DBA, Table Owner	Privileges you have granted to others for your tables.
USER_VIEWS	Table Owner	Your views, complete with the SQL code that you used to create them. Here's a great opportunity to share your views with a captive audience.

The PUBLIC user was created by Oracle7 to handle situations in which all users are allowed to see your table. PUBLIC simplifies your life by allowing you to grant privileges to PUBLIC rather than to many individuals. Anything granted to PUBLIC is automatically given to any newly created users, which may not seem fair to those with more seniority. See Chapter 10 for details on granting privileges for tables.

Looking at Data Dictionary Views with SQL*Plus

This section deals with two useful queries you use to take a quick look around in the data dictionary views. The first query is how you list out all the data dictionary views that are available for you to explore. The second query is how you list out all the Oracle user names that are defined to the Oracle7 database you are using.

List useful data dictionary views

The following steps show how to query a data dictionary view and show part of the results.

1. Start up SQL*Plus.

See Chapter 1 for a reminder of how to do it.

2. Type in the following SQL*Plus command and press Enter:

```
select TABLE_NAME from ALL_SYNONYMS
  where TABLE_NAME like 'USER%'
  or TABLE_NAME like 'ALL%'
order by TABLE_NAME;
```

The query's WHERE clause (everything between where and order by in the command above) narrows down the results by restricting the query to those data dictionary views that begin with USER or ALL. These two groups of data dictionary views (about 125) are very useful. There are another 250 not-so-useful views stored in the ALL_SYNONYMS data dictionary view.

Oracle7 lists the results of your query. The following shows a partial listing that you receive when running the query:

```
TABLE_NAME
_____

ALL_CATALOG
ALL_CLUSTERS
ALL_CLUSTER_HASH_EXPRESSIONS
ALL_COL_COMMENTS
ALL_COL_GRANTS_MADE
ALL_COL_GRANTS_RECD
ALL_COL_PRIVS
ALL_COL_PRIVS_MADE
ALL_COL_PRIVS_RECD
ALL_CONSTRAINTS
ALL_CONS_COLUMNS
ALL_DB_LINKS
ALL_DEF_AUDIT_OPTS
ALL_DEPENDENCIES
ALL_ERRORS
ALL_INDEXES
ALL_IND_COLUMNS
ALL_OBJECTS
ALL_REFRESH
ALL_REFRESH_CHILDREN
ALL_SEQUENCES
```

These views are just a few of the data dictionary views available. You are restricted to seeing what you have privileges to see. So, unless you're the DBA you can probably see just a small slice of the whole database pie. Chapters 10 and 11 go on and on about the subject of privileges, grants, and how they fit together. Chapter 19 also has a section on security, which could also have practical uses at airport terminals.

List all Oracle users

Follow these steps to find out what users are hanging out in your database.

1. **Start up SQL*Plus.**

   Remember, Chapter 1 has the details.

2. **Type in the following SQL*Plus command and press Enter:**

```
select * from all_users;
```

An essential tool for SQL*Plus

This DESCRIBE command saves you time because it generates a complete list of all the columns and their datatypes for any table, view, or synonym you choose. You can abbreviate DESCRIBE to DESC or DESCR. For example, to use the command for a table called ARTIST, type:

```
desc artist
```

Oracle7 replies with something like this:

Name	Null?	Type
ARTIST_ID	NOT NULL	NUMBER(3)
FIRST_NAME		VARCHAR2(10)
MIDDLE_NAME		VARCHAR2(10)
LAST_NAME		VARCHAR2(16)
JR_SUFFIX		VARCHAR2(3)
SALUTATION		VARCHAR2(4)
FIRM_NAME		VARCHAR2(50)
ADDRESS		VARCHAR2(50)
CITY		VARCHAR2(18)
STATE		VARCHAR2(18)
ZIP		VARCHAR2(12)
PHONE		VARCHAR2(16)
FAX		VARCHAR2(16)
EMAIL		VARCHAR2(33)
SPECIALTY		VARCHAR2(33)

As a bonus, SQL*Plus remembers your SQL command while you type in the DESCRIBE command. Someone, of course not *you*, may forget the exact spelling of a column while typing a query. This forgetful person can use DESCRIBE to view the column names and then resume editing a query, without starting over.

Oracle7 replies with a list of users. On my own Personal Oracle7 database, the list looked like this:

USERNAME	USER_ID	CREATED
SYS	0	26-SEP-95
SYSTEM	5	26-SEP-95
SCOTT	8	26-SEP-95
DEMO	9	26-SEP-95
CAROL	12	03-MAY-96
AMY	13	04-MAY-96

Your results will vary, of course, because your database certainly does not have an identical list of user IDs.

Perusing Data Dictionary Views with PO7 Navigator

Open the Personal Oracle7 (PO7) Navigator. You do this in Windows 95 by selecting it from the Programs menu, as shown in Figure 7-1. A database connection is an icon that, when clicked, starts up the Oracle7 database and logs you in as a particular Oracle user ID. If a database connection already exists, you're ready to take a look at the data dictionary views. If no database connection exists, see Chapter 9 on how to create one.

Adjust database connection properties

The default setup for a database connection shows you only what you own — that is, the tables, views, indexes, and synonyms that you created yourself. To see the data dictionary views, follow these steps, which revise the properties of the database connection and include the data dictionary views along with your own tables, views, and so on.

1. **Click the database connection you wish to use in the PO7 Navigator window.**

   If the database has not already started, it does so. You see a few pop-up windows telling you what the database is doing. When the database connection is complete, the connection icon looks like two plug ends connected together. The original icon looks like a plug and an extension cord ready to be connected together.

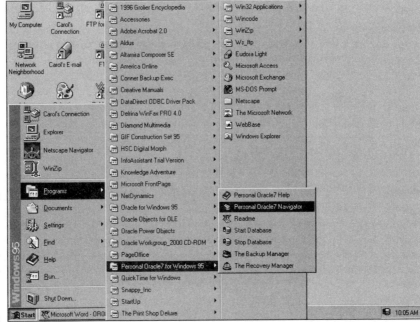

Figure 7-1:
Select the
PO7
Navigator
from your
myriad
programs.

2. **Right-click the mouse to view the pop-up menu for the connection (see Figure 7-2) and select Properties from the pop-up menu.**

   Another window appears with your user name as the title. This is the User Property Window.

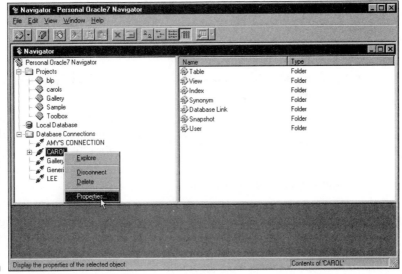

Figure 7-2:
Select
Properties
in the pop-
up menu to
adjust your
database
connection.

In Oracle7.3, the window is divided into two tabs. Click the Settings tab and then continue to Step 3.

3. **Click the two check boxes in the lower half of the window to show objects owned by SYS and SYSTEM (see Figure 7-3).**

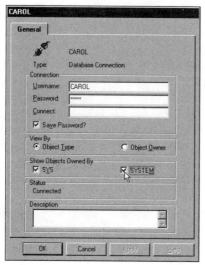

Figure 7-3:
Make sure
that the
checks
show up in
the check
boxes for
SYS and
SYSTEM.

4. **Click the OK button to close this window and return to the main PO7 Navigator window.**

View data dictionary views

After adjusting the database connection, follow these steps to view the data dictionary views.

1. **Click the database connection you wish to use in the PO7 Navigator window.**

   If the database has not already started, it does so. You see a few pop-up windows telling you what the database is doing. When the database connection is complete, the connection icon looks like two plugs connected together.

2. **Double-click the View icon.**

   Double-clicking on the View icon on the right side of the PO7 Navigator window brings up a listing of all the views available, including the data dictionary views.

3. Click the Name column heading (optional).

Clicking on the Name heading in the PO7 Navigator window sorts the table names in alphabetical order. Click once to put the names in ascending order. Click again and the names are in descending order. Figure 7-4 shows the PO7 Navigator window with the table listings.

4. Scroll to a data dictionary view and double-click it.

Scroll down to the data dictionary view you want to look at and click on the name. For example, scroll to and double-click on the USER_TAB_GRANTS_MADE view.

The contents of the USER_TAB_GRANTS_MADE table appear on your screen as shown in Figure 7-5. See Chapters 10 and 11 if you want to know where these privileges originated.

You follow these steps to look at the contents of any of the data dictionary views. Use Table 7-1 above to help you decipher all the information you have at your mouse-tip.

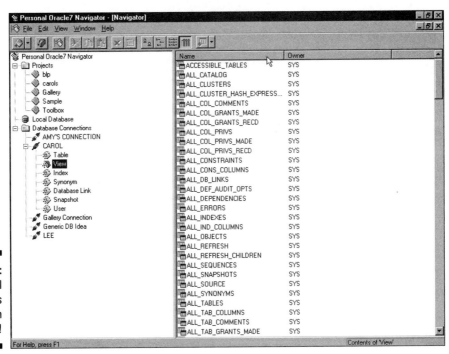

Figure 7-4:
Look at all the views you can browse!

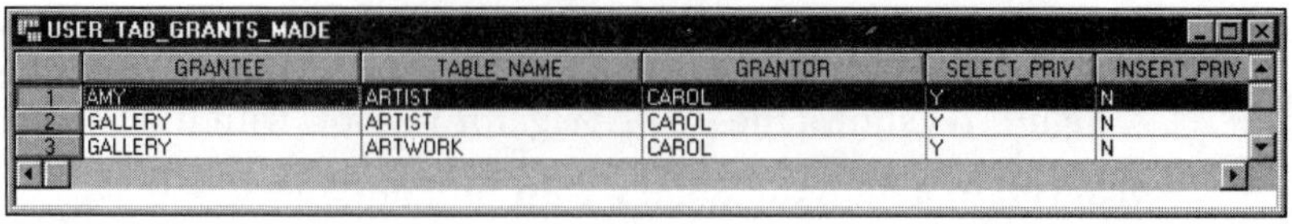

Figure 7-5:
Looking at
one of the
many data
dictionary
views
available to
you.

	GRANTEE	TABLE_NAME	GRANTOR	SELECT_PRIV	INSERT_PRIV
1	AMY	ARTIST	CAROL	Y	N
2	GALLERY	ARTIST	CAROL	Y	N
3	GALLERY	ARTWORK	CAROL	Y	N

USER_TAB_GRANTS_MADE

Chapter 8
Oracle's User

● ●

In This Chapter

▶ Discovering the use of the users

▶ Observing your role in life

▶ Conjuring users

▶ Using Personal Oracle7 Navigator

▶ Changing your password

▶ Making a connection with your database

● ●

I'm not saying this is true for you, but for me, a strong sense of who I am really helps me get through life. This chapter is all about you and your identity. In Oracle7, you log in with a user ID and a password — your Oracle7 identity. Your Oracle7 identity, or Oracle7 user ID, gets assigned one or more roles (a collection of abilities) by your DBA. This chapter covers how your Oracle7 identity was created and how you can (if you are the DBA) create others. Even if you are not the DBA, you can use the information in this chapter to help you understand how you, as an Oracle7 user, fit into the picture.

Role Playing

Here's a fun fact about Oracle7: Every table in Oracle7 was created by one Oracle7 user ID. The Oracle7 user ID that created the table is called the table's *owner*. The owner can do anything to the table, including dropping it from a (virtual) moving train. Every Oracle7 user has the potential to create tables, because any user can be assigned the role (group of abilities) that allows the user to do so. The database administrator (DBA) stratifies users into roles, which limit or expand their capabilities. The DBA, with infinite wisdom, decrees which users are also owners and which are merely tourists who can look around but cannot vote in a local election.

My point is, being an Oracle7 user is not bad, like being a drug user or something. In fact, being an Oracle7 user can be pretty cool. (This is your brain on databases.) Perhaps you work in an office sharing accounting database tables with 20 other staff members. You have your own Oracle7 user ID. Your coworkers each have their own Oracle7 user IDs as well. One Oracle7 user ID (possibly not any of you, but someone in the MIS department) has created all the tables you use. This Oracle7 user ID (the one who created the tables) owns all those tables and therefore is called, lo and behold, the table owner. Oracle7 allows users like you to share tables with their owners, provided the owner gives you permission to do various activities with the tables. For example, the owner might allow you to only look at the data and not change anything on one table. On a different table, your Oracle7 user ID might be allowed to add new rows or modify the data in existing rows. Each of these actions has a specific privilege that the table owner grants to you.

To understand how what kind of user you are affects what you can do with Oracle7, you first have to understand what kinds of users Oracle7 has.

What kind of users are there?

Asking, in a database context, the age-old question "Who am I and what is my role in life?" brings us to Oracle7 *roles*. Oracle7 assigns five basic roles that define what you may and may not do within the confines of the database. In addition, the DBA can create as many other roles as necessary. Roles become time-saving tools for table owners because the table owner can assign a set of privileges once to a role instead of assigning all the privileges to individual Oracle7 user IDs. Chapter 10 tells you all about how these kinds of roles are used.

Here are the five basic roles that come as standard Oracle7 equipment:

- **DBA:** The Grand Poobah of all roles. In Oracle7's world, more than one DBA can exist. Incredible, but true. The Oracle7 DBA can create new Oracle7 user IDs, add disk space to the database, start and stop the database, and create roles and synonyms that are for use by all other Oracle7 users. The DBA can also export tables that belong to any user.

- **EXP_FULL_DATABASE** and **IMP_FULL_DATABASE:** Romulus and Remus of the Oracle7 realm, these two can make a copy of the entire universe and duplicate it elsewhere. What power! Few are chosen for these honored positions. Usually, the DBA adds these roles to his or her own plate.

- **RESOURCE:** This is the role that makes you an owner (that is, as soon as you create a table to own). All the movers and shakers in the database have this role, which lets you make tables, indexes, views, and synonyms. You can export and import your own tables. You can drop, modify, re-create, adjust, bend, and create relationships for your own tables. You can assign (grant) privileges (such as the ability to read or modify your table) to other users. However, even though you can do all this to your own tables, you cannot do anything to another user's tables unless that table's owner has given *you* privileges.

✓ **CONNECT:** The people who use the database for anything are in this role. The CONNECT role gets you in the door, nothing more. You are not allowed to create any tables. The only way that you can do anything once you have connected to the database is by receiving additional privileges from owners. Owners can allow you to look at their tables, add data, modify, and delete data from their tables by granting you the privileges.

The DBA can also give you more privileges by assigning you to additional roles that have been created for the purpose of giving a set of privileges to any user who is a member of that role.

What kind of user are you?

If you share Oracle7 at your workplace and you have a pocket protector on, you may have the authority to create tables. If you're not sure, ask the DBA this question: "I just created this table with 10,000 rows. Now how do I get rid of the pesky thing?" and see how fast the DBA runs over to your desk. If the DBA is at your desk in under ten seconds, you have the power to create tables. Otherwise, you probably don't.

But if the DBA doesn't give you an indication of what your user role is, how can you find out? By using either SQL*Plus or the PO7 Navigator.

The SQL*Plus method

Here's how you find out your role in the great theater of life using SQL*Plus. Type this command:

```
select GRANTED_ROLE, DEFAULT_ROLE from USER_ROLE_PRIVS;
```

After you press Enter, Oracle7 gives you the results, which will look something like the following:

GRANTED_ROLE	DEF
CONNECT	YES
RESOURCE	YES

In this example, you have two roles, the CONNECT role and the RESOURCE role. This means that you can log into Oracle7 and you can really have fun by creating your own tables and other tasks. Refer to the list in the previous section for more of an explanation.

If you see other roles, they are probably associated with jobs you do that require you to log into Oracle7 screens. As long as you have the RESOURCE role, which lets you create tables, you're in business.

The PO7 Navigator method

Here's how you can find out what your user role is by using the PO7 Navigator:

1. **With the PO7 Navigator window up, click the icon labeled Local Database in the left window.**

    This brings up a list of objects (tables, indexes, and so on) in the right window. Double click on the User icon in the right window.

    Oracle7 displays all the user names in the right window.

2. **Right-click your user name and select Properties from the sub-menu, as shown in Figure 8-1.**

3. **Click the Role/Privilege tab to see what roles you do and don't have.**

    Oracle7 got dramatic and made the role icon (next to each role name) look like a theater mask, as you can see in Figure 8-2. I really don't think we Oracle users would wear masks like that, but I didn't write Oracle, just the book about it.

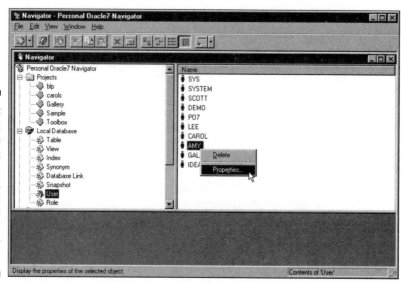

Figure 8-1: Looking at the properties of a user. You'd think Oracle7 was a real estate broker or something.

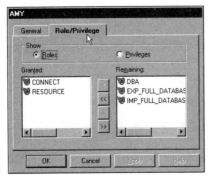

Figure 8-2:
Available
roles are
on the right.
Assigned
roles are on
the left.

Connected as PO7

You can change your own roles. See Chapter 10 for complete instructions. In fact, you get connected into Oracle7 as the DBA after you click on the icon called Local Database, which means that you can click on any of the user IDs and look at their roles and even change them.

4. Save your changes.

Click OK to save your changes and leave the window.

Creating a New User from Scratch

Creating a new life is a big responsibility — you have to feed it and change it every day for years. Creating a new user in Oracle7, on the other hand, carries some responsibilities, but generally won't get you up in the middle of the night stumbling for a bottle and a burp cloth.

Oracle7 offers two ways to create new users: with SQL*Plus or with the PO7 Navigator. If you want to use SQL*Plus, keep reading; if you want to use the PO7 Navigator's utility, skip ahead to the section "Using a wizard to help you conjure up a user."

The SQL*Plus method to create a new user

Creating a new user requires a short foray into the world of SQL*Plus. This involves going to the operating system level of talking to your Oracle7 database, so please be very careful. This book contains a wealth of information on SQL*Plus and the commands that you can use within it. Chapter 1 shows you how to start up SQL*Plus. Chapter 4 shows you a lot of the commands you use when working in SQL*Plus to look at your tables and your data. Chapter 9 shows you how to create tables and Chapter 16 shows you how to create indexes. For creating primary keys and foreign keys, look at Chapter 17. This is not a complete list by any means! Browse through the Table of Contents or the Index for more references to SQL*Plus.

Follow these steps:

1. **Start up SQL*Plus as the database administrator (DBA).**

   If you're not the DBA, then you cannot create a user, so you just have to follow along. See Chapter 1 for instructions on starting up SQL*Plus. On most systems, you know SQL*Plus is ready when your cursor is a vertical bar next to a line that starts with SQL>.

   You are now ready to conjure up a brand-new identity, a user ID, in Oracle7's universe. This user ID can create all your tables, add data to the tables, create forms and reports, and so on, depending on the authority you grant. You must also choose a password.

2. **Create the new user.**

   Type the following, substituting as directed below and pressing Enter:

   ```
   create user username identified by password;
   ```

   Replace *username* with the user name (also called the user ID) and replace *password* with the actual password. The password is a combination of numbers and letters. The semicolon at the end is the signal that this is a complete command, ready for execution. The semicolon is not part of the password.

   Oracle7 replies:

   ```
   User created.
   ```

3. **Assign one or more roles.**

   For more on roles, check out the "What kind of users are there?" section earlier in this chapter. At a minimum, assign the CONNECT role, which allows the new user to log in to Oracle7. To assign the CONNECT role, type this in and press Enter:

   ```
   grant CONNECT to username;
   ```

   Oracle7 replies:

   ```
   Grant succeeded.
   ```

4. **Type** exit; **and press Enter.**

Once you have created the user ID, you can connect to that user ID whenever you wish to create new tables, to make changes to the structure of existing tables, or to make more tables related to the ones you've already created.

Remember to write down the name and password you just created and keep them in a secure and hidden place (not taped to your monitor).

Using a wizard to help you conjure up a user

All right then, here's an easy way to create a new user life in Oracle7 using the PO7 Navigator:

1. **Double-click Local Database icon on the left side of the main PO7 Navigator window.**

   Oracle7 connects to the database and displays some icons that you need to continue.

2. **Click the User icon on the left side of the window.**

   This shows you a list of the current users that are defined in your database.

3. **Right-click the User icon and select New from the pop-up menu that appears, as shown in Figure 8-3.**

Figure 8-3:
All Oracle7's users are shown wearing little blue suits and carrying briefcases. What is Oracle trying to tell us?

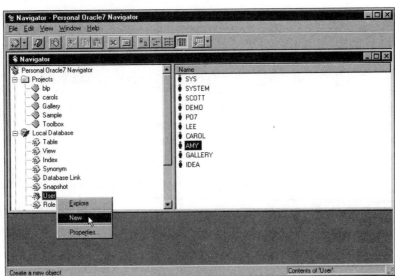

This brings up the Create User dialog box, and it should resemble Figure 8-4. (The Oracle 7.3 version is the New User Properties window, which looks just a little different.) This window is not really a wizard, but it should be, because creating new life is definitely in the realm of wizards.

Figure 8-4:
Creating a
new user is
a snap
with this
Create User
dialog box.

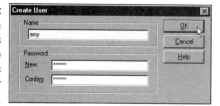

4. **Type a new name for the new user ID.**

5. **Type the password in both the New box and the Confirm box.**

Write down the name and password you just created and keep them in a safe and secure place. In Oracle 7.3, you can click on the Roles/ Privileges tab and assign roles right away. See Chapter 10 for detailed instructions on how to assign roles.

6. **Click the OK button and your work is done.**

Oracle has rules about what you can name a user ID. See the "Choosing a name for your new baby" sidebar for details and advice on names for user IDs and for passwords.

Choosing a name for your new baby

What's in a name? Don't ask me. I named my kid Blue. But I got more conventional and gave him the middle name Skyler. Then I got psychic and gave him another middle name: Mercury. Worked for me.

As the DBA, you have the responsibility of creating all the new user IDs for your Oracle7 database. When setting up a name for a new user, you have to follow the rules. You can use up to 30 characters. A letter and single-digit number each count as one character. The same rules apply to setting up passwords. My advice is to use a single word or acronym for a new user name. You will appreciate this later when you have to type the name as the identifier in front of every table you've created.

Changing Your Password

Whether you are a DBA or not, you may be required to select a password for your Oracle7 user ID. The password, like the user name, can be up to 30 characters long. Here are my own recommendation:

✔ Choose a password that you can easily remember and that has a number in it. For instance, take your middle name (Skyler), then add a number or two (Skyler1). A password that contains both numbers and letters is hundreds of times more difficult for a hacker to crack!

✔ Change your password as often as you are told to. If no one tells you anything, tell yourself to change it every two months.

The following section shows how to change your password using SQL*Plus. If you have PO7 Navigator, you can skip to the following section, "Changing Your Password in PO7 Navigator."

Changing your password in SQL*Plus

You should check with your DBA before changing your password to see if the DBA needs to know about it. After the DBA creates your user ID and password, the password is kept secret and cannot be seen, even by the DBA. Both you and the DBA can change your password using the following steps:

1. **Start up SQL*Plus.**

   See Chapter 1 for a reminder on how to do it.

2. **Type the following command and press Enter:**

   ```
   alter username identified by newpassword;
   ```

   Replace *username* with your user name and replace *newpassword* with your new password.

   Oracle7 replies:

   ```
   User altered.
   ```

3. **Leave SQL*Plus.**

   Type exit and press Enter.

That's all there is to it.

Changing your password in PO7 Navigator

You are your own DBA in PO7, so you can change the password of any of the users defined to the database. Here are the steps (which are very similar to the steps for creating a new user):

1. **Double-click the Local Database icon on the left side of the main PO7 Navigator window.**

   Oracle7 connects to the database and displays some icons below that you need to continue.

2. **Click the User icon on the left side of the window.**

   A list of user names appears in the right window.

3. **Right-click the little blue-suited-man icon next to your user name in the right window and select Properties from the sub-menu.**

   This brings up the User window with your user name on top. Here you see an outlined area in the middle of the window that is labeled Password.

4. **Type a new password in the New box.**

5. **Type the new password again in the Confirm box.**

   Write down the name and password you just created and keep them in a secure and hidden place.

6. **Click the OK button to complete the job.**

   PO7 Navigator accepts the change and returns you to the main window.

Finished. Very easy, wasn't it?

Creating a Database Connection for Yourself

A database connection in PO7 Navigator lets you quickly connect to the appropriate user ID. When you use Personal Oracle7 in its stand-alone mode, you may never need to create more than one user for all your needs. If you use Personal Oracle7 at work, you may need to match an Oracle7 user ID that is in a larger database and may end up with several user names in your Personal Oracle7. Create a database connection for each new user ID you create.

I recommend that you create at least one user ID that is different than the default user ID for PO7 even if you use PO7 alone in your room. After you create that user ID, follow the instructions in this section to create a database connection for that user ID. Looking at lists of tables and other objects (such as indexes) that you create will be more convenient because you won't see all the system tables and indexes mixed in with yours.

After you create the database icon, the icon appears on the main window every time you go into the PO7 Navigator, and you can double-click on the icon to start up the database and log in.

Follow these steps to create your very own database connection icon:

1. **In the PO7 Navigator main window, select File⇨New⇨New Database Connection.**

   PO7 Navigator opens up the Create Database Connection dialog box. Oracle 7.3 calls the box New Database Connection Properties. You are now ready to establish a reusable database connection.

2. **Type a name for the connection, the user ID, and the password, which appears as a line of asterisks.**

   Leave the Connect line blank, as you see in Figure 8-5. Oracle 7.3 left the Connect line out.

Figure 8-5:
A database
connection
can have
any name
and
appears on
your main
PO7
Navigator
window.

Create Database Connection	
Name	OK
Amy	Cancel
Connection	Help
Username: amy	
Password: ******	
Connect:	Configure...
☑ Save Password?	

3. **Click the OK button.**

   You see a couple of status windows telling you that Oracle7 is opening the database. Once opened, the PO7 Navigator creates the new connection for you. The hard drive usually makes some noise, and then the window closes. You see the connection appear under Database Connections. Wow!

The steps you just performed need not be repeated. Once you establish the user ID and the database connection, they are there for your use anytime.

Now that you have a connection defined, all you have to do to log into the database with that user ID is click once on the connection name. You are definitely dangerous now.

Part III
Putting Oracle7 to Work

The 5th Wave By Rich Tennant

WE'VE TRIED EVERYTHING, BUT SHE STILL GETS THIS SHARP JABBING PAIN IN THE BACK OF HER NECK FROM WORKING AT THE COMPUTER ALL DAY.

In this part...

This section is kind of like puberty. You have a brand-new body of knowledge and now you're learning the fun and responsibility of putting it all into practice.

You get revved up in the first chapter in this section by creating your very own tables. Learn how the experts do it!

Next, find out about all your choices for creating a secure working environment for your database tables. I give you some common-sense guidelines to help you make wise decisions about security using Oracle7 roles and privileges.

After creating tables and loading them with data, you'll want to show off that data in nice-looking reports. SQL*Plus has a lot of reporting tools that are not evident at first glance. Find out how to tap the hidden report-writing talents of SQL*Plus.

Have you ever considered using your database from a distance, such as across the Internet or across the room? Find out what the possibilities look like in Chapter 13.

All this work you've done deserves tender loving care and protection. How would you feel if you lost it all and had to start over? Don't get caught with your data showing. Back up now or lose sleep later.

Chapter 9
Defining Tables, Tablespaces, and Columns

• •

In This Chapter

▶ Pondering the possibilities of tablespaces

▶ Technical talk about columns

▶ Creating a table with SQL

▶ Special SQL words for when you bang your thumb

▶ Wizarding a table with Personal Oracle7 Navigator

• •

*T*his chapter is full of good stuff, so fasten your seat belts. You're about to discover where to put tables, how to name your columns, and what datatypes to assign them. You can also learn how to make tables with SQL code or the Personal Oracle7 (PO7) Navigator. Get ready: You're flying now!

Tablespace: The Final Frontier

Tablespaces are the portions of the database that are reserved for your tables. Your database administrator (DBA) may not have told you a thing about tablespaces. On the other hand, this same DBA may come whining to your desk that you've just brought the database to its knees by using all the space in the SYSTEM tablespace. Read on to find out what you actually did.

If you are allowed to create tables, you are assigned a default tablespace, which is where all your tables go. This default tablespace is sort of like your own private science lab: If your DBA has done a good job, your default tablespace is tucked away in a safe corner so that your incredible genius can blossom without disturbing anyone. Here, you have the liberty to ponder endlessly such burning issues as which fork should you use first or what to do if the little umbrella is missing from your mai tai.

You may, however, have to lower yourself to paying attention to where your tables go. You can tell Oracle7 where to put the tables as you make them. To see the syntax you need for telling Oracle7 where to stick your table, see the "Making Your Own Table with SQL" section in this chapter.

How do you decide whether you need to pay attention to where your tables actually go? And how much structure (meaning the mapping out of tables into tablespaces) do you need, anyway? You really need very little structure when working on a PC. Just take a look at your PC desktop and then take a look at someone else's. I bet they both look rather chaotic. Anyway, if you're working on a PC, let Oracle7 take care of the structure for you.

If you are responsible for planning the table structure for the database or your part of the database, you can create a single large tablespace for an entire set of tables rather than creating many small tablespaces. I recommend being conservative about the number of tablespaces you create. Every tablespace you add increases the work you have in managing the database. When you have many tablespaces, you may run into a problem where the database overall has enough space to hold all your data but cannot use the data because you placed a table into a tablespace that is out of room. Tables cannot span multiple tablespaces. Remember, you should always consult your DBA about table placement.

A Word or Two about Columns

Oracle7 needs tables, and tables need columns. Even if a table contains no rows, it must have columns. When creating columns, you'll want to consider names, datatypes, and null values.

Chapter 2 covers the naming conventions used for columns as well as for tables, indexes, and other database items. This section goes into more detail about column datatypes and about null values in your data.

Defining columns in Oracle7

Columns get defined during the process of creating a new table in the database. You must name the column, and then you tell Oracle7 what kind of data goes into the column by specifying the datatype of the column. In a nutshell, Table 9-1 shows all of your choices when defining columns in Oracle7. You may want to mark the table to reference later.

Table 9-1	The Complete Guide to Datatypes	
Datatype	*Parameters*	*Description*
VARCHAR2(n)	n=1 to 2,000	Text string with variable length. Specify the *maximum length (n)* when defining the column. This datatype holds letters, numbers, and symbols in the standard ASCII text set (or EBCDIC or whatever set is standard for your database). If your data is shorter than the maximum size, Oracle7 adjusts the length of the column to the size of the data. If your data has trailing blanks, Oracle7 removes the trailing blanks. VARCHAR2 is the most commonly used datatype.
NUMBER(p,s)	p=1 to 38, s=-84 to 127 or FLOAT	Number. Specify the *precision (p),* which is the number of digits, and the *scale (s),* which is the number of digits to the right of the decimal place. For example, a number with a maximum of 999.99 is defined as number (5,2). FLOAT specifies that you can have the decimal point anywhere in the number. Oracle7 truncates data that does not fit into the scale. For example, you define the columns as number (5,2) and then you add a new row into the table, telling Oracle7 to put the number 575.316 into this column. The number that actually gets stored in the column is 575.32, because Oracle7 automatically truncates the decimals at the hundredths, which is the scale defined for that column. If you define a column as number (3,0) and then add a row with data 575.316 in that column, the actual number stored is 575.
LONG	none	Text string with variable length. Maximum length is 2 gigabytes, so LONG is for very large data. There can be only one LONG datatype column per table, and it must be at the end of the table. A LONG datatype cannot be used in any part of the SQL query except in the SELECT clause. A LONG datatype cannot be used in the WHERE, GROUP BY, or ORDER BY clauses in SELECT statements. You cannot search for characters within a LONG datatype column. See Chapter 3 for examples of WHERE, GROUP BY, and ORDER BY.

(continued)

Table 9-1 *(continued)*

Datatype	Parameters	Description
LONG	none	A lot of other restrictions on use of the LONG datatype exist. Read the manual for all the rules and regulations. My advice: Use this one only when you absolutely need it for very large chunks of data that do not need text searching done on them. Otherwise, the limitations of the LONG datatype get in your way. Use VARCHAR2 when you need to do text searching.
DATE	none	Valid dates range from January 1, 4712 BC to December 31, 4712 AD. DATE is stored internally as a 7-byte number and, by definition, also includes the time in hours, minutes, and seconds.
RAW(n)	n=1 to 255	Raw binary data of variable length. You must specify the maximum length *(n)* when defining the column. The RAW datatype is used for small graphics or formatted text files, such as Microsoft Word documents.
LONGRAW	none	Raw binary data of variable length. The maximum length is 2 gigabytes. The LONGRAW datatype is used for larger graphics, formatted text files, such as Word documents, audio, video, and other non-text data. You cannot have both a LONG and a LONGDRAW column in the same table.
CHAR(n)	n=1 to 255	Text string with fixed length. The default length is 1. You can specify the maximum length *(n)* when defining the column. If you add data to this kind of column and the data is shorter than (*n*), Oracle7 adds blanks on the end of the data to make it a fixed length. For example, your column is datatype CHAR(10). You insert a row with HENRY in the column. HENRY is five characters long. Oracle7 takes HENRY and adds five blanks to the end of it and then stores it in the database that way. This is the main difference between CHAR and VARCHAR2. CHAR pads the data with blank spaces and VARCHAR2 strips off blank spaces. See Chapter 21 for more discussion of problems that can occur with the CHAR datatype.

What is a null?

When the column of a row *has no data*, the column is described as being *null* or having a *null value*. Use null when you do not know the value of the data. For example, if I put together a table for the fish in my aquarium, I may have a null value (no data) in the DEATH_DATE column of the row for Wesley. This means that either Wesley is alive or I don't know when he died.

Null values are allowed in columns of all datatypes. There are only two instances in which null values are not allowed:

✔ Primary key columns

✔ Any column defined with the NOT NULL constraint

As another example to show you the definition of a null value, imagine that your checkbook register has a column where you place a little X when you reconcile your bank statement with the register. I'll label the column that gets the X with the name CLEARED. When a check clears your account, you actually don't know about it until you receive your statement. Imagine that check number 2001 just cleared your account. Your check register has no value (null) in the row for check number 2001, yet the check was cleared. Therefore, the check register column CLEARED, when it has no X, could mean that the check has not cleared, or it could mean that the check has cleared and you don't know about it. The lack of data (no X,

or null value) indicates that the state of the CLEARED column for check number 2001 is *unknown* at this time.

Do not use null to represent zero. Zero is a known quantity. Zero can be added, subtracted, and generally used in calculations. Null values cannot be added, subtracted, or used in calculations. When a null is added to 10, the results equal null. Saying it a different way: Add some unknown quantity to 10 and you get another unknown quantity.

Nulls do not equal nulls or any other value. For example, the following statement is evaluated by Oracle7 as false *even when there is a null value in the* SELLING_PRICE *column:*

SELLING_PRICE = null

In the example, the word "null" represents a literal null value. (You might be comparing two columns that contain nulls and the same logic holds.) Oracle7 gets around this problem (which is a standard SQL requirement) by giving you the IS NULL and IS NOT NULL operators. Rewrite the statement above as follows. Oracle7 evaluates the following statement as true:

SELLING_PRICE is null

Likewise, Oracle7 evaluates the following statement as false:

SELLING_PRICE is not null

The most commonly used datatypes are VARCHAR2, DATE, and NUMBER. The CHAR datatype is commonly used for coded data of a constant length, such as state abbreviations.

The other datatypes are rather specialized and used infrequently (unless you're creating a database with delivery-on-demand CD music selections or something fun like that).

Nulls or not nulls

When designing columns, you'll need to consider whether or not to allow *nulls* in the columns. Here's the rule: Primary keys (the unique identifier for a table) cannot contain nulls. Otherwise, anything goes. I advise allowing nulls everywhere except primary keys. Even if your brain knows that the column will always contain data, exceptions to rules always exist. If you define the column to not allow nulls, you may be in a bind if you are adding a new row that really has no value for that column.

If you do choose to define the column so that no nulls are allowed, you can do it by adding the NOT NULL constraint to the column in the create table statement (see the next section).

See Chapter 17 for information on how to change a column's null value setting (nulls allowed to nulls not allowed and vice versa).

Creating and Dropping Your Own Table with SQL

So you want to create a table of your very own, eh? You've come to the right place. Go to SQL*Plus (refer to Chapter 1 if you don't know how) and type the following create table command:

```
CREATE TABLE tablename
(column datatype (p[, s])[null/not null] [primary key],
 column datatype (p[, s])[null/not null] [primary key],
 column datatype (p[, s])[null/not null] [primary key],
 column datatype (p[, s])[null/not null])
[tablespace tablespacename]
```

Items in square brackets are optional. If you don't specify NULL or NOT NULL, the default is NULL. If you don't specify the primary key parameter, no primary key will be created for the table. The letter p stands for number or precision and s stands for scale. See Table 9-1 for definitions. If the tablespace parameter is omitted, Oracle7 places the table in your default tablespace. After you are done, hit the Enter key, and Oracle7 responds with

```
Table created.
```

This create table code creates a table for the fish in my aquarium. I can track all kinds of information about my fish with this table. The pieces of information that I wish to track for each fish are:

✔ The name of the fish.

✔ The name of the aquarium I have the fish in. (This is just in case I get several aquariums.)

✔ The birthday of my fish.

✔ When the poor thing died (if it has died).

✔ Its color.

✔ The breed of fish.

✔ Male or female or unknown sex.

✔ A comment about why the fish died, or any other comments, such as where I bought it or what its favorite color is.

Each of these items becomes a column in the FISH table. Here's the actual SQL code for creating the table:

```
create table FISH
(NAME_OF_FISH VARCHAR2(10) NOT NULL PRIMARY KEY,
AQUARIUM_NAME   VARCHAR2(10) NULL,
BIRTH_DATE     DATE NULL,
DEATH_DATE DATE NULL,
COLORS VARCHAR2(10) NULL,
BREED VARCHAR2(10) NULL,
SEX CHAR(1) NULL,
COMMENT_TEXT VARCHAR2(100))
TABLESPACE USER_DATA
/
```

Now that you've created your own table, can you get it out of your life? No problem! Just drop it. This drop command works better on databases than with my dog: "Drop it, boy, drop it!" Here's the Oracle7 DROP command:

```
DROP TABLE tablename;
```

Tablename is (naturally) the name of the table you want to remove.

Use the DROP command only when you are certain that you can't fix the table and you don't need the data, because you can't restore the table using ROLLBACK after it is dropped. The only way to restore the table is from a backup copy. See Chapter 3 for a discussion of the ROLLBACK command.

DROP and DELETE are very different commands. DROP removes the table definition from your database completely, without a trace. DELETE removes the *rows* from a table but leaves the table itself intact.

See Chapter 4 for instructions on how to delete rows using SQL*Plus and PO7 Navigator.

PO7 Navigator's Wizard for Tables

When you want to create a brand-new table, use the PO7 Navigator. This section shows you how.

1. **Go to PO7 Navigator.**

   See Chapter 1 for instructions, if you need them.

2. **Connect to the database.**

   Double-click on the database connection of the Oracle7 user ID (owner) creating the table. This brings up a list of icons under the user icon labeled Table, Index, and so on.

   See Chapter 8 for instructions on creating a database connection if you don't know how.

3. **Right-click the Table icon in the left window and click New from the sub-menu that pops up, as shown in Figure 9-1.**

   The New Table dialog box appears, as shown in Figure 9-2.

4. **Select the Create table manually option button and then click OK.**

   The manual method is simpler than the Use table wizard method.

   This brings up the Create Table window, as shown in Figure 9-3.

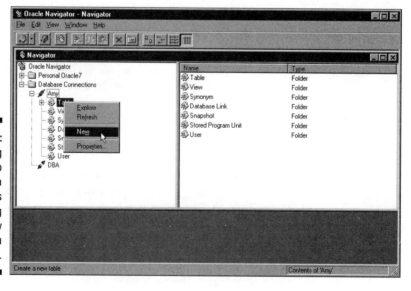

Figure 9-1: Getting ready to make a table means selecting the New Table menu item.

Figure 9-2:
Select the
manual
table
creation
process.

Figure 9-3:
Naming a
table is like
creating a
new life in
the Oracle7
world.

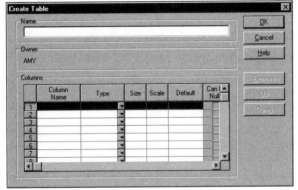

Oracle7.3 has a slightly different look, with two tabbed sections, one (the General tab) for the name, and one (the Design tab) for the columns.

5. **Name the table.**

   Click in the Name box and type the name of the table. Chapter 2 has a list of naming standards for tables.

   In Oracle7.3, after you name the table, click on the Design tab before continuing.

   After naming your table, define all the columns that are to be a part of the table. Each one is defined in the area of the window called (Oracle7 was especially intuitive on this) Columns.

6. **Name the column.**

   Enter a column name into the Column Name field. The first column goes into row 1, the second into row 2, and so on.

7. **Assign the datatype.**

   Make a selection from the datatypes in the drop-down Column Type list. See the list of databases in this chapter describing all the choices you have. VARCHAR2 is the most commonly used datatype for text information.

8. Adjust the size.

Adjust the size of the column by typing in the size you want in the Size field. Oracle7 measures size in number of characters or digits. For example, a column for a person's last name might be defined with a size of 20, because most people have last names that are less than 20 letters long.

9. Adjust the scale.

Scale is only used for columns with the NUMBER datatype. (See Table 9-1 for more about scale.) Otherwise you can leave the field blank.

10. Fill in the default value (optional).

The *default value* is the data that goes into the column when any new rows are added to this table.

For example, you assign a default value YES to the ADD_TO_MAILING_LIST column in your NAME_AND_ADDRESS table. Unless you specifically put in a value of NO (or MAYBE, or something else) in the ADD_TO_MAILING_LIST column when you insert new rows, every new row gets a YES in the ADD_TO_MAILING_LIST column.

The default value can be a phrase, word, letter, number, date, or whatever fits the datatype of this column.

Use your mouse to move the draw bar on the bottom of the Columns area to the right, revealing the next set of specifications for your column. Figure 9-4 shows this area, with important features labeled.

11. Allow nulls or not.

Leave the Can be Null? check box blank if this column is optional and can be left blank. Click on the check box (making it checked!) if required information must be entered into this column. For instance, in the fish example, what good is your chart without each fish's name?

12. Require unique column data or not.

The Unique? check box question is somewhat misleading, because the question *only applies to columns that are not the primary key*. A *primary key* is a column or set of columns that contain data uniquely identifying each row. A primary key is always unique by definition.

Making a check mark in the Unique? check box for the primary key column or columns seems logical. Unfortunately, Oracle7 interprets this as a request to create both a primary key constraint and a unique index. When Oracle7 tries to create both the key and the index, it fails and sends you an error message saying:

```
ORA-02261: such unique or primary key already exists in
           the table.
```

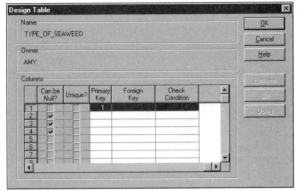

Figure 9-4:
The second
half of
column
definitions
revealed.

You don't see the error message until you complete the table definition and click the OK button, by the way, which makes it even more confusing.

To avoid getting the error, use the following chart to decide whether to check or not to check. Oracle7.3 may not give you the error, but still follow this chart for best results.

Unique Data Needed in column?	Primary Key Column?	Unique? is Checked or Unchecked?
No	No	Unchecked
Yes	No	Checked
Yes	Yes	Unchecked

Congratulations! You have completed the definition of a column.

There are two more boxes, labeled Foreign Key and Check Condition.

The Foreign Key box can either be defined now as you create your table, or later when you are ready. See Chapter 17 for full instructions on adding the Foreign Key to your table (the instructions are good for both creating a new table and changing an existing one).

The Check Condition box is an advanced, optional feature of Oracle7 not covered in this book. Just leave the box blank.

Repeat Steps 4 through 11 for each column until you have defined them all.

13. Rearrange columns (optional).

Figure 9-5 shows the three buttons you can use to move columns up or down in the matrix. Generally, I recommend that you *make the primary key columns the first columns in the table.* This makes your table more compatible with other databases, such as Paradox, which require the primary key to be first. Otherwise, arrange the columns any way you please. It makes no difference to Oracle7.

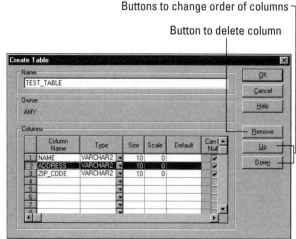

Buttons to change order of columns ┐

Button to delete column

Figure 9-5:
Rearrange
the order of
your
columns
here, if
needed.

Some designers like to arrange columns all in alphabetical order. Others like to arrange them in a "logical" order, like name, address, city, state, and so on. Arranging them the latter way is better if you use SQL*Forms or other tools that generate data entry screens using the order of your columns as a guide. These tools set up the data entry screen so that the user enters each column in the order it appears in the database table. The closer your columns match the order in which you want people to enter the data, the easier modifying the data entry screen created by your tool will be.

14. Click OK when you're done.

As in life, the only constant in Oracle7 is change. After a table has been created, its structure can change. To learn about changing tables using SQL*Plus and the PO7 Navigator, see Chapter 17. Also, Chapter 16 shows you how to add or change primary and foreign keys.

Chapter 10

Security Options: Roles, Profiles, and Grants

. . . .

In This Chapter

▶ Finding your built-in security blankets (The Nankie Phenomenon)

▶ Role playing

▶ Examining user profiles (Is this my good side?)

▶ Creating and assigning roles with SQL (The Director's Office)

▶ Designing roles in Navigator

. . . .

*D*atabase designers can get bogged down in security. The concern over safety often starts genuinely: Somebody in your office reads about a hacker in Australia who figured out the password to a protected file and ended up printing a love note in the newspaper. What you don't find out until much later is that the kid was the son of the office's vice president, who talks in his sleep.

Anyway, this chapter is devoted to showing off the Oracle7 security features at your disposal. You can't control what the office vice president says in his sleep, but you can control what role he is assigned and the table privileges assigned to that role.

Security Blanket Included

Here's what you get as standard security in the Oracle7 database world:

✔ All tables have an *owner* — the user that created the tables.

✔ If you're the table owner, the DBA and you are allowed to:

  • View the data in the table.

  • View and modify the table structure (column names and so on).

- Add and delete rows.

- Add, change, and remove data in any table row or column.

- Modify the structure (add, change, remove columns).

- Remove the entire table.

- Create table synonyms, views, indexes, primary keys, and relationships.

- Grant and revoke permission to any user or role to perform the preceding tasks.

These security measures you have are kind of like the relationship Dr. Frankenstein had with his little creation — they can get out of hand. Here's an interesting fact about security: If you query a table you don't have permission to see, you get this error message:

```
ORA-00942: table or view does not exist
```

This message has panicked many an innocent database user and designer, which is why three entire sections of Chapter 21 help you figure out what part of security caused this message. I call the first section "Solution 1: That Table Does Too Exist!" Don't miss the fun!

Meanwhile, this chapter contains a wealth of information about creating a reasonable security scheme for your Oracle7 database and deciphering the meanings of terms like *role* and *profile*.

Armed guards versus open arms

You may spend more time designing and implementing the security system than you do building the rest of the database system. A broad spectrum of security approaches exists. The strictest approach is when users have multiple passwords. The most lackadaisical approach is when every user logs on as the DBA, and the ID and password are conveniently posted in public.

Here's a typical security approach:

✔ One common login ID, and no additional password, is required for read-only access to the database.

✔ Roles for designers allow them to create and remove tables.

✔ Roles for users allow them to update certain tables, or allow them access to groups of tables for each functional area.

Roles, grants, and profiles are for Oracle7 databases that are shared among many users. You don't need roles if you work with your own private database, unless you have multiple personalities.

You can go totally overboard devising roles for every conceivable situation, mixing and matching the roles like my family's socks — which usually does not work. A little common sense and intuition go a long way when you're devising roles. Remember, simpler is usually better.

Roles Meet the Real World

Roles help you to easily keep track of who can do what in the database. To illustrate, I'll show you how roles existed in the olden days — back when I was your age.

Suppose that you are in charge of an office that has 35 employees, 15 of which are salaried and 20 of which are hourly. Two of the office managers are hourly. The rest of the managers are salaried. You want all hourly employees to enter their time card information in the TIMECARD table; then you want all the managers to review and adjust the pay rates on the PAY_RATE table. Figure 10-1 shows how you grant table permissions directly to each employee in the pre-role era of Oracle version 6 and below.

Now that Oracle7 exists, you can create two roles:

- ✔ The *manager* role can view and change pay rates.
- ✔ The *hourly employee* role can enter time card data.

The two roles overlap, as shown in Figure 10-2, because managers can also be hourly employees. Using Oracle7, you can grant the table permissions to two roles instead of to each individual employee.

Figure 10-1:
Ancient
Oracle
practices,
including
granting
table
permissions
directly to
users.

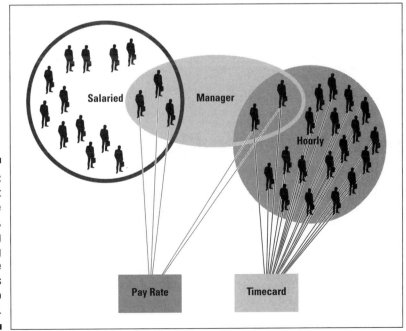

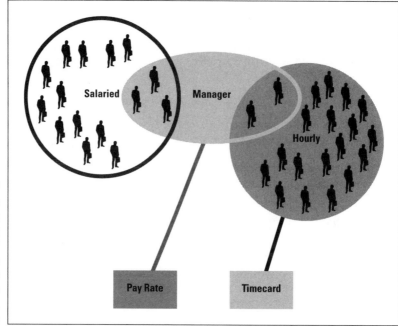

Figure 10-2:
The modern
streamlining
of Oracle7
lets you
grant table
permissions
to roles.

At first glance, a clever person might exclaim, "Wait just a darned minute! Oracle has increased my workload: Now I assign the employees roles and grant table permissions to roles." This is a clever observation but inaccurate in the long run. You may not notice the advantages of the role system until you start making changes. Without roles, when you add a new table that is used along with the TIMECARD table, you give table permissions to 20 employees. With roles, one permission is needed. You get the idea?

Profiles: The Power Players

Another way to control access to your database, besides assigning roles, is through the use of profiles. You may have a particularly paranoid boss. To relieve paranoia, first offer to check under your boss' bed and in the closets. If this tactic does not relieve the problem, offer to construct a tinfoil hat that blocks evil thought patterns and cosmic rays. I'm not kidding!

You or your boss may actually have a valid security concern about unauthorized people wreaking havoc in your lovely tables. Perhaps you want to be certain that when people leave for lunch they are quickly logged off the database. You may want to limit a user's total Central Processing Unit (CPU) time so that the Query From Heck that generates a results table ten times the size of the entire database isn't executed.

You can assign profiles to users, roles, and groups of users to limit access to system resources. You can tell Oracle7 to limit:

- ✔ Idle time
- ✔ CPU time
- ✔ Storage space
- ✔ Hang time in high surf (just kidding)
- ✔ Concurrent sessions per user
- ✔ Connect time
- ✔ Logical reads per session
- ✔ Other stuff

If you're still reading this section, you may want to actually look up the section on the `CREATE PROFILE` command available to the DBA in your Oracle7 Administrator's Guide documentation. Assigning profiles to each role that you create allows you to further customize what each role's abilities and limits are within the database.

The `CREATE PROFILE` command allows you, as DBA, to control the use of your database by various individuals assigned certain roles in your database. For example, you might limit the role you name `VAMPIRES` to ten CPU seconds per session — so the users don't suck the system dry. The role you name `MUTANT_CLONES` should probably have a limit on concurrent sessions so users don't start multiplying like rabbits.

Dive In: Creating and Assigning Roles with SQL

If you have Personal Oracle7 or if you are the DBA, creating and assigning roles is one of the simplest things you can do in SQL, something you can get right in there and do. Sometimes the DBA allows people who create tables to also create roles — check with your DBA to find out. To create a role in SQL, simply type

```
create role rolename;
```

where `rolename` is, obviously, the name of the role. Oracle7 responds with `Role created` if you've done your job correctly. To assign (or grant) someone a role, simply type

```
grant rolename to username
```

where *username* is — you guessed! — the Oracle user ID of the person to whom you are granting the role. Oracle7 responds with `Grant succeeded`. To assign table privileges, simply type

```
grant privilege, privilege, privilege on tablename to
rolename
```

where each `privilege` is replaced by a privilege. Select, insert, update, or delete are the most commonly used privileges, although others fall into the domain of the DBA and so are not covered by this book. Once again, Oracle7 responds with `Grant succeeded`.

Only the DBA can create roles, unless the DBA has granted this privilege to another user or role. Only the table owner can grant privileges (unless the table owner has given this right to another user or role, or someone has bribed the head waiter).

Imagine that you want to create two roles for your employees. One role, called `HOURLY`, gives employees access to the `TIMECARD` table, where they can log hours worked. Only hourly employees need this role. The other role, called `MANAGER`, lets a manager review and change the pay rate for an employee, which is stored in the `PAY_RATE` table. Here's the SQL code to create these two roles with the Oracle7 replies:

```
create role HOURLY;
Role created.
create role MANAGER;
Role created.
```

Next, you assign your employees to each role. One user, `JONES`, is both a manager and an hourly employee. Here are the two commands for Jones' roles, with the Oracle7 replies:

```
grant HOURLY to JONES;
Grant succeeded.
grant MANAGER to JONES;
Grant succeeded.
```

Now, for the final coup-de-grace, you assign the appropriate table privileges to each role.

```
grant select, insert, update, delete on TIMECARD to HOURLY;
Grant succeeded.
grant select, insert, update, delete on PAY_RATE to
            MANAGER;
Grant succeeded.
```

Working with Roles in the PO7 Navigator

This is so easy it's scary! Here's how to create and assign roles using PO7 Navigator.

1. **Start up PO7 Navigator.**

   See Chapter 1 if you need a refresher on how to do it.

2. **Create a database connection for the DBA.**

   Oracle comes pre-loaded with a DBA user ID called SYSTEM. You can use this user ID, or another user ID that has been created and given the DBA role on your Desktop Oracle7. Refer to Chapter 8 for explicit instructions about how to create a database connection.

3. **Connect to the DBA database connection.**

   Just click on the DBA database connection that is listed in the left window of the main PO7 Navigator screen.

4. **Right-click the Role icon on the right side of the window (the left side for Oracle 7.3) and then select New from the pop-up menu that appears, as shown in Figure 10-3.**

   The Create Role dialog box appears, as shown in Figure 10-4. In Oracle 7.3, the dialog box is called New Role Properties.

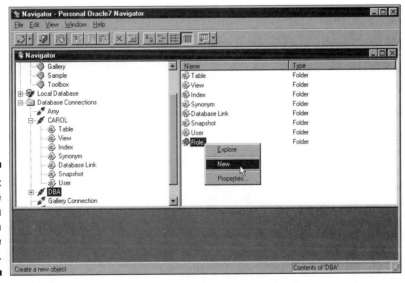

Figure 10-3: Select the New menu to create a new role (tricky, eh?).

Figure 10-4:
Creating a
role
couldn't be
easier.

5. **Type the role name and click OK.**

Now that you have created the role, you, as the DBA, can assign this new
role to other user IDs. Table owners can begin granting table privileges to
this role also. Here are the steps for assigning a role to a user.

1. **Start up PO7 Navigator.**

   Refer to Chapter 1 for instructions if you need them.

2. **Connect to the DBA database connection.**

   You created this connection in the previous few pages.

3. **Select a user.**

   Double-click the User icon on the right side of the PO7 Navigator
   window. This brings up a list of all the user IDs in the database, as
   shown in Figure 10-5.

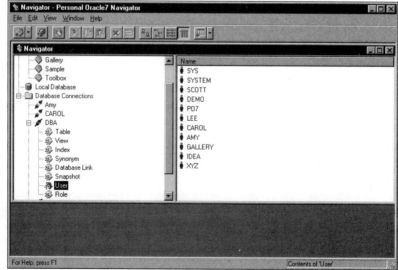

Figure 10-5:
The DBA
has a list of
all Oracle7
user IDs.

4. Select a user ID.

Right-click the user ID that will receive the new role. Then select Properties from the little pop-up menu. This brings up the user properties window.

5. Assign the new role.

Click the Role/Privilege tab near the top of the window. The window now shows the current list of roles and privileges for this user, as shown in Figure 10-6. The window has a list of all the granted roles on the left and a list of all the remaining roles that can be assigned on the right.

To assign a role, select the role in the right window and then click the little < button that is between the two windows to move it to the left window.

Figure 10-6:
Looking at the roles and privileges of one Oracle7 user.

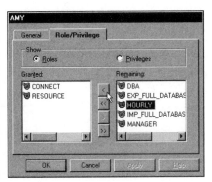

6. Click the OK button.

When you want to remove a role, simply follow these same steps, except instead of moving the role from the right to the left in the final step, move the role from the left to the right.

TIP

A role can have an assigned password, which means that a user must enter an additional password to access the role. Use this password-protected role only for high-security areas, such as the recipe tables for your famous banana bread.

Roles can sometimes be confusing, but they are a great way to enforce security. Once you set up the roles initially and get the appropriate table privileges granted, adding and removing users to the roles is easy. Using roles instead of granting table privileges directly to each user ID saves time in the long run.

Chapter 11

Views and Synonyms — Do You See What I See?

1 n this chapter, you can read about alternate ways to view tables in Oracle7. You can also learn how to make tables look as though they have different names, or have fewer columns and rows. You can learn how to combine tables into single larger tables without actually duplicating data. All of these tricks make security easier to plan.

The things in this chapter are kind of like sunglasses at the beach: They're not essential, but using them makes viewing swimsuits, or the lack thereof, much easier. Sunglasses also let you block out the incredible glare from the white Maui sand, which keeps blowing onto your keyboard, and the glares from the people you are staring at.

A View Is Like a Table — Almost

Views have one primary purpose: They rearrange the way you see a table, a portion of a table, or a group of tables without actually creating any copies of the underlying data. Imagine that you have a really great comprehensive table called NAME_AND_ADDRESS. This table contains the name and address of every customer you have ever done business with. The table also contains the name and address of every potential customer who filled out a questionnaire at your store.

Your sales department uses the NAME_AND_ADDRESS table to go after new leads to drum up new business. In fact, salespeople get frustrated because they have to weed out all the hundreds of names that are current or past customers from the hundreds of prospects.

Your accounting department uses the NAME_AND_ADDRESS table as its master mailing list. People in accounting send Christmas cards to all your past clients. The accounting department also gets tired of having to constantly separate the rows of current and past clients from the rows of potential clients.

Views help you solve the dilemma of sharing one table among two different interest groups. You can create two views of the NAME_AND_ADDRESS table. A view is a window into the underlying table. A view changes the outward appearance of the table without actually changing the data in the table. One of the views you create has only potential future clients in it. You name it PROSPECT and instruct your sales department to use the new view instead of the NAME_AND_ADDRESS table. From the salespeople's points of view (pardon my pun), you have given them a customized table for their own special needs. Your sales staff now knows you really love them.

Next, you create another view called CLIENT, which is limited to current and past customers. You ask your accountants to use this view in lieu of the NAME_AND_ADDRESS table. The accountants buy you a new desktop pen set to show their appreciation.

The two views you created each contained a subset of the data in the underlying table. The next section looks at the different ways to create views that contain subsets of a table's data.

You can also create views that span several tables and make them appear to be a single table. These kinds of views are explored in the subsequent sections of this chapter.

You can use views just like tables in queries, reports, and online forms. Here are restrictions for using views:

- ✔ If the view combines multiple tables, you can view the table data, but sometimes you can't update the data.

- ✔ In general, the user creating a view should own all the referenced tables. If some of the tables belong to other users, complex rules regarding updates through the view exist. Views that are for query only are not a problem.

Views that Narrow

The basic command for making a new view looks like this:

```
create [or replace] view viewname as
select column, column, etc. from tablename
where where clause;
```

Just about any valid query can be used in the select portion of the command. Once created, Oracle7 replies with

```
View created.
```

You can change a view by revising the query and adding the *or replace phrase* (in brackets above) to the command. Oracle7 replaces the existing view or simply creates a new view if one does not already exist.

To remove a view, drop it:

```
drop view viewname;
```

Oracle7 tells you that it took care of it:

```
View dropped.
```

Sometimes, a view becomes invalid because changes have been made to the underlying table. In these cases, the next time you use the view, you will get an error message indicating the problem. For example, if the underlying table was dropped, Oracle7 says:

```
ORA-04063: View "owner.viewname" has errors.
```

Owner is the view owner, and *viewname* is the name of the view.

See Chapter 22 for a report that pulls out the query that was used to create a view. This can be handy if you lost (or never kept) your original CREATE VIEW command.

This chapter has lots of examples to give you a good feel for the versatility of views. Enjoy yourself.

Your top-secret spy agency has a table called SPY_MASTER that contains counterintelligence agent names. You want your secretary to run a report listing these agents and their code names, sorted by country. You also want to be the only one able to view or change the names in the table.

You create a view called `UNCLASSIFIED_AGENT` that includes the agent code names and the country to which they are currently assigned. You grant permission for your secretary to see this view. Figure 11-1 shows the table and the view. The view is like a window that lets you see into one part of the table and contains only two of the three columns. You'd better be nice to your secretary!

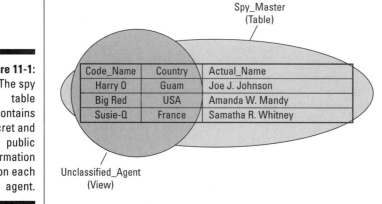

Figure 11-1:
The spy
table
contains
secret and
public
information
on each
agent.

The code for creating the `UNCLASSIFIED_AGENT` view goes like this:

```
create view UNCLASSIFIED_AGENT as
select CODE_NAME, COUNTRY
from SPY_MASTER;
```

Your company payroll table contains the pay rate for each employee. You want to give managers the ability to view and modify only their subordinates' pay rates. The table, `EMPLOYEE_PAY_RATE`, includes the employee's ID number and pay rate and the manager's ID number. You set up a view that looks at the manager accessing the table and matches that manager's ID with the employee IDs. It looks to the managers as if only their staff is in the table, as shown in Figure 11-2. You call the view `EMPLOYEE_PAY_RATE_BY_MANAGER` and give each `MANAGER` role permission to see and change data in this view.

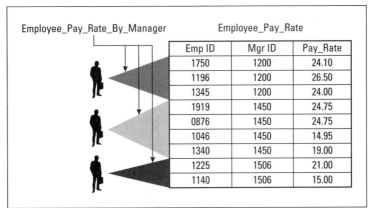

Figure 11-2:
Managers
get their
own view of
the
EMPLOYEE_
PAY_RATE
table.

You can set up the code for creating this view in two ways. The first way creates a set of views, one for each manager. The SQL code looks like this:

```
create view MGR_1450_EMPLOYEE_PAY_RATE as
select * from EMPLOYEE_PAY_RATE
where MGR_ID = 1450;
```

The second way to set up the code requires a little more preparation. Another table — the MANAGER table, connecting the manager's ID with the actual Oracle7 user ID — is required. The SQL for the view looks like this:

```
create view EMPLOYEE_PAY_RATE_BY_MANAGER as
select * from EMPLOYEE_PAY_RATE
where MGR_ID =  (select MGR_ID from MANAGER
                 where USER = MANAGER.ORACLE_ID);
```

The example above has a column called USER in the last line. Where did the USER column come from? Oracle7 has a small set of columns that are available in every table, even though they are not actually contained in any table's definition. These columns are like ghost columns — you can see them but they're not really there. Oracle7 calls them *pseudocolumns*. USER is one of these pseudocolumns.

On a similar note, Oracle7 has a small table called DUAL that is owned by the SYSTEM user ID and is accessible to all. DUAL always has one row and one column. Now that I think about it, I wonder why Oracle called the table DUAL — it should be called SINGLE! See the next section for a discussion on pseudocolumns and the proper use of the DUAL table.

Pseudocolumns and the DUAL *table*

The column named USER is a pseudocolumn — a column that Oracle7 defines for convenience. You can treat pseudocolumns just like any other column in queries, but you cannot change pseudocolumn values.

DUAL is a real table in Oracle7 that you can use any time you want to retrieve a single row of pseudocolumns or a single row of literal values that require no table access.

Here's a little list of some of the pseudocolumns available to you:

- ✔ USER: Oracle7 ID of current user logged on. USER is useful for security validation, because if you forget what user ID you've used, you can type

```
select USER from DUAL;
```

  The results tell you the user ID:

```
USER
----------------
AMY
```

- ✔ SYSDATE: Current date and time. SYSDATE is in Oracle7's standard date format. You can use SYSDATE to date stamp rows or add today's date to a report. Here's how:

```
select to_char(sysdate,'mm/dd/yyyy hh:mi:ss') from dual;
```

  The results show the current date and time in the specified format:

```
TO_CHAR(SYSDATE,'MM/DD/YYYYHH:MI:SS')
-------------------------------------
11/13/1996 01:49:35
```

- ✔ ROWID: The unique location of a row. ROWID contains a hexidecimal number for the block, row, and file where the row is stored. ROWID is the fastest path to retrieving a row, but you cannot use it as the table's primary key because it can change if you relocate the table.

- ✔ ROWNUM: This is a number assigned sequentially to rows retrieved from a query. The first row returned is assigned ROWNUM 1, the second row is assigned ROWNUM 2, and so on, which is useful for limiting the total rows returned in a query where ROWNUM is less than 100.

Views That Tie Everything Together

This section shows you how to use views to expand and combine multiple tables. Views can be used to group common information from several tables into a single table without duplicating data. You retrieve the underlying data from the original tables when the view is used, which means that any change made to the original tables is automatically used for the views.

You have created a table called COUNTRY in which each country has a number ID assigned called COUNTRY_ID. The COUNTRY_ID appears as a foreign key in other tables, such as your CUSTOMER_ACCOUNT table. A foreign key connects one table to another. See Chapter 5 to read more about the foreign key concept.

The CUSTOMER_ACCOUNT table uses the COUNTRY_ID from the COUNTRY table for the customer's location. Figure 11-3 diagrams the table layout.

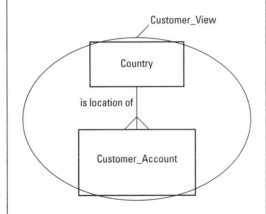

Figure 11-3:
The diagram for tracking your customers.

You need a view that combines the COUNTRY_NAME and the CUSTOMER_ACCOUNT tables so that you have a simple and convenient way to create reports. This view allows you to create reports as if you only had one table with all the information in it. Writing a query on one table is easier, so this saves you time and effort. This view can be especially handy when others need to write their own queries and are not experts like you on the subtleties of foreign keys. Figure 11-4 shows the data that appears in the tables and how it goes into the view.

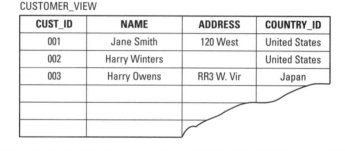

COUNTRY

ID	COUNTRY NAME
01	United States
02	Great Britain
03	Japan

CUSTOMER_ACCOUNT

CUST_ID	NAME	ADDRESS	COUNTRY_ID
001	Jane Smith	120 West	01
002	Harry Winters		01
003	Harry Owens	RR3 W. Vir	02

CUSTOMER_VIEW

CUST_ID	NAME	ADDRESS	COUNTRY_ID
001	Jane Smith	120 West	United States
002	Harry Winters		United States
003	Harry Owens	RR3 W. Vir	Japan

Figure 11-4:
Sample
data for the
two tables.
The view
combines
the tables.

Here's the SQL code to create this view:

```
create view CUSTOMER_VIEW as
   select CUST_ID, NAME, ADDRESS, COUNTRY_NAME
   from CUSTOMER_ACCOUNT,
        COUNTRY
   where COUNTRY.COUNTRY_ID = CUSTOMER_ACCOUNT.COUNTRY_ID;
```

PO7 Navigator's Wizard Does Views

When you create a view in the PO7 Navigator, you can select columns from a window, so you don't need to remember all the column names. When you join tables, using the PO7 Navigator is a bit more complicated, but not too bad. Here's how to create the CUSTOMER_VIEW view that I describe in the preceding section. Refer to Figure 11-3 for a bird's eye view of the tables. Try not to get too carried away with the binoculars, or else your neighbors will catch you peeking and call the cops. The view combines the CUSTOMER_ACCOUNT table with the appropriate COUNTRY_NAME from the COUNTRY table. Figure 11-4 shows the view with sample data.

Start out by firing up the PO7 Navigator and connecting to the user that will own the view (database connection). Refer to Chapter 1 for information on how to start PO7 Navigator and connect to a database. Then follow these steps to create the view:

1. **Right-click the View icon and select New from the sub-menu, as shown in Figure 11-5.**

   The Create View dialog box, where you do all the work, appears (see Figure 11-6). The Oracle 7.3 version has two tabbed sections.

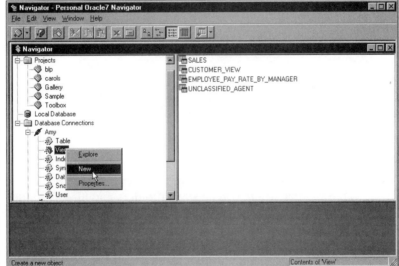

Figure 11-5:
Creating a view from scratch takes a little time, even in the PO7 Navigator.

2. **Type in the name of the view. In Oracle 7.3, click the Design tab after you type in the name of the view. This brings up a section that looks like the lower part of Figure 11-6.**

3. **Select the database.**

   Click the down arrow at the end of the Database box to see your database selections. Click <Default> (or another choice, if appropriate). Usually, you select <Default> for the database box. If you are accessing tables that are actually stored in a different database, this is where you'd select the database connection that points to the other database. Chapter 13 talks about database connections to outside sources.

   The Table and View icons appear. The view you create can be based on tables, views, or a combination of tables and views.

Click here to expand (+) or contract (-) tables

Name view here   Scroll up and down here

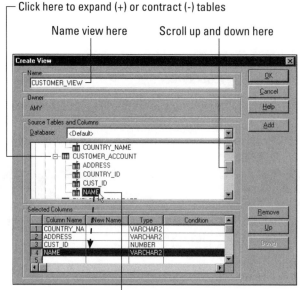

Figure 11-6:
You select
columns by
hunting and
pecking
with the
mouse.

Double-click column to add it to view

This window with the Table and View icons looks and works a lot like
the window where you view your folders and files in Windows 95
Explorer. Figure 11-6 shows the window, with important features
labeled.

4. **Double-click the icons until you find the owner, table, and column
   you want to include in the view.**

5. **Double-click each column to be included in the view.**

   When you double-click a column, it appears in the Selected Columns
   box. You can select columns from one or more tables.

6. **Continue to select columns from tables and views until you have
   selected all the columns you need.**

7. **Get the columns in the order you want them.**

   Change the order of the columns by clicking on the column you wish to
   move in the Selected Columns section of the window and then using the
   buttons on the right side (the bottom in Oracle 7.3) of the windows
   labeled Up and Down. Remove columns with, you guessed it, the
   Remove button. Add more columns by double-clicking on each column
   you want in the Source Tables and Columns section of the window.

8. Set conditions for the view.

If your view contains more than one table, telling Oracle7 how the two tables relate to one another is really important. Use the Condition box to type in the connection between the tables. (See the preceding section about creating views that join tables together in SQL*Plus for examples.) The general format is

```
tableA.columnA = tableB.columnB
```

Writing a condition is like writing the WHERE clause in a query.

Continuing with the CUSTOMER_VIEW example, here's how to set the conditions:

- Select the COUNTRY_NAME column.

- Tab over to the CONDITION column.

- Click and drag the dividing line between the CONDITION and the SOURCE columns to widen the CONDITION.

- Type the condition that connects the two tables. Figure 11-7 shows the example condition:

```
CUSTOMER_ACCOUNT.COUNTRY_ID = COUNTRY.COUNTRY_ID
```

The Condition box has other uses. Anything that you ordinarily put into the WHERE clause can go here. Here are some other examples to give you the idea:

- Only choose rows for the State of Wisconsin:

```
STATE_CODE = 'WI'
```

- Get employees who were hired over 5 years ago:

```
HIRE_DATE < ADD_MONTHS(SYSDATE, -60)
```

9. Click on the OK button.

You're done!

The condition that you type into the Condition box looks like the condition you put in a WHERE clause in a query. A limit on the width of this column exists — it doesn't allow for long condition clauses. Are you in any condition to be messing with the computer right now?

You can look at the complete SQL command that PO7 Navigator created for the view by right-clicking on the view and selecting Properties.

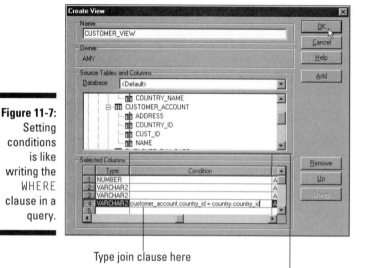

Figure 11-7:
Setting
conditions
is like
writing the
WHERE
clause in a
query.

Type join clause here

Click and drag dividers to give more room in Condition box

The PO7 Navigator does not modify views. To modify a view, remove the view the same way as you remove a table (see Chapter 9). Then go through the preceding steps as if the view were brand-new.

Synonyms: Nicknames for Tables and Views

No, it's not that spice on sticky buns. A *synonym* is an alternate name. You can make a synonym for a table, a view, even another synonym. Once created, the synonym can be used as if it were a table. Like views, synonyms do not duplicate data—they are only a different route to the same data. Darn! Now I'm getting hungry!

Here's how you create a synonym for a table:

```
create synonym ABC for TABLENAME;
```

Replace ABC with the synonym name and replace TABLENAME with the actual table name.

Where synonyms fit in the order of the universe

Oracle7 answers a set of questions to find a table for you:

1. **Does the table have the owner ID attached to it?**

   If so, Oracle7 goes directly to that table owned by that owner. For instance, if you put TEST.CUSTOMER in your query, Oracle7 looks for a table named CUSTOMER owned by TEST.

   If not, Oracle7 goes to the next step.

2. **Does the current user own a table with this name?**

If so, Oracle7 uses it. If not, it goes to the next step.

3. **Does the current user have a private synonym with this name?**

   If so, Oracle7 uses it. If not, it goes to the next step.

4. **Is there a PUBLIC synonym with this name?**

   If so, Oracle7 uses it. If not, Oracle7 sends an error message.

Public synonyms can be created for use by everyone. Usually, only the database administrator (DBA) can make a public synonym. However, like any other privilege in the database, your DBA can bequeath the ability to create public synonyms to you or to a role to which you belong. The SQL code for creating the public synonym is nearly the same, but you add the word PUBLIC and the owner of the table into the command:

```
create PUBLIC synonym ABC for owner.tablename;
```

Replace ABC with the actual synonym name and owner.tablename with the actual owner and the actual table name. Here's an example:

```
create PUBLIC synonym STATE_CODE for BOBM.STATE_CODE_LIST;
```

The synonym name does not have to match the table's name. If you are creating PUBLIC synonyms, they must be unique among all public synonyms.

Another kind of synonym that any user who creates tables can do is called the *private synonym*. A private synonym has all the same features as a public synonym except that it is *for the use of the synonym owner only* and not for everyone else. Private synonyms are not used very often.

One good use of the private synonym is to create yourself a shorthand name for a table. For example, you have named a table some long name like `CA_GRANT_STEP_ELEMENT_TYPE`. Now you are experimenting with a query in SQL*Plus using this table. Your fingers get into wrestling matches trying to type the table name over and over. Create a private synonym that you can use in place of the table name for your queries:

```
create synonym STEP for CA_GRANT_STEP_ELEMENT_TYPE;
```

Good uses for synonyms

Here are ways to use synonyms to your advantage:

- Create a synonym for a table that has a long name you are tired of typing. For example:

```
create synonym EE for EMPLOYEE_TRUST_FUND_ACCOUNT;
```

- Use public synonyms for centrally located lookup tables. The code for the synonym and the grant to allow all users to view the data looks like this:

```
create public synonym STATE_CODE for CENTRAL.STATE_CODE;
grant select on STATE_CODE to PUBLIC;
```

- Modify screen terminology, which gives two groups of users two different perspectives on the same information. For example, people in the sales department call a customer a *client* and have a fit when they see a table called `CUSTOMER` in their database. The table is shared with the people in the accounting department, who would rather die than call a customer a client. You create a synonym called `CLIENT` and make sure that the sales department uses it. You are subsequently revered as a wise and ancient sage, and promoted and worshipped accordingly. Little do they know that the underlying table for the `CLIENT` synonym is still the same old `CUSTOMER` table! The accounting department folks (who are always right, or so they say) continue to use the `CUSTOMER` table.

- Make multiple sets of tables that mirror each other but have different owners. Larger companies, where a need for both a test phase database and a production phase database exists, use this method.

Combining a grant and a synonym

A common mistake that Oracle7 users make when creating PUBLIC synonyms is assuming that now their tables can be shared with other Oracle7 users. *Creating a PUBLIC synonym for a table does not automatically allow other users to view or change the data in your table.* You must still grant the appropriate privileges, using the GRANT command described in Chapter 10. You do not grant privileges on a synonym — you always grant privileges on a table or view.

The rest of this section discusses the subtle and strange ways that synonyms (private and public) can behave. This part is for geeks who work in large offices where they have to keep track of hundreds of tables and dozens of user IDs. If you continue reading, you might accidentally force yourself to retain some residual information in your brain cells. You could wind up knowing too much.

Still reading? Okay, here goes. Imagine you have two mirrored (identical in structure but not in data) sets of tables in a single database. Both sets of tables are identically named but owned by two different Oracle7 user IDs, TEST and PROD. Synonyms can be designed to control which set of tables any particular user ID gets to see and use. With the identical SQL code, one user accesses the test data while another accesses production data. Here's a sample of the SQL code:

Log in as user A, who works with the TEST tables, and create these synonyms:

```
create synonym CUSTOMER for TEST.CUSTOMER;
create synonym ORDER_ITEM for TEST.ORDER_ITEM;
```

Log in as the DBA and create these synonyms so that all other users work with PROD tables:

```
create PUBLIC synonym CUSTOMER for PROD.CUSTOMER;
create PUBLIC synonym ORDER_ITEM for PROD.ORDER_ITEM;
```

Log in as PROD and grant privileges on the tables:

```
grant select on CUSTOMER to PUBLIC;
grant select on ORDER_ITEM to PUBLIC;
```

Log in as TEST and grant privileges:

```
grant select on CUSTOMER to PUBLIC;
grant select on ORDER_ITEM to PUBLIC;
```

The following SQL code reaches different tables, depending on who is executing them:

```
select * from CUSTOMER;
```

Because no owner ID is added to the table name, user A, who has a private synonym for CUSTOMER, sees the TEST table. User B, who has no private synonym, gets the public synonym, which allows him to see the PROD table. At this point, you will have successfully amazed and baffled the entire office staff.

You can do some amazing tricks when you understand the subtleties of synonyms. Besides, knowing how synonyms work helps you decipher some of the more frustrating errors that can be caused by misunderstanding the way that Oracle7 handles synonyms.

Chapter 12

Reports: The Hidden Talent of SQL*Plus

. . . .

In This Chapter

▶ Formatting reports

▶ Grouping and summarizing

▶ Using fun and fancy extras

. . . .

*I*n a perfect world, database programmers would get to play with data all day long and not be bothered by the demands of others. You can keep tinkering in hopes of one day achieving oneness with all data. Of course, your boss probably doesn't work in a perfect world. He or she probably expects you to do something with all those numbers in your database. Yesterday. The nerve . . .

Fortunately, Oracle7 can help you out. You can use SQL*Plus to spit out those reports — summarized, sorted, grouped, signed, sealed, and delivered. You can even use SQL*Plus to do a couple of higher-level things on reports to dazzle your boss. And you can do it all quickly, leaving you time to resume your quest. Om . . .

Getting a Decent-Looking Report from SQL*Plus

Some commands that are especially for SQL*Plus are not SQL at all. They are basically environment settings that take effect during a SQL*Plus session. The most useful commands let you lay out a report that looks pretty decent. The kind you might get away with showing to the Board of Directors.

Here's a short description of some of the most useful commands for creating reports in SQL*Plus.

Adjusting the size and heading for a column

The COLUMN command allows you to change the heading of a column and several other things that by default are derived from the column itself.

```
COLUMN c HEADING h FORMAT f WORD_WRAPPED
```

Replace c with the actual column name.

Replace h with the column heading you want. If the name includes spaces, enclose it in double quotes.

Replace f with the format you want. The format parameter defines how many characters wide the report column will be and defines the appearance of numbers. For text columns, use A(n), where n is the number of characters. For number columns, use a pattern of 9's and zeros. For example, the format 990.00 lines up dollar amounts very well. For date columns, you cannot define the appearance of the date. You can define the width of the report column to match the format of the date. You define the data format itself in your SELECT clause by using the TO-CHAR function. See "Formatting Dates" in Chapter 20 for details.

WORD_WRAPPED is optional. If used, long text columns wrap to the width you specify in the format and break where there's a new word instead of exactly at a certain number of characters.

```
COLUMN SELLING_PRICE HEADING "Sales Price" FORMAT 9,990.00
```

A query selecting this column appears like this:

```
Sales Price
-----------
   1,050.99
```

The COLUMN command stays in effect as long as you stay in SQL*Plus.

Adding a title to your query

A title makes a query look like a regular report. There are two versions of the TITLE command. The first one lets you put a simple line of text at the top of your report.

```
TTITLE justify "title text"
```

Replace *justify* with CENTER or RIGHT or LEFT to justify the text of the title. Replace *title text* with whatever you want to say. Enclose it in quotes.

The second version gives you a lot more flexibility. You can format pieces of the title on the left, center, and right sides all in one title. You can include columns that are in your query in the title. You use this version of TITLE most often when you have a report that is sorted and grouped by categories. See the "Summarizing, Grouping, and Ordering In Queries" section in this chapter for an example.

Sending SQL output to a file

Here's a very useful command. This is how you write the results of your query to a file. Later, you can go get the file and print it. Hard copy is so much more convincing than pixels on a screen.

```
SPOOL filename
```

Replace *filename* with the actual file name you want. If you do not specify a suffix in your file name, SQL*Plus automatically tags a suffix on the file name. On a PC, the suffix is *.lst.* On other systems, the suffix is usually *.lis.*

Once spooling starts, SQL*Plus sends everything to this file. To stop the spooling, issue this command:

```
SPOOL OFF
```

Spooling also ends as soon as you exit SQL*Plus. You cannot edit a file that is in the middle of spooling, either. You get a blank file. Remember to stop spooling before you edit the file.

Summarizing, Grouping, and Ordering In Queries

I could write a whole book on this topic, but here's my distilled, in-a-nutshell, use-it-or-lose-it summary.

Sorting the results of your query

Sorting query results is very easy. Use the ORDER BY clause, which comes at the end of your query.

The general format is

```
ORDER BY column [ASC / DESC ] , column [ASC / DESC ] ...
```

List the columns in the order in which you want them sorted. The default order is ascending, so you can either add the ASC parameter or leave it off. To sort in descending order, add the DESC parameter next to each column that is to be sorted in descending order.

Here's a simple example that gets all the columns from the ARTIST table and sorts the results by the last name of the artist.

```
Select * from ARTIST
ORDER BY LAST_NAME;
```

A shortcut for the ORDER BY clause lets you list the columns by their position rather than their name. For example, if you want to sort by the first three columns in your select statement, simply write ORDER BY 1, 2, 3.

Summarizing instead of showing details in your query

You can use the basics of summarizing in two ways. One way is to create a report that shows nothing but the summary, which is what this section discusses. The other way is to show a summary at the end of a report or at certain break points within the report, which is what the next section discusses.

You want a total count of all the tickets sold for a benefit dinner. The TICK-ETS table has one row for each ticket printed. One column, called STATUS, reads SOLD when you sell the ticket and OPEN if the ticket has not yet sold. Here's the query:

```
select count(status)
from TICKETS
where STATUS = 'SOLD';
```

The count function is one of many functions available to you in SQL*Plus.
Oracle7 shows you 103 tickets sold:

```
count(status)
-------------
103
```

Oracle7 has many different summary commands. Oracle7 calls them *group
functions*. Among the most commonly used summary commands are

- ✔ AVG — Average value of a column, ignoring nulls.
- ✔ MAX — Maximum value of a column.
- ✔ COUNT — Number of rows where the column being counted is not null. If
  all are null (or if none match the query criteria), COUNT equals zero.
- ✔ SUM — Total sum of the column.

Group functions act upon the rows returned from your query, not on the
whole. For example, if you want to count all the managers in your employee
table, add a WHERE clause that eliminates all but the managers from
your query.

Grouping rows and showing totals on break points

To round out the SQL report, you need three things combined and coordi-
nated to make a report with details, breaks, and summaries.

First, your query includes an ORDER BY clause. Second, you must tell
SQL*Plus what columns to use as break points. Third, you must tell
SQL*Plus what to do at the breaks. The easiest way that I can explain this to
you is to use an example.

You own the planet Earth. You want a list of the names of all the cities on
Earth, broken down by continent and by country. Then you want a count of
the total cities in each country and on each continent and a total count of all
the cities. Your minions scurry to comply. Here is what their SQL*Plus script
looks like:

```
break on report on continent skip 2 on country skip 1
compute count of city on report
compute count of city on continent
compute count of city in country
select continent, country, city
from EARTH
order by continent, country, city;
```

I've included the first eight Earth cities you put into your database, just so
you can get an idea of what your report looks like. Here it is:

```
CONTINENT              COUNTRY      CITY
-----------------      ------------ --------------------

EUROPE                 ENGLAND      LONDON
                                    MANCHESTER
                       ************ --------------------
                       count                           2

                       FRANCE       NICE
                                    PARIS
                       ************ --------------------
                       count                           2

*******************                 --------------------
count                                                  4


NORTH AMERICA          CANADA       TORONTO
                       ************ --------------------
                       count                           1

                       USA          CHICAGO
                                    LOS ANGELES
                                    NEW YORK
                       ************ --------------------
                       count                           3

*******************                 --------------------
count                                                  4


                                    --------------------
count                                                  8

8 rows selected.
```

Look through the SQL reports in Chapter 22 for good examples of SQL*Plus reports.

Dazzle Your Friends with These Commands

Here are a few hints that will blow 'em away.

Defining a variable

Define a variable so that you can run the same SQL query for varying results. Just use a variable name in the query's WHERE clause and you have a nice flexible reporting tool. You can use the variable anywhere that you use a column. Always refer to the variable with a preceding ampersand (&) and single quotes around it. Here's a sample:

```
select NAME, SALES_CALL_DATE from CUSTOMER_ACCOUNT
where SALES_CALL_DATE <= TO_DATE('&CUTOFF_DATE');
```

When you run the query, Oracle7 asks you for a date:

```
Enter value for cutoff_date:
```

You type in a regular date in the Oracle7 format:

```
01-jul-96
```

Oracle7 goes on its merry way and produces the report:

```
NAME                           SALES_CAL
------------------------------ ---------
Jane                           15-JAN-96
Joe                            11-FEB-96
Harry                          21-APR-96
```

Changing the page length and width

Two parameters adjust the page size. You can adjust the default page size so that it fits on your computer screen. When creating a report that prints out on letter-size paper, adjust the page size so that page breaks are at the bottom of the page.

```
SET PAGESIZE 60
```

This code changes the number of lines per page to 60.

```
SET LINESIZE 132
```

This command changes the number of characters per line to 132, which is usually what you want for printing landscape-style reports.

Experiment with these settings by spooling and printing test reports. Your printer may need a slightly different setting.

Making two queries appear on one page

```
SET EMBEDDED ON
```

This code requests no page break between queries, which can be really handy if you have a detailed report and you want to use a separate query to summarize things at the end of the report.

```
SET EMBEDDED OFF
```

This code returns you to default mode, which puts a page break between every report.

Hiding the query

Maybe to appear more intelligent or avoid blame, you want to put the results of your query in a report showing everyone the query you created to produce the report. Use the ECHO command to handle this. The default mode depends on your system. Usually, the default is OFF, meaning you don't see the SQL code that created your report. To check the setting, type

```
SHOW ECHO
```

Press Enter, and Oracle7 replies with the current setting of the ECHO command:

```
echo ON
```

If ECHO is ON, turn it OFF by typing:

```
SET ECHO OFF
```

Oracle7 does not reply with a message after you press Enter.

Change ECHO to OFF before you spool to a file so that you can receive only the output and not the query. After you are done spooling, you can reset ECHO by typing:

```
SET ECHO ON
```

SQL*Plus gives you many more tools. These basic ones can enhance your skills in creating useful reports through SQL*Plus.

Chapter 13

Sharing and Getting Data Out of Oracle7

In This Chapter

▶ Breaking the database barrier

▶ Linking across the Internet

▶ Bringing data in from the outside

▶ Getting data out to share

*T*he idea of distributing a database all over the world is not a new one. This *client/server* technology is the key element in the World Wide Web. This chapter covers only a tiny corner of that world by looking at the way Oracle7 connects databases within SQL*Plus. Read tons about how databases and the Web intertwine in *Creating Cool Web Databases* (IDG Books Worldwide), which I co-authored with Joseph Sinclair.

If you have no need to connect one Oracle7 database to another, maybe you have been wondering, "How do I move my old database stuff into this nice shiny new Oracle7 database?" Or, on the other hand, perhaps your question is "What can I do to get my Oracle7 data out and put it into this other cool tool?"

This chapter explores all three situations:

✔ Moving items from Oracle7 to Oracle7

✔ Moving items from other databases into Oracle7

✔ Moving items from Oracle7 to other databases

Breaking the Database Barrier

You can reach out across the Internet or an intranet to retrieve data from another Oracle7 database. The primary differences between the *Internet* and *intranet,* besides one letter in the middle, are the distances they cover and who has access to the them. Both are clusters of computers joined together with one or more networks made up of cable wire, phone lines, or other connecting technologies. A typical intranet spans one or two floors of an office building, or sometimes a few blocks of nearby buildings. Intranets are generally private and for in-house use only. The Internet, on the other hand, spans the globe and is public.

Oracle7 has built-in features in SQL*Plus that allow you to use an intranet or the Internet to connect directly to another Oracle7 database. You can even run a query that joins two tables located on two separate databases.

In other words, you and others in your office are probably closer than you may think to sharing data between multiple Oracle7 databases. If you are all connected to a local network (intranet) for printing and e-mail, that same network can be used to send and receive data between two databases. Just plug in *SQL*Net* — an Oracle7 product that lets you run SQL*Plus or other tools from one computer that gets information stored in an Oracle7 data-base on another computer — on both machines, do some tweaking, and away you go. Figure 13-1 illustrates an Oracle7 database on an intranet running in client/server mode; SQL*Net acts as the conduit on both ends of the network.

Figure 13-1:
Oracle7
connecting
to another
Oracle7
database
across an
intranet.

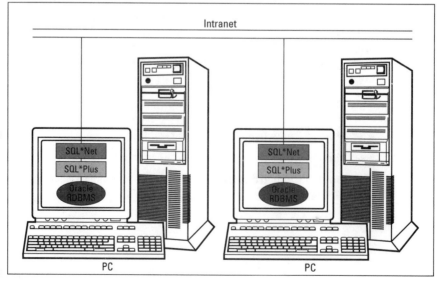

Techno-junkie alert: Here's the SQL*Plus code

Racing across time and space in search of new unspoiled territory, the bold Oracle7 user tests the waters with newfound SQL*Net, which casts its lines out on both ends of a cross-database connection. Simply put, SQL*Net is a kind of translator, because each Oracle7 database only talks to its own personal SQL*Net, and the SQL*Net does the talking to other SQL*Nets. So to get two Oracle7 databases to talk to each other, you have to get one database to tell its SQL*Net to tell the other SQL*Net to tell the other database something. The whole process is a lot like negotiations at a Jimmy Carter peace talk.

This section describes how to connect two databases together. One database is called the *local database*. That's the one you start up SQL*Plus on and run the following commands in. The database you connect to is called the *remote database*. Before you can connect to another database using SQL*Net and SQL*Plus, you must meet these conditions:

- ✔ **SQL*Net must be on the local computer.**

  You must install, configure, and run SQL*Net on the computer where your local Oracle7 database resides, tasks too great for the scope of this book. See Chapter 23 for information on where to get SQL*Net and where to get help using SQL*Net.

- ✔ **SQL*Net must be on the remote computer.**

  You must install, configure, and run SQL*Net on the computer where the remote Oracle7 database resides (the one with which you intend to make a connection). See the preceding bullet for my disclaimer about SQL*Net.

- ✔ **You must start both the local database and the remote database.**

  See Chapter 1 for information on how to start up the local database. To start up the remote database, you must log into the remote computer as if you were using it locally and then start up the database the same way you started your local database. Another alternative is to ask the DBA who runs Oracle7 on the remote computer to "pretty please with sugar on top" start Oracle7 on the remote computer for you.

- ✔ **You must know a valid Oracle7 user ID and password on the remote database.**

  See Chapter 8 for instructions on how to create a new Oracle7 user ID if you need one. Again, create an Oracle7 user ID on the remote database the same way you did it for the local database. Do it by first logging into the remote computer as if you were a local user. The most polite (and politically correct) method is to ask the DBA of the remote database to create a new Oracle7 user ID for you.

Now, make the connection happen by creating a database link between the two databases.

Run this SQL code at your local database in SQL*Plus:

```
create database link LINKNAME using 'CONNECT_STRING';
```

Replace *LINKNAME* with the actual link name, and replace *CONNECT_STRING* with the actual connection string that tells SQL*Net how and where to connect. One part of the connect string is the Oracle7 user ID and password you use to log into the remote database.

When you send the database link command, the remote database sees you as if you had logged in using SQL*Plus like any other Oracle7 user. To use the link, simply use the LINKNAME as a suffix to the table name. For example, you want to query the CAR_INVENTORY table in the remote database. Your link is called DETROIT. The SQL code looks like this:

```
select CAR, TOTAL_ON_HAND
from CAR_INVENTORY@DETROIT;
```

Your local Oracle7 knows that this table resides on the remote database, so Oracle7 sends the entire query to SQL*Net, which in turn sends it to the remote database. SQL*Net receives the query and transmits it to the remote database as if you had just typed it into SQL*Plus on the remote database. The remote database runs the query and returns the answer to the local database using the same SQL*Net connections in reverse.

Client/server technology with Oracle7

You can also use SQL*Net to create a *client/server* environment on your office intranet. Figure 13-2 shows how several PCs (clients) get connected to a single Oracle7 database on the mainframe (server). Each client connects to the server as if the database is right on the client's desktop. Client/server has become an industry standard, not only for relational databases but for many other kinds of software as well. Notice that each client requires its own copy of SQL*Net to make the connection, while the server needs one copy of SQL*Net to receive many connections.

Client/server technology helps you if you plan to run a multinational corporation with centralized database core functions. Distributed processes run locally and still update central database tables. If all of this makes sense, why are you reading this book? Actually, I'm flattered that you're reading this book!

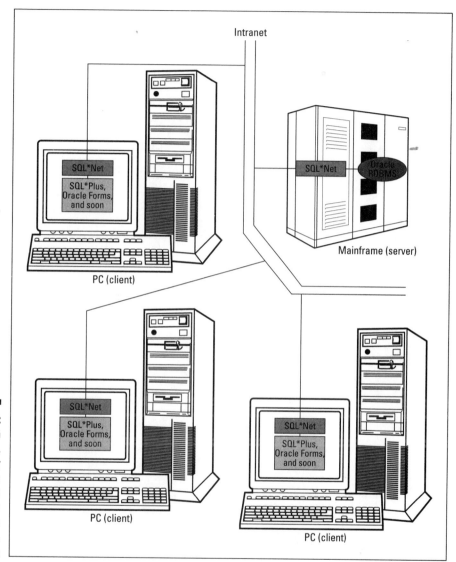

Figure 13-2:
With
Oracle7,
many
clients can
connect to
one server
across an
intranet.

As the Internet becomes more and more popular, the technology for connecting Oracle7 to other Oracle7 databases via the Internet has changed. A
new standard, called *Open Database Connection* (ODBC) has rocked the
relational database world. Before ODBC, you could only connect one
Oracle7 database to another Oracle7 database. The same was true of other
brands of databases as well. Each had its own proprietary connection with
SQL*Net (the one for Oracle7). Today, using ODBC software, you can
connect your Oracle7 database to other ODBC-compliant databases and
software.

Figure 13-3 shows the way that ODBC opens the door to a world of new software tools, from databases to Web page design tools. I'd like to make a few points about this illustration:

✔ Rather than use SQL*Plus, this setup uses Oracle Forms. Other Oracle7 tools — such as Oracle Reports — can also use this configuration.

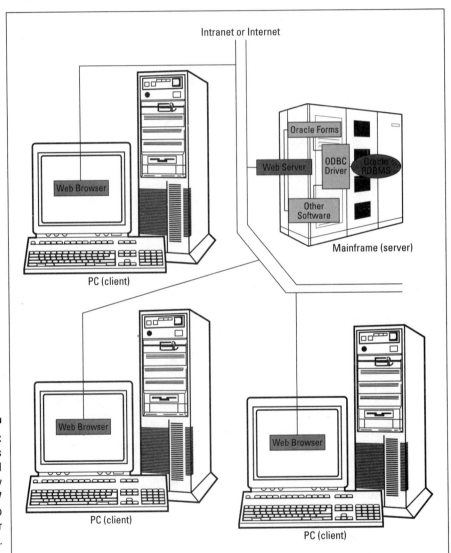

Figure 13-3: ODBC has changed the way Oracle7 connects to other software.

Intranet fun with remote database connections

Many businesses link offices with an intranet, which resembles the Internet architecture. The intranet structure shares data inside an organization. Small isolated databases suddenly become resources for each other. The possibilities are endless when you combine Internet technology to the intranet network that may already exist in the office.

✔ Notice the box labeled "Other Software." Because ODBC is an industry-wide standard, any software vendor can now write software that utilizes an Oracle7 database. A dozen new software tools already take advantage of the ODBC connection for use with standard Web browsers like Netscape Navigator.

✔ This setup can be used either with an intranet or on the Internet.

✔ No additional software (besides a standard Web browser like Navigator) is required on the client.

✔ Although I do not show it in this illustration, both the client and the server computers need not be PCs and/or mainframes.

Chapter 23 explores some of the new ODBC tools available to use with Oracle7. Take a look at this brave new world.

Pulling Data Out of Oracle7 with SQL*Plus

Some people never need to pull data out of their Oracle7 databases except as printed reports. However, most of us want to know how to get data out of Oracle7 in a specific format so that we can use it elsewhere. This section shows you a method I've developed that works very well for extracting data from Oracle7.

Oddly enough, Oracle7 does not provide any kind of extraction tools for getting data out of Oracle7 in a format that is usable to other databases. Oracle7 gives you the EXP and IMP commands (see Chapter 14 for more information) for backing up tables or loading them into another database. Still, Oracle7 has no utilities for exporting Oracle7 tables into any non-Oracle7 formats.

Sometimes you need data in a format that some other software can read. Most spreadsheets, word processors, and desktop databases accept data from outside sources if the data is in a plain text file with these features:

- ✔ Each line in the file contains one row.
- ✔ Each column has data surrounded by double quotation marks.
- ✔ Each column is separated from the following column by a comma.

Oracle7 calls this kind of text file a *comma-delimited file*. You can use SQL*Plus to create a comma-delimited file. Here's how:

1. **Create a file containing a query, selecting all the columns you wish to extract.**

2. **Add SQL*Plus commands to put in quotation marks and commas.**

3. **Add SQL*Plus commands to remove page breaks and column headings and adjust column width.**

4. **Add SQL*Plus commands to spool the results into a file.**

5. **Save the script file.**

6. **Log on SQL*Plus and run the script file.**

This creates a comma-delimited file where every column's data is surrounded by double quotes. What a lot of work!

I bet you're wondering why Oracle7 does not give you a simple SAVE AS command where you select the format you want. Me, too! The method described here is tedious but it works. Also, see Chapter 22 has a script that you can use to generate the initial select statement that includes all the columns in a table automatically. That saves a little time.

Let me use an example to show you how to create the script you need. This example extracts the data from all the columns and all the rows of the TYPE_OF_SEAWEED table. I chose this table because it has only a few columns and because it has a variety of different datatypes, giving me the opportunity to show you how to handle each different datatype. Figure 13-4 shows the contents of the TYPE_OF_SEAWEED table.

Figure 13-5 shows the end results of the SQL*Plus script I created. The end product has three lines, one for each row, and each column's data is enclosed in double quotation marks followed by commas.

Figure 13-4:
The TYPE_OF_SEAWEED table has three rows and five columns.

Figure 13-5:
A comma-delimited file created from the TYPE_OF_SEAWEED table.

The sample SQL*Plus script shown here also appears on the CD at the back of the book. Appendix B tells you where to find this script on the CD. Here is the entire script:

```
set feedback off
set pagesize 0
set termout off
set linesize 1000
set heading off
set echo off
column NUMBERCOL format a12
column CHARCOL1 format a42
column CHARCOL2 format a12
column DATECOL format a12
spool comma.txt
select  '"' || to_char(TYPE_ID) || '",' NUMBERCOL,
     '"' || DESCRIPTION_TEXT || '",' CHARCOL1,
     '"' ||EDIBLE || '",' CHARCOL2,
     '"' ||to_char(PER_POUND) || '",' NUMBERCOL,
     '"' ||to_char(LAST_CHANGE_DATE,'mm/dd/yyyy') || '"' DATECOL
from TYPE_OF_SEAWEED
```

(continued)

(continued)

```
order by TYPE_ID;
spool off
set feedback on
set pagesize 24
set termout on
set linesize 80
set heading on
set echo on
```

That's a lot of code. Here are some notes about the code:

- ✔ Each column that you selected has a double quote concatenated (linked) to it on either side. Concatenation to number and date columns requires that you convert them into character datatypes using the `TO_CHAR` function.

- ✔ Each column except the final one also has a comma concatenated to it on the end.

- ✔ I used a date format of mm/dd/yyyy. You can use any date format you choose.

- ✔ Assign each column an alias and use that alias in a `COLUMN` command to define the width of the column. I chose to use the same alias for the two number columns, so the same column command applies to both columns.

- ✔ The `SET` commands at the beginning of the script cause the spooled file to contain only the data you select and no extraneous noise that Oracle7 sometimes throws in. These commands also keep the output that goes into the file from scrolling on your computer screen.

- ✔ The `SET` commands at the end of the script cause your SQL*Plus session to reset itself to normal. This way any further queries or SQL*Plus commands you enter behave as you would expect them.

Once you have created a script like this, repeating it for other tables is pretty easy. Save the file in a safe place for future use. Your sycophants will consider you a savior and a genius if you share this with others. Much groveling will ensue. Bootlicking will be in order and noses shall be brown. Tell them to go buy their own copy of *Oracle7 For Dummies!*

*Pushing Data Into Oracle7 With SQL*Plus*

What about those times when you want to go the other way — getting data from some other kind of database, such as Microsoft Access, into Oracle7?

For example, what do you do when have a plain text file with data you use for mailing labels or form letters that you want to convert into your Oracle7 database?

Oracle7 provides a program that runs from the command line, called SQL*Loader. Unfortunately, I find this tool to be extremely difficult to use no matter how often I use it. Instead, I find that the most practical way to add new data from other databases is to get the data into a text file, edit the data into a series of insert commands, and run it in SQL*Plus.

First, prepare your data by putting it into a comma-delimited file format where

↙ Every column's data is surrounded by single quote marks.

↙ Every column, except the last one, is followed by a comma.

↙ Every new line contains a new row of data.

Figure 13-6 shows an example of this kind of file. Most desktop databases provide an option for exporting or saving a table in this kind of format. With this kind of file and a good word processor, you can create a set of INSERT commands that work beautifully with Oracle7 in these situations.

Figure 13-6:
A comma-delimited file from a word processor.

Next, use your word processor to add a phrase to the front of each line:

```
insert into tablename (column, column, column, ...) values (
```

The INSERT command can be on two lines, because SQL*Plus is not sensitive to line breaks.

In the example, the text file in Figure 13-6 gets loaded into the TYPE_OF_SEAWEED table. For this file, you would put the INSERT INTO TYPE_OF_SEAWEED command phrase on the front of every line:

```
insert into TYPE_OF_SEAWEED (TYPE_ID, DESCRIPTION_TEXT,
EDIBLE ,  PER_POUND, LAST_CHANGE_DATE) values (
```

After this, add the following two characters at the end of every line:

```
);
```

These characters (the closing parenthesis and the semicolon) tell SQL*Plus that you have reached the end of a command and it should be executed. The end results look like the file in Figure 13-7.

Figure 13-7:
A file with a
series of
insert
commands.

```
Commas.txt - Notepad                                    _ □ ×
File  Edit  Search  Help
insert into TYPE_OF_SEAWEED (TYPE_ID, DESCRIPTION_TEXT,
EDIBLE ,  PER_POUND, LAST_CHANGE_DATE) values (
'4','Rooted, fluted leaves','EDIBLE','1.5','01-JAN-97');
insert into TYPE_OF_SEAWEED (TYPE_ID, DESCRIPTION_TEXT,
EDIBLE ,  PER_POUND, LAST_CHANGE_DATE) values (
'5','Floating, all green','EDIBLE','5.5','19-NOV-96');
insert into TYPE_OF_SEAWEED (TYPE_ID, DESCRIPTION_TEXT,
EDIBLE ,  PER_POUND, LAST_CHANGE_DATE) values (
'6','Rooted, varigated color','INEDIBLE','7','');
```

The file shown in Figure 13-7 is also on the CD-ROM included with the book. See Appendix B.

To run the file, which now contains a series of insert commands, follow these steps.

1. **Start up SQL*Plus (the instructions are in Chapter 1).**

2. **Type** `set echo on` **and press Enter.**

   This allows you to see what SQL*Plus reads from the file.

3. **Type** `spool filename` **and press Enter.**

   Use a file name with which you can spool the whole session so that you can easily inspect it for errors later.

4. **Type** `start filename` **and press Enter.**

   This time, use the name of the file you edited that has all your comma-delimited data in it. Oracle7 responds by reading the file and executing each insert command, and then replies:

```
1 row created.
```

Et voila, presto! You are finished. You now have inserted a whole bunch of data from some outside source.

When using this method, keep in mind a few notes of caution:

✔ All dates must either have the default Oracle7 format of "dd-mon-yy" or have the TO_DATE function added to them. For example, dates might look like this:

```
to_date('01/15/96','mm/dd/yy')
```

✔ Data that contains single quotes must be changed. Put an additional single quote in front of the single quote in the data. Oracle7 interprets this properly. For example, your data might look like this:

```
'Mom''s Diner'
```

When put into the database, it looks like this:

```
Mom's Diner
```

✔ If your data contains ampersands (&), you must add the following SQL*Plus command before you run all the inserts:

```
set define off
```

This tells Oracle7 to leave the ampersands as they are. Otherwise, Oracle7 thinks you are defining a variable.

You can return to the state you were in before you did all the inserts, by typing

```
ROLLBACK;
```

Press Enter. Oracle7 replies with

```
Rollback succeeded.
```

Chapter 14

The Five Ws of Safeguarding Your Data

. . . .

In This Chapter

▶ Why back up

▶ What to back up

▶ When to back up

▶ What backup weapon to use

▶ Where to hide your backups

. . . .

*Y*ou've heard this story, I'm sure: A poor soul plans to back up his disk drive on Wednesday, but on Tuesday the system crashes and it takes him a month to recover. Another good one: A rookie drops her table instead of deleting a few rows. She has no way to recover because she has no backup.

No, the five Ws is not a singing group. And if it were, this chapter would not be about their backup band. This chapter covers the five Ws of backups — who, what, where, when, and how. I know, I know. The last one is an H, but because it has a W in it, I am taking the liberty of including it in the five Ws. Some of the methods under *what* and *how* describe shortcuts you can use to speed up the process. I concentrate on Personal Oracle7 in this chapter. More backup options exist for other versions of Oracle7, but they are complex and require much study to use properly. If you're interested in those, you might want to take a class.

Why Back Up — Onward and Upward!

Back up to save face. Do you want to be caught with your pants down because you did not back up? Worse yet, do you want to get caught backing up with your pants down?

When I refer to *back up*, I'm referring to different methods that accomplish similar tasks. Backing up your database essentially means making a duplicate copy of all, or a portion of, your database — kind of like wearing a belt and suspenders.

Many good reasons to back up your database exist. The reason that motivates me the most is that backing up saves me a lot of time in the long run. Losing data because you did not back it up costs you time: time to figure out what is missing; time to get another copy; time to remember all the things you did for the last month; time to re-create everything that you cannot replace. Time to get real about backing up your data.

If you use a PC, periodically backing up your entire PC hard drive helps you to recover quickly from hardware problems. How often is "periodically"? It depends on how much you use your computer. For someone who uses it daily, I'd recommend backing up at the end of each week. On the other hand, if you are a casual PC user, sitting down once or twice a week to play or work or perhaps surf the Internet, I'd recommend backing up once a month.

Backing up an entire database allows you to keep a snapshot of the database structure and data. Backing up portions of the database lets you shorten the amount of time invested in backups, while safeguarding parts of the database.

What to Back Up

Here are my guidelines for a backup plan. Ultimately, you are the judge. I am the executioner. We can hang the jury.

- ✔ Back up the whole database on a regular basis. For critical database systems that support a business operation on a daily basis, back up nightly. For normal daily use, back up once a week. For occasional use, back up once a month.
- ✔ During database development, when you create and drop tables frequently, back up the table owner before making major changes.
- ✔ Use backups to transfer whole groups of tables from one database to another.

When to Back Up (Back Up Before You Go Off the Cliff)

Generally you don't wait until you crash to fasten your seat belt. Planning a back up schedule and sticking to it pays off in the long run. No system is immune to losing data. I've seen systems with full backup capabilities get zapped by lightning, which burned up a crucial disk drive. Exactly when to back up depends on what kind of system you're running. If you use common sense and lean a bit to the conservative side, you'll have a good strategy for timing backups.

Some of the choices you have when using Oracle7 include:

- ✔ **Backup Manager:** Copies the entire database in a compressed format to disk or tape. You shut down the database to run a full database backup and then restore using the Recovery Manager.

- ✔ **Export utility:** Copies selected tables or projects (groups of tables) to a file. You use the Import utility to restore data.

- ✔ **Tablespace backups:** Copies selected tablespaces while the database is running. The database must be running in ARCHIVELOG mode. This is a very exotic technique, so I do not cover it in this book. The tablespace backup is generally only used by large organizations in which the database is online 24 hours a day. Tablespace backups require careful study and just cannot be covered in a few paragraphs.

- ✔ **Recovery logs:** You can design your recovery logs so that the database recovers activities up to the minute when a failure occurs. I don't cover this technique in this book. You should get expert help before implementing this kind of a recovery scheme.

- ✔ **Audit utility:** Not exactly a backup utility, this utility allows you to track all activity on tables. Auditing can be incredibly detailed. You don't really need the Audit utility unless you are wearing a tin foil hat to ward off evil thought rays and cosmic debris. I'm not covering the utility in this book because the audit trail can eat up disk space in a hurry. You can get a pretty good description of this in the Oracle7 manual.

Which plan should you use? Again, that depends on your situation. Imagine you are a musician who just produced a CD of your music. You're setting up a cool Web site with promotional materials on your home PC, and you're using Oracle7 to keep track of the CD distribution and accounting. You work about an hour a day on the PC, between rehearsals, radio spots, and signing autographs. I recommend you use Oracle's Backup Manager to back up the database weekly. I also recommend you back up your PC at the end of each week, using software that backs up only changed files to disk, zip drive, or tape.

On the other hand, what if you work in a federal office and you decide to enhance a set of tables with new features? You plan to add new tables and modify the existing ones. I recommend that you use the Export utility or EXP command to save all tables before you start making changes. Checkered tablecloths and potted plants may be good changes.

How to Back up (Choosing Your Backup Weapon)

The three backup tools I'm covering in this book work in Personal Oracle7. They include the Backup Manager, the Export utility, and the EXP command. The EXP command is available on all platforms. The other two work with Personal Oracle7.

Backup Manager

Backup Manager reminds me of a supervisor I had when I worked as a civil servant. The Backup Manager utility comes with Personal Oracle7. To run the utility, follow these steps:

1. Select Backup Manager from the Personal Oracle7 program menu.

The Oracle7 Backup Manager dialog box appears, as shown in Figure 14-1.

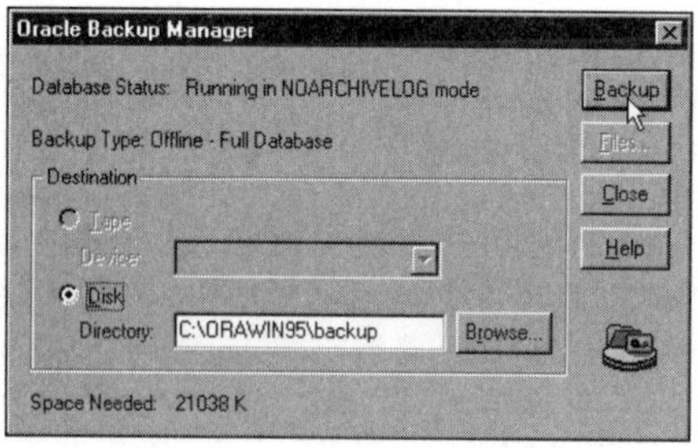

Figure 14-1:
The Backup Manager has a little beeper that goes off when you back up — kind of like those big trucks.

Oracle Backup Manager

Database Status: Running in NOARCHIVELOG mode

Backup Type: Offline - Full Database

Destination

○ Tape
  Device

● Disk
  Directory: C:\ORAWIN95\backup Browse...

Space Needed: 21038 K

Backup
Files...
Close
Help

2. Choose a location directory where you want to store your backup.

3. Click Backup.

The database shuts down automatically if you start the backup while running the database.

When you restore your database from a backup, the database returns to the exact state it was in when you performed the backup. If your backup is a week old, you lose all changes made during the current week.

What if your hard drive crashes?

If your hard disk crashes and you're in the process of restoring all your software, first try to start up Oracle7, which has built-in recovery steps that handle a lot of situations. Oracle7 often is able to restore your database. If you cannot start up Oracle7, use the Recovery Manager to restore your database. Use the Automatic recovery selection in the Recovery Manager window, and Oracle7 recovers the database back to your most recent backup made with the Backup Manager.

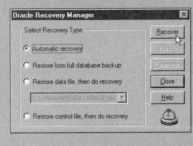

Export utility

This utility is a part of PO7 Navigator. You must create a *project* to use this feature. A project is a group of database items, like tables, views, or users. Once grouped into a project, you can export these items. Exporting a project creates a copy of the entire project in a file.

Building a project for export

Follow these steps to create a new project, and add a table to the project.

1. **Start the PO7 Navigator.**

   Refer to Chapter 1 if you don't know how. When PO7 Navigator starts up, you immediately get the main window of the Navigator.

2. **Start a New Project.**

   Right-click the Projects icon on the left side of the PO7 Navigator window and select New from the sub-menu that pops up.

   The Create Project dialog box appears, as shown in Figure 14-2. Fill in the project name in the File name box. This is an actual file name and must comply with naming standards for your operating system. For example, in Windows 95, the file name can be up to 35 characters long. Click the Save button on the right side of the Create Project dialog box when you are done.

Figure 14-2:
Creating a project makes a file that you name in the Create Project dialog box.

This brings up a window box labeled with your new project's name. In Figure 14-3, the project is named MyProject.zpj because I called the new project "MyProject."

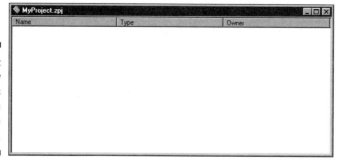

Figure 14-3:
Your new project is empty the first time you see it.

3. **Exit the project window.**

   Click the Close button (the usual Windows 95 "X" in a little square) in the upper-right corner of the window. This returns you to the PO7 Navigator main window.

4. **Add tables, views, users, or other elements that pertain to your project.**

   Here's how to add a table to the project.

   • Double-click the Local Database icon in the left side of the PO7 Navigator main window. This brings up a list of icons in the right half of the main window. Table, View, Synonym, and User are a few of the icons found here.

   • Double-click the Table icon. This brings up a list of all the tables in the database in the right half of the PO7 Navigator window. Use the scroll bar with your mouse to look through the list of tables, as shown in Figure 14-4.

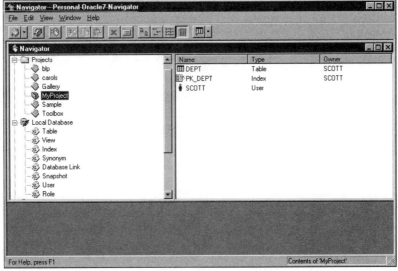

Figure 14-4:
Working
with the
icons in the
PO7
Navigator
makes
creating a
project
easy.

• Click and drag the table you want over to your Project icon. Release the mouse to place the table into the project.

To add other items, repeat the last two steps with a different icon, such as the Index icon or the View icon.

5. Take a look at the contents of your project.

To see everything you have put into the project, click on the Project icon. A list, like the one in Figure 14-5, appears.

Export the project

Export the project you have created in PO7 Navigator by following a few steps.

1. Start up the PO7 Navigator.

If you are not there right now, start it up. (Chapter 1 tells how to start it.)

2. Start up an Export.

Right-click the icon of the project you want to export on the left side of the PO7 Navigator-window and select Export from the sub-menu that pops up. This brings up the Export – Save As window.

3. Save the export file.

The Export – Save As window is just like a standard Windows 95 window that pops up when it's time to save a file. (See Figure 14-6.) Choose the directory where you want the export file to reside and type the name in the File name box.

Click here to sort by table name

Click and drag icon to add to project

Click here to sort by owner

Figure 14-5:
Here's what
your project
looks like
after adding
a few items.

Scroll bars

Figure 14-6:
When you
export a
project you
create a
new file
in which
copies of
all the
items in a
project are
stored.

4. Save the file.

Click the Save button in the lower-right part of the Export – Save as
window to save the file. Oracle7 exports the data and after finishing
pops up an information window telling you the job was done, as shown
in Figure 14-7.

Figure 14-7:
PO7 sends
you a nice
signal that
all is well.

This completes the steps for exporting a project using PO7 Navigator. You can back up the file you have created like any other file on your PC. Later, if you want to restore your project to the state it was in when you created the exported file, you can use the IMP command (see the next section on how) to restore the project.

EXP *and* IMP *commands*

The EXP and IMP commands, like my old Maui Cruiser, have been around since the Dark Ages and still run like champs. Run the EXP and IMP commands from the command line in any operating system, so you don't need PO7 Navigator to use them.

EXP pulls tables or entire *schemas* (all tables, indexes, and other database objects owned by one Oracle7 user ID) out of the database in a compressed file format that is only readable by Oracle's IMP command.

The full database export

You can use EXP to export the entire Oracle7 database as well. A full database export is another alternative way to back up your database. Oracle7 recommends that you do a full database export every time you do a full system backup (such as a backup of all files to tape). On a practical note, you should not always do this step, because it takes extra time.

To restore from a full database export, use IMP, just as you would with any other file created by EXP.

You should only do a full database import (IMP run with the file created by a full database export from EXP) when a failure on the disk completely wipes out your database or when you want to actually create a brand new database on another computer. Consult with an expert before attempting this one.

IMP reads a file created by EXP and restores the tables, indexes, or whatever database objects are in the file back to the database. You are prompted for choices and can restore all or only specified objects as you wish.

Exporting with the EXP command

Let's start with a step-by-step look at the EXP command.

1. **Start up the EXP utility.**

   From Windows 95, select Run from the Start menu. Then type in:

   ```
   exp
   ```

   Tough, huh? EXP prompts you for information.

2. **Log on to the database.**

   Oracle7 asks you for a user name by saying:

   ```
   Username:
   ```

   You type your user ID and press Enter. Next, Oracle7 asks you to enter a password by saying:

   ```
   Password:
   ```

   Type in your password and press Enter. Notice the cursor moves but Oracle7 does not display the letters on the screen. This protects your password from being seen by all those people who keep looking over your shoulder.

   Oracle7 checks your user name and password and tells you that you are now connected to the database. For example, if you're running Personal Oracle7 on your PC, Oracle7 sends this message:

   ```
   Connected to Personal Oracle7 Version 7.2.2.3.1
   ```

   Naturally, your version number may differ.

3. **Set buffer size.**

   The buffer size tells Oracle7 how much data to pull out of the database at a time. The default is usually acceptable unless you are exporting a very large (more than 10,000 rows) table. In the case of large tables, set it to the maximum value. This makes the fetching process run faster. Sometimes I tell my dog, "Fetch, Buffer," but he ignores me. In cases other than very large tables, use the default.

Oracle7 prompts you for buffer size by saying:

```
Enter array fetch buffer size: 4096 >
```

Accept the default (4096) by pressing Enter or type the number you chose and then press Enter.

4. **Set Export file location and name.**

Oracle7 prompts you for a file name and suggests a default name by saying:

```
Export file: EXPDAT.DMP >
```

Accept the default by just pressing Enter or type a file name of your own and then press Enter. Remember, Oracle7 creates the file in the current directory unless your file name includes the directory path name.

5. **Choose the type of export you wish to do.**

You have three choices:

- **Full database export:** You only see this choice if you are the DBA. See the sidebar "The full database export" for a description of the full database export.

- **User export:** This one lets you export all the database objects (such as tables, indexes, views, grants, and so on) that belong to one user. If you are the DBA, you can export several users. If you are not the DBA, you can only export your own user ID.

- **Table export:** This one lets you export one or more tables that you own. A table export also exports database objects that belong to the table, such as indexes, grants, primary key and other constraints, and of course, the data.

Oracle7 asks you to choose an export type and suggests a default of tables (3) by saying:

```
(2)U(sers), or (3)T(ables): (2)U > 3
```

Accept the default by pressing Enter, or type in your choice and press Enter. (The above prompt is missing the first choice because the user running EXP is not the DBA.) If you chose 2 (User export), Oracle7 asks you different questions after this point. The remaining steps assume that you chose 3 (Table export).

6. **Decide whether to export data with your tables.**

Oracle7 asks you if you want to export data and suggests that you do by saying:

```
Export table data (yes/no): yes >
```

Normally, you want the table data. Sometimes, however, you want only the structure with no rows. This can be useful if you intend to use the export file for creating a new table in a separate database.

Accept the default (yes, Oracle7, please export my table data) by pressing Enter, or type no and press Enter to not export table data.

7. **Decide whether to use compression on your table data.**

Once again, normally you do want to compress the table data. Read up on table extents in Chapter 18. Compressing extents means that the table takes up less room and some space that was wasted in the table's structure gets freed up. I can think of only one reason to not compress the extents: when you have deliberately created a table with a lot of empty space in anticipation of a large number of rows to be inserted later. It's like calling ahead to a busy restaurant and making reservations. Now, Oracle7 asks you about it and sets the default to yes (do compress extents):

```
Compress extents (yes/no): yes >
```

Accept the default by pressing Enter, or type no and press Enter to not compress extents. Oracle7 responds by sending you an informational message:

```
About to export specified tables ...
```

8. **Name a table for exporting.**

Oracle7 asks you for a table name by saying:

```
Table to be exported: (RETURN to quit) >
```

Type in a table name and press Enter. For example, if you were exporting the CUSTOMER_ACCOUNT table, type:

```
CUSTOMER_ACCOUNT
```

Press Enter. Oracle7 responds by exporting a copy of the table and placing it into the export file. It informs you of the deed and tells you how many rows it exported. In the example of the CUSTOMER_ACCOUNT table, here is what Oracle7 said:

```
. . exporting table     CUSTOMER_ACCOUNT  4 rows ex-
        ported
```

Then Oracle7 immediately asks for another table name by saying:

```
Table to be exported: (RETURN to quit) >
```

9. **Repeat Step 8 until all tables are exported. Then press Enter without typing a table name to stop the export.**

   Oracle7 completes the export and sends a message saying:

   ```
   Export terminated successfully.
   ```

   In Windows 95, the above message flashes on the screen briefly and then the window closes. The message flashes very quickly, and reading the message is difficult .

After the export is finished, you can use the file to retrieve individual tables or all the tables by running the IMP utility.

Importing with the IMP command

The IMP command lets you bring into your database any item (table, index, user, and so on) that was saved in an export file. You might import a table if you have made changes to the data that you don't like and you want to revert to the older, unchanged data. Another time to import is when you have lost data because of some errors or a database failure.

1. **Start up the IMP utility.**

   From Windows 95, select Start⇨Run and then type imp.

2. **Log into the database, typing your user name and password when prompted.**

Copying tables — a fast alternative to exports

You may need a quick way to save a table if, for instance, you want to repeatedly experiment with a program or routine. You may need a base copy of the table that you use to restore the table before beginning a new round of tests. You use the CREATE TABLE ... AS command in SQL*Plus to help you with this. Here's the code:

```
create table CUSTOMER_BACK UP as
select * from CUSTOMER_ACCOUNT;
Table created.
```

This code copies the CUSTOMER_ACCOUNT table structure and its contents into a new table called CUSTOMER_BACK UP.

When you want to replace the rows in the CUSTOMER_ACCOUNT table, delete the rows and insert backup rows:

```
DELETE FROM CUSTOMER_ACCOUNT;
14 rows deleted.
insert into CUSTOMER_ACCOUNT
    select * from
    CUSTOMER_BACK UP;
14 rows created.
```

3. Name the export file to use.

IMP connects to the database and looks for a file named expdat.dmp in the current directory. If it finds one, it assumes you wish to use it. Otherwise, IMP issues two error messages (IMP-0002 and IMP-00021) and gives you a chance to type in the file name. Oracle7 prompts you:

```
Import file: EXPDAT.DMP >
```

Type in file name, including full path if not in the current directory.

4. Set buffer size.

Oracle7 asks:

```
Enter insert buffer size(minimum is 4096) 30720 >
```

Accept the default (30720) or type in a number, and then press Enter.

5. Select to import or just look.

Oracle7 asks:

```
List contents of import file only (yes/no): no >
```

Accept the default or type Yes to just look, and then press Enter.

6. Decide whether you care about errors.

Oracle7 asks:

```
Ignore create error due to object existence (yes/no): no
        >
```

If you know the table exists and you want to add rows to it using the import, type Yes. If you want the import to stop with an error message if it cannot create the table, type No. Then press Enter.

7. Decide whether to import grants.

Oracle7 asks:

```
Import grants (yes/no): yes >
```

Accept the default (yes) or type in no, and then press Enter.

8. Choose to import or not import data.

Oracle7 asks:

```
Import table data (yes/no): yes >
```

Accepting the default yes brings in the data. Answering no imports only an empty table. Make your choice, and then press Enter.

9. Decide whether to import entire file.

Oracle7 asks:

```
Import entire export file (yes/no): yes >
```

Leave blank to import everything in the file or type no to import parts you specify. Press Enter. If you type no, then Oracle7 prompts you for a user name and table names that you want to import and imports them one at a time, prompting along the way. When you have imported all you want, leave the prompt line blank and hit Enter to complete the import session.

If you accept the default yes, then Oracle7 completes the import session by informing you of its progress as it imports all the tables and other items (indexes, grants, etc.) from the export file.

In either case, after the import is completed, Oracle7 says:

```
Import terminated successfully.
```

Where to Hide Your Backup Tapes

Once you have created backup tapes, your next big decision is where to store them. If you have teenagers, don't place your backup tapes near food. Make sure that your hiding place is safe from that funny swirly stuff that floats around in the air, and from the evil thought patterns and cosmic rays that emanate from the Remote Troll Planet that controls your TV. Better get one of those little foil hats to ward off those cosmic rays. Put one on your teenager — he'll thank you later.

Hide back up tapes in a drawer that is not metal and not near magnets. *Don't forget where you put the tapes.* The first office I worked in as a computer geek kept backup tapes in the vice president's garage. I'm not kidding!

Part IV
Tuning Up and Turbocharging

The 5th Wave   By Rich Tennant

Determined to help Wanda find her lost file, Del connects his "Royco 100 Fish Finder" to her hard disk.

©RICHTENNANT

In this part...

Y ou're running like a Cadillac — cruising with your
Oracle7 schema (set of related tables) with all its
related queries, scripts, and online screens in perfect
harmony. Then, out of the blue, the engine starts to
sputter. Now your cruising machine gets sluggish and
sometimes won't even get out of first gear. What
went wrong?

This section covers things that go wrong in Oracle7 and
how to fix them. Oracle7 has a handful of little bugaboos
that haunt every database after a while. A little tuning up
here and there can get your database engine back into
racing form.

Chapter 15

What's Slowing Your Query Down?

• •

• •

*P*erhaps you write SQL code in your spare time. If so, you actually have no spare time. I suggest you get a life. On the other hand, you may use some additional software programs that generate all your queries for you. Everything goes well until one day you create a query that runs so slowly you consider taking it out and shooting it. The database administrator (DBA) starts yelling in your face. You take three Excedrin and grab the manuals.

This chapter is all about performance tuning, or speeding up your query. I cover the bases with useful information for tuning up your SQL code. This chapter and the others in this section will have your code flying like never before.

Baby Steps versus Giant Leaps

A SQL query or command can run slowly for many reasons. To discover important performance clues, ask yourself a couple of questions: "When did the problem start?" and "What did I change just before I started having trouble?"

When you create a complex SQL statement, you may be wise to take small bites out of the whole goal and then test each one as you go along. These steps can help you develop good habits for creating tricky SQL statements:

1. **Build the statement one table at a time. Choose the main table and build the beginning statement using only the main table.**

2. **Test your beginning statement and make corrections.**

3. **Add another table, test the statement, and make corrections.**

4. **Continue adding tables, testing, and correcting until the SQL statement is completed.**

Often you can catch trouble spots in your code when you gradually build the code. Taking baby steps gives steady, forward progress. Giant steps, in which you create an entire SQL command at once, tend to fall short.

SQL*Plus has a command to help you figure out whether you've improved the response time for your query. The next section discusses this command, called timing.

Set SQL*Plus Timing On

The timing command in SQL*Plus gives you great feedback on the performance speed of your SQL command. To turn the timing on, simply type:

```
set timing on
```

This is an *environment command* in SQL*Plus, meaning that it changes how SQL*Plus displays the results of your queries and other commands. An environment command stays on until you reset it or leave SQL*Plus. There are many environment commands. Some are described in this chapter, and others are described in Chapter 12.

To turn the timing setting on in SQL*Plus using Personal Oracle7 Navigator, start up SQL*Plus (refer to Chapter 4) and follow these steps:

1. **Select the Options menu at the top of the window.**

2. **Select Set Options (Environment in Oracle 7.3).**

   This opens a window for setting all your environment settings, as shown in Figure 15-1.

Figure 15-1:
You can
handle the
SQL*Plus
settings
easily in the
Navigator's
pop-up
window.

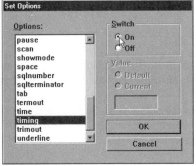

3. **Scroll to and select the timing setting and then click the On button. (In Oracle 7.3, first click the Current button, then click the On button.)**

4. **Click OK.**

After you do that, every SQL command you execute is followed by statistics. If you're running Oracle7 on a PC, you see something like this:

```
real: 550
```

This is the real time in thousandths of a second. Other operating systems show different statistics, such as the CPU time or buffers used.

The first time you run a SQL command, Oracle7 reads new data into its buffers. The data stays in the buffers until the end of the session or until Oracle7 runs out of buffers and reuses the one with this data. Consequently, when you use the timing statistics to compare variations on similar queries, make sure that you run each of them a second time. By doing this, you get timing statistics that do not include the initial loading of the buffers.

Now you have a method for testing out the changes you make to your query in an attempt to speed it up. You can look at the slow query's timing statistics, make changes to the query, and compare this changed query's timing statistics. As a starting point, the next section dives into parts of the query you can explore to determine what is slowing your query down.

Looking at the SELECT Clause — Too Much or Too Little

When your query does not work efficiently, you can take specific steps to inspect and adjust it to work efficiently. The sections here go through your query piece by piece. Each section points out the most common causes of inefficient SQL code and shows how to correct the situation.

Picking apart the FROM *clause for little flaws*

The FROM clause contains a list of all the tables from which you retrieve data. I think FROM clause is a perfect name for this clause, don't you? Oracle7 goes out of its way to say in its documentation that the order in which you choose to name your tables in the FROM clause is of no significance. Then, in very fine print, buried somewhere in the manuals, Oracle7 comes clean and explains a little-known quirk of the Oracle7 engine that helps you create better, faster SQL.

In most cases, Oracle7 ignores the order of the tables in the FROM clause. However, when Oracle7 needs a tiebreaker, it looks at the FROM clause. It chooses to use the index on the last table in the FROM clause and to ignore the index on the other table. If you list the larger table first, performance suffers, because Oracle7 does not use an index on this large table. That means it will scan the entire contents of the table. So you may want to rearrange the order of the tables in your query, placing large tables at the end.

When listing tables in the FROM clause, list them in *ascending* order according to the number of rows to be retrieved from each table when the query runs.

You are an alien visiting Earth on spec for your home company. You set up database tables for 100,000 new clients (CUSTOMER_ACCOUNT) who have shown interest in your unusual product and for the 50 countries (COUNTRY) that these clients live in. COUNTRY_ID links the two tables together. A query listing the customers and countries could take two forms.

The wrong way to query would be something like this:

```
select C.COUNTRY, A.NAME
from CUSTOMER_ACCOUNT A, COUNTRY C
where A.COUNTRY_ID = C.COUNTRY_ID
order by COUNTRY, NAME;
```

The right way to query would look like this:

```
select C.COUNTRY, A.NAME
from COUNTRY C, CUSTOMER_ACCOUNT A
where A.COUNTRY_ID = C.COUNTRY_ID
order by COUNTRY, NAME;
```

Why is the latter approach better? Because the FROM clause in the second query places the larger table (the CUSTOMER_ACCOUNT table) last and the smaller table first.

Missing table joins: The WHERE *clause monster*

When you write a query, the WHERE clause has two main functions:

- ✔ Listing criteria that narrow down the rows chosen (such as a date range)
- ✔ Specifying connections between two tables (matching foreign and primary keys)

If your query contains more than one table and the second function (specifying connections) is missing or incorrect, SQL*Plus does not issue an error message. Instead, SQL*Plus figures you know what you're doing and processes your query as if you wanted to match every column in the first table with every table in the second. If one table has ten rows and the other has 20, your end result has 200 rows. That's probably not what you intended! This method of matching all rows with each other is called a *Cartesian join*.

A *Cartesian join* is a set of all the possible combinations of every row in two or more tables. Its namesake is the French philosopher and mathematician René Descartes, who founded much of modern geometry. As you might imagine, a Cartesian join is usually the result of an error in your query and causes your query to return many more rows than intended, and as a result slows down your response time.

A Cartesian join occurs in these two cases:

- ✔ Two tables are named in the FROM clause and are not related to each other in the WHERE clause.
- ✔ The relationship that is defined is incorrectly formed.

Figure 15-2 shows how a Cartesian join looks with two small tables.

As the amount of data increases, the size of the Cartesian join monster grows exponentially. The number of rows produced by a Cartesian join is equal to the number of rows in each table multiplied by the number of rows in the other table.

If the query results seem to show up as repeated rows, you very likely have a Cartesian join. Review the WHERE clause for relationships between tables.

You hastily prepare a query of all your customers whose names begin with *A,* and their countries, but you forget to place the relationship portion of the WHERE clause into the query.

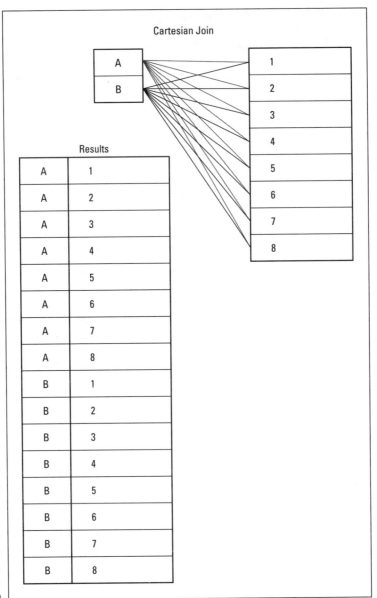

Figure 15-2:
A Cartesian
join can
grow into a
CPU-eating
monster.

The right way to handle table connections in your WHERE clause in this example is:

```
select C.COUNTRY, A.NAME
from CUSTOMER_ACCOUNT A, COUNTRY C
where A.NAME like 'A%'
and A.COUNTRY_ID = C.COUNTRY_ID
order by COUNTRY, NAME;
```

The wrong way to connect tables might look like this:

```
select C.COUNTRY, A.NAME
from COUNTRY C, CUSTOMER_ACCOUNT A
where A.NAME like 'A%'
order by COUNTRY, NAME;
```

The first query works because you have included a proper phrase in the WHERE clause to tell SQL*Plus how to connect the two tables.

Extra table joins: Overkill that slows you down

Be careful when you create queries that join more than two tables. A common mistake is to include a condition in the WHERE clause that is unneeded and repetitive, which can happen when a hierarchy of tables exists.

Avoid extraneous joins in hierarchical table relationships. Follow relationship lines in diagrams as an aid.

Dissecting a WHERE clause

The WHERE clause can have many parts. Oracle7 looks at the WHERE clause as a list of conditions strung together like train cars. The connector between each train car is the word AND or the word OR. Parentheses also help Oracle7 determine how to connect the conditions. In a long query with many tables, the WHERE clause gets long and seems complex. Just remember that it always breaks down into a list of conditions. Each condition stands on its own and contains either a relationship that defines how two tables are joined or a data test that must be satisfied. Each line of the following code is an example of a condition in a WHERE clause.

```
BIRTHDATE < TO_DATE('01-JAN-75')
A.CUST_ID = B.CUST_ID
STATE_CODE  IN ('HI','FL','TN')
```

You have three tables: CONTINENT, COUNTRY, and CITY. Each table's primary key builds on the previous one. Figure 15-3 shows the relationships among the tables. The line between the CONTINENT table and the CITY table is unneeded and should be omitted. However, this line shows how easily you can make an error when working with several related tables. The CONTINENT column is a foreign key column in the CITY table. You can interpret it as a foreign key to either the COUNTRY table or the CONTINENT table. Refer to Chapter 5 for a thorough explanation of primary keys and foreign keys.

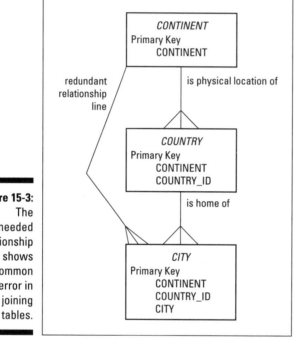

Figure 15-3:
The unneeded relationship line shows a common error in joining tables.

As you write a query, you add a condition that relates the CITY table with the CONTINENT table. This is an unneeded condition that makes Oracle7 do more work when it runs the query — and slows performance.

Here's your example with the proper joins in the WHERE clause:

```
select CITY.CONTINENT, CTRY.COUNTRY_NAME, CITY.CITY
from CONTINENT CON, COUNTRY CTRY, CITY
where CITY.COUNTRY_ID = CTRY.COUNTRY_ID
and CITY.CONTINENT = CTRY.CONTINENT
and CTRY.CONTINENT = CON.CONTINENT
order by 1,2,3
```

This incorrect one contains extraneous joins in the WHERE clause:

```
select CITY.CONTINENT, CTRY.COUNTRY_NAME, CITY.CITY
from CONTINENT CON, COUNTRY CTRY, CITY
where CITY.COUNTRY_ID = CTRY.COUNTRY_ID
and CITY.CONTINENT = CTRY.CONTINENT
and CITY.CONTINENT = CON.CONTINENT
and CTRY.CONTINENT = CON.CONTINENT
order by 1,2,3
```

The first query works better because it requires SQL*Plus to do less work in connecting the three tables together and still gets the right results.

The ORDER BY *clause reduces Oracle7 to a crawl*

The ORDER BY clause determines how Oracle7 sorts the rows it returns to you as the result of your query. The ORDER BY clause does not limit you to any particular column. In fact, you can include columns that have functions, such as concatenation or addition, on them as well. Be aware that anything in the ORDER BY clause that is not indexed slows performance.

Review your ORDER BY clause for columns or expressions that are not indexes, because these slow performance. Resolve the performance problem by rewriting the ORDER BY clause to use indexes or by creating another index on the column or columns that you use. See Chapter 17 for an in-depth discussion of indexing.

Your sales staff just notified you that sales have decreased. You want to see the trend over the last 30 days, so you sort your query by descending date. The date you want in your report is converted to YY/MM/DD format, which is your preference.

The right way allows SQL*Plus to use the index on SALES_DATE:

```
select to_char(SALES_DATE,'YY/MM/DD'), SALES_AMOUNT
from DAILY_SALES
WHERE SALES_DATE BETWEEN
TO_DATE('01-JAN-96') and TO_DATE('31-JAN-96')
ORDER BY SALES_DATE
```

The wrong way has an `ORDER BY` clause that uses no index:

```
select to_char(SALES_DATE,'YY/MM/DD'), SALES_AMOUNT
from DAILY_SALES
WHERE SALES_DATE BETWEEN
TO_DATE('01-JAN-96') and TO_DATE('31-JAN-96')
ORDER BY to_char(SALES_DATE,'YY/MM/DD')
```

The first query works much faster because an index is used to retrieve data. Without an index, the data is retrieved by reading through every row in the table.

The danger of NOT

All the phrases or parts of your `WHERE` clause contain some kind of *logical operator* such as `=` (equal) or `<` (less than). `NOT` is tacked on to reverse the logic of any of these operators. `NOT` is used explicitly by adding parentheses around a phrase and placing `NOT` just in front of it, like this:

```
... where not (STYLE = '4-door')
```

`NOT` is contained implicitly in one logical operator — the `NOT EQUAL` operator. In other words, `NOT` is there even though you don't type the word into your query. Here are the three forms that you can use to write `NOT EQUAL`:

```
<>
```

This is the preferred method, because it is accepted by all the variations of Oracle7 across all hardware platforms.

```
!=
```

This form of `NOT EQUAL` does not translate between all platforms! Use the first form of `NOT EQUAL` (`<>`) instead.

```
^=
```

Again, this form of `NOT EQUAL` does not always translate between platforms. Use the first form of `NOT EQUAL` (`<>`).

You have great flexibility when using the `NOT` logical term in your query's `WHERE` clause, but you pay a price for using `NOT` — Oracle7 cannot use an index on any phrase that contains `NOT`. Without an index to use, a query slows down. So don't use the `NOT` logical term in the `WHERE` clause. Just imagine if your doctor said, "You only have three days to live — NOT!"

Here's an example of a query that works without NOT:

```
select * from COUNTRY
where COUNTRY_ID <= 100
```

Here's the same query using NOT:

```
select * from COUNTRY
where NOT (COUNTRY_ID > 100)
```

The first example runs faster than the second even though both get the same results. The first one allows Oracle7 to use an index that exists on the COUNTRY_ID column, while the second one prohibits use of the index.

IN *versus* EXISTS: *Important facts you should know*

Sometimes you compare a column to a list of values. A common way to create the list is to create a sub-query inside your where clause. The basic method involves figuring out a sub-query that creates a list and then including that in the where clause as a sub-query.

There are two general formats for a sub-query in a WHERE clause. The first one uses the IN logical operator and looks like this:

```
... where column in (select ... from ... where ... )
```

The second format uses the EXISTS logical operator and looks like this:

```
... where exists (select 'X' from ... where ...)
```

Most people use the first format because it is a lot easier to figure out. The second format actually gives you much better performance, if you take the time to learn how to create it. You will find that nearly every sub-query you create using the IN logical operator can be converted to use the EXISTS logical operator.

In the second format, the sub-query starts with select 'X'. This looks strange, but it is correct. EXISTS looks directly at the WHERE clause and does not even care what data you pull from the table you have in the sub-query. EXISTS uses a *correlated sub-query,* which is why it is more difficult to construct.

Chapter 12 discusses the correlated sub-query. Refer to that chapter for a good explanation of how to construct a correlated sub-query.

When you replace IN with EXISTS, you gain performance speed. Oracle7 saves time when it uses EXISTS because it evaluates the main query first and runs the sub-query only until it finds a match. With IN, Oracle7 suspends processing of the main query while executing the sub-query to make a list. Oracle7 stores that list in an indexed temporary table and then resumes processing of the main query. While there are exceptions, Oracle7 usually performs queries that use EXISTS faster than those that use IN. Therefore, examine your WHERE clause for the IN condition. In most cases, you can replace the IN condition with EXISTS.

Here's an example of a sub-query using EXISTS:

```
select *
from COUNTRY C
where exists (select 'X' from CITY
              where CITY.COUNTRY_ID = C.COUNTRY_ID)
```

Here's the same query using IN for the sub-query:

```
select * from country C
where C.COUNTRY_ID in (select CITY.COUNTRY_ID from CITY)
```

The first one gets the same results (the same rows retrieved) as the second one but runs faster because it uses EXISTS rather than IN.

Whenever possible, also replace NOT IN with NOT EXISTS. Even though both have NOT in them (which can slow performance down because it prevents the use of indexes), NOT EXISTS performs faster than NOT IN.

SQL gets fancy

This chapter really just scratches the surface of all the subtleties of SQL*Plus and the SQL language. If you have a taste for more, perhaps you'd be interested in another book, *SQL For Dummies,* by Allen G. Taylor, published by your favorite and mine: IDG Books Worldwide, Inc.

Chapter 16

Speeding Up Queries with Keys and Indexes

- -

- -

*E*very table should have a *primary key,* as a general rule. In this chapter, you discover how to create a primary key with either Personal Oracle7 Navigator or SQL*Plus. Choose your weapon. Stand back to back, go ten paces, turn and . . .

Speeding up a slow query is a dilemma faced by almost anyone who works with Oracle7 for a while. Oracle7 has a brain called an Optimizer that has the job of deciding how to go after the data you request in your query. In most cases, a slow tortoise query gets transformed into a speedy rabbit query by adding an index to an important column in the query. In this chapter, you find out how to create the keys and the indexes and about loopholes that prevent the Optimizer from using the fresh new index.

Why Create an Index?

Speed, speed, speed is the main reason to create an index. When you run a query in Oracle7, you tell Oracle7 what parts of which tables you want to see. Oracle7 looks at its own resources and decides the most efficient way to get the data to you. An index helps Oracle7 get the data faster.

What is a row ID?

Each row ID contains the physical location of the row and is the fastest retrieval method that Oracle7 uses. If Oracle7 knows a row ID, it knows the location of that row and can go directly to it without any delay. The row ID consists of several hexidecimal numbers that identify the storage space used for a single row from a single table. Every row has a row ID. You can query on a row ID like any column, but you cannot modify the ID.

You may be tempted to use the row ID as a foreign key in other tables. You can copy the row ID into a normal column and then use it for looking up data from the table. This retrieval method may seem logical, because it is the fastest way to the table's data. However, Oracle7 and I recommend that you do not use row ID this way because the row ID of a row may change. When a table gets reorganized, such as during export and import of the entire table or database, the row ID changes. The foreign key connections that use that row ID are suddenly invalid.

Oracle7 does not sift or sort your table's rows based on any index. As you add rows to a table, you always add them to the end of the current rows. Sometimes, you move a row from its original position to the end of the current rows. This happens if a row gets updated with a lot of data at once that does not fit into its current space in the table. Therefore, the table rows become jumbled up in sequence, even if you had entered them in order originally.

Oracle7 keeps indexes as independent objects in the database. An index is a lot like a table when you look at its internal structure, and consists of rows of data. The columns in the index include a copy of the indexed column(s) and the *row ID* of the corresponding row in the table that is indexed.

Unlike tables, indexes are kept in perfect sorted order by the index columns. Every new row added to a table creates a row in the index. The row in the index is added in its sorted order, which allows Oracle7 to use very fast search algorithms on the index. After the row is found in the index, the row ID is used to retrieve the table row.

What can you use an index for? Lots of stuff.

✔ **Faster queries:** You can make an index on columns you use for searches. For example, if you have an online screen that allows searches by last name, add an index on the LAST_NAME column of the table. This kind of index does not require unique values.

 ✔ **Unique values:** Oracle7 automatically generates an index to enforce unique values in the primary key of a table. You can use this feature for any column or set of columns that requires unique values in your table.

 ✔ **Foreign keys:** Foreign keys are used frequently in queries. You can speed up the performance of foreign keys by adding an index on them.

Adding, Changing, and Removing a Primary Key

When you name a column or set of columns as the primary key, Oracle7 automatically creates an index on that primary key, which has two positive effects.

The first positive effect is that the primary key, by definition, must have a unique value for every row added to the table. The unique index on the primary key enforces this rule. Every row added must pass the test and have a unique primary key.

The second positive effect is that you often use the primary key to find a row in the table. An index on the primary key makes finding a row faster and more efficient.

The index that Oracle7 creates assumes the original name of the primary key. If you did not name the primary key, Oracle7 names the index using the following naming convention:

```
SYS_nnnn
```

Oracle7 replaces *nnnn* with a sequential number.

If you use PO7 Navigator to create the primary key, the following naming convention is used:

```
PK_tablename
```

PO7 Navigator replaces *tablename* with the actual table name.

You can define the primary key for a table when you create it or after you create the table. (Refer to Chapter 9 to find out how to define the primary key for a table when you create it.) Here is how you add a primary key after you create the table.

When you add a primary key to an existing table, Oracle7 verifies that all the rows in the table have unique primary keys before it allows you to successfully add the primary key. If rows have duplicate primary keys, you must find them and either change the keys or eliminate the duplicate rows. See Chapter 22 for a SQL query that lists duplicate keys for you, and also for another SQL command to eliminate duplicate rows.

Adding, changing, and removing a primary key using PO7 Navigator

PO7 Navigator has a nice dialog box for creating and changing tables. You can also use this dialog box to add, modify, or remove the primary key of a table.

1. **Start up PO7 Navigator.**

2. **Click the table owner's database connection icon in the left window.**

   You connect to the database as the owner of the table you wish to work on.

3. **Double-click the Table icon in the right window to view a list of tables in the right window.**

4. **Find the table name in the right window, right-click on it, and select Design (select Properties in Version 7.3) from the pop-up sub-menu, as shown in Figure 16-1.**

   The Design Table dialog box appears. In Version 7.3, click the Design tab to see the Design dialog box.

5. **Use the mouse to position your cursor on the row where you see the name of the first column of the primary key, and then tab to the right until your cursor rests in the column labeled Primary Key.**

6. **To add a new primary key, single-click to add this column to the primary key.**

   You see a sequence number appear in the column. The first column you select becomes number one and should correspond to the first column in the primary key.

7. **Click the Can be Null? box to remove the check.**

   Null values are now prevented in the primary key. Version 7.3 accepts this change, but the next time you look at the Design window, the check box reappears. This appears to be an error in the Design window itself, because the NOT NULL constraint is there; it's just not registered in the Design window. If the column is already NOT NULL when you arrive in the Design window, you may get this message:

```
ORA-01442: column to be modified to NOT NULL is already
          NOT NULL
```

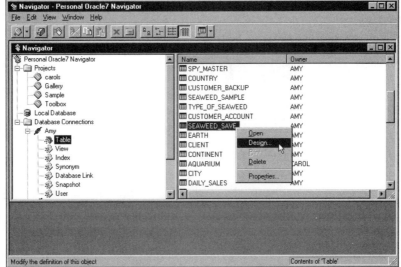

Figure 16-1:
You can
add a
primary key
as an
afterthought
in PO7
Navigator.

If that happens, click OK, which returns you to the Design window.
Then click the Can Be Null? check box so that it is checked (instead of
unchecked). This will prevent the error message.

8. **Verify that the Unique box has no check mark.**

Primary keys are unique by definition, so do *not* check the Unique box
for primary key columns. If you do, Oracle7 tries to create two identical
indexes, one for the primary key and one for the unique columns,
which causes both to fail.

9. **Repeat Steps 5 through 8 for each additional column of your
primary key.**

10. **Click OK in the Design Table dialog box when you are done.**

Oracle7 builds the index required to enforce your primary key. Oracle7
checks every row in the table. If any of the rows have duplicate values
in the primary key, you see an error message like the one in Figure 16-2.
Version 7.3 sends a slightly different message:

```
ORA-02437: cannot enable (tablename, keyname) - primary
        key violated
```

You'll need to fix the data so that every row has a unique primary key.

Figure 16-2:
Oops! Your
table
contains
duplicate
values in
the primary
key
columns.

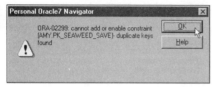

Removing a primary key with PO7 Navigator

Every once in a while, you may make a mistake. I have heard that some people who are below the status of Oracle7 Priestess make mistakes. I know you didn't mean to.

When you remove a primary key in PO7 Navigator, you automatically remove all foreign keys that refer to this primary key. Remember that you get neither a warning nor a list of what you changed.

Here's how to remove a primary key. Versions 7.2 and 7.3 are supposed to work the same way, according to the documentation. I found I could not remove the primary key using Version 7.3. If you have this problem, you must use SQL*Plus to remove the primary key.

1. **Follow Steps 1 through 5 in the "Adding , changing, and removing a primary key with PO7 Navigator" section.**

2. **Double-click in the Primary Key column.**

   The primary key is removed.

3. **Click OK in the Design Table dialog box after you are finished.**

   Oracle7 removes the primary key constraint and the index.

Changing a primary key with PO7 Navigator

The only way to change a primary key is to remove it and then create a new one.

1. **Follow the steps in the "Removing a primary key with PO7 Navigator" section earlier in this chapter.**

   Now you are ready to create a new primary key.

2. **Add the new primary key by following Steps 6 through 10 in the "Adding, changing, and removing a primary key using PO7 Navigator" section of this chapter.**

Adding, changing, and removing a primary key with SQL*Plus

A primary key is a constraint that you can place on a table. A *constraint* is a rule used to validate data placed in columns when a row is added to a table. The constraint also validates changes to data.

Adding a primary key with SQL*Plus

You can add the primary key constraint using the ALTER TABLE command:

```
alter table tablename
add primary key (column1, column2, ...);
```

Replace *tablename* with the actual table name. Replace *column1, column2,* and so on with the actual columns in the primary key. Separate each column by a comma. The columns do not need to be next to one another in the table or in any particular order.

Here's a specific example, where I add a primary key to the COUNTRY table. The key consists of only one column, the COUNTRY_ID column.

```
alter table COUNTRY
add constraint PK_COUNTRY
primary key (COUNTRY_ID);
```

Oracle7 builds the index required to enforce the primary key. Oracle7 checks every row in the table. If any of the rows have duplicate values in the primary key, you see an error message similar to the following one. The text in parentheses is the name of the primary key that Oracle7 created. Version 7.2 gives you this error message:

```
ERROR at line 1:
ORA-02299: cannot add or enable constraint
(AMY.SYS_C00511)- duplicate keys found
```

Version 7.3 gives you a slightly different error message, but the meaning is the same. If Oracle7 succeeds, you see this message:

```
Table altered.
```

Removing a primary key with SQL*Plus

To remove a primary key, use this ALTER TABLE command:

```
alter table tablename drop primary key cascade;
```

Replace *tablename* with the actual table name.

The *cascade* parameter is an optional parameter that tells Oracle7 to drop not only the primary key but also any foreign key constraints that use the primary key. If you use this parameter, you need to re-create the foreign keys. SQL*Plus does not tell you which foreign keys are removed, so be careful!

Changing a primary key with SQL*Plus

To change a primary key, you actually remove the original primary key and then create a new one. Here's a sample of the code you use to remove the primary key on the COUNTRY table and then add a new primary key:

```
alter table COUNTRY drop primary key;
```

Oracle7 responds with this message:

```
Table altered.
```

Next you type

```
alter table COUNTRY add primary key (COUNTRY_ID);
```

Again Oracle7 responds with

```
Table altered.
```

Foreign Keys are Created and Indexed Separately

When you name a column or set of columns as a foreign key, Oracle7 creates a constraint, but an index is not required. I recommend that you create an index for every foreign key you create. This section shows you how to create a foreign key constraint. The "Creating Your Own Indexes" section later in this chapter shows you how to create an index, including one for a foreign key.

When you add a foreign key to an existing table, Oracle7 goes to the table referenced by the foreign key and then makes sure that each row in your table has either a null or a valid key in the columns that are foreign keys. If it finds any that are bad, you cannot create the foreign key. In that case, you have to sniff out those bad foreign keys. Be on the alert for Limburger, garlic, or Roquefort. It may be a sign of a foreign key gone very bad. Sometimes keys are missing in the reference table. Other times, you need to change the foreign key table.

See Chapter 22 for a SQL query that lists invalid foreign keys and another SQL command that eliminates them.

Adding, changing, and removing a foreign key with PO7 Navigator

To add a foreign key, use the same PO7 Navigator dialog box that you used to create and change a table. You can also use the dialog box to remove the foreign key. The steps are very similar to those used for the adding, changing, and removing of a primary key.

Adding a foreign key with PO7 Navigator

1. **Start the PO7 Navigator.**

2. **Double-click the table owner's database connection icon in the left window.**

   You connect to the database as the owner of the table you wish to work on.

3. **Double-click the Table icon to view a list of tables in the right window.**

4. **Find the table name in the right window and right-click it, and then select Design (choose Properties in Version 7.3) from the pop-up sub-menu.**

   The Design Table dialog box appears. In Version 7.3, click on the Design tab to see the Design portion of the dialog box.

5. **Use the mouse to position your cursor on the row where you see the name of the column of the foreign key.**

   Tab to the right until your cursor rests in the column labeled Foreign Key. See Figure 16-3 to review this part of the dialog box.

6. **Type the name of the table whose primary key is referenced as a foreign key in this table.**

   Do *not* use PO7 Navigator to create a foreign key that contains multiple columns. PO7 Navigator is not smart enough to figure that one out. For these kinds of foreign keys, use SQL*Plus.

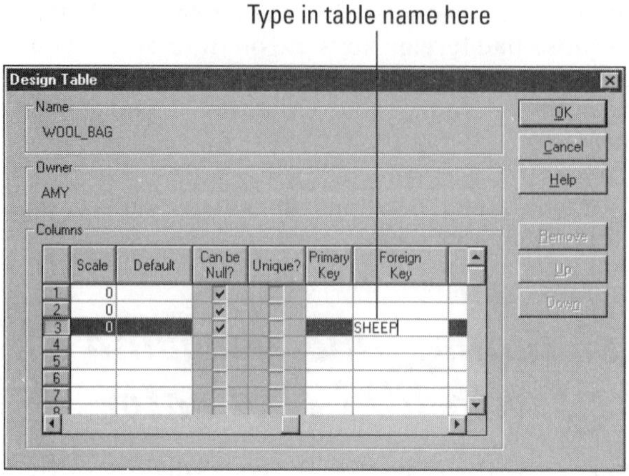

Type in table name here

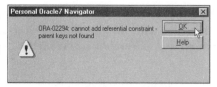

Figure 16-3:
Write in a
table name
to create a
foreign key.

7. **Click the OK button in the Design Table dialog box when you're finished.**

   Oracle7 builds the foreign key constraint that is used on every row of data. If Oracle7 finds any invalid foreign key values — other than nulls, which it ignores — you get the error message shown in Figure 16-4. You must fix the data so that every row has either nulls or a valid key in the Foreign Key column. Oracle7.3 gives you a slightly different error message, but it means the same thing.

Figure 16-4:
The error
message
you get
when
foreign keys
don't fit.

The foreign key you define in PO7 Navigator gets transformed. Initially, you only type the table name. If you return to the table definition later, you can see that PO7 Navigator expands the table name to include the owner, the table, and the key column name. You may have to adjust the width of the Foreign Key column to read the entire contents. Figure 16-5 shows what the column looks like.

Move vertical column dividers (click and drag)

Figure 16-5:
The Foreign
Key column
with the
text
showing.

Design Table

Name
SEAWEED_SAMPLE

Owner
AMY

Columns

	an t Null	iqu	Primary Key	Foreign Key
1			1	
2	✔			
3	✔			
4	✔			
5	✔			AMY.CUSTOMER_ACCOUNT(CUST_ID)
6				
7				

OK
Cancel
Help

Remove
Up
Down

Removing a foreign key with PO7 Navigator

You may need to remove a foreign key if you change or drop the referenced table. In fact, if you try to drop a table that is referenced in a foreign key of another table, you get an error message:

```
ORA-02266: unique/primary keys in table referenced by
enabled foreign keys
```

To avoid this, either remove the primary key with the cascade option or remove the offending foreign key:

1. **Follow Steps 1 through 5 of the "Adding a foreign key with PO7 Navigator" section.**

2. **Press the backspace key to delete the table name, which removes the foreign key.**

3. **Click the OK button in the Design Table dialog box after you're done.**

   Oracle7 drops the foreign key constraint.

Changing a foreign key with PO7 Navigator

Just like changing the primary key, you actually remove the foreign key and then create a new one. Foreign keys are kind of like my parents — they just refuse to change.

1. **Follow the steps to remove the foreign key.**

   Now you are ready to create a new foreign key.

2. **Add the new foreign key by following Steps 6 and 7 of the "Adding a foreign key with PO7 Navigator" section.**

3. **Click the OK button after you're done.**

Oracle7 drops the old foreign key constraint and adds the new one.

Handling a foreign key with SQL*Plus

This is the step that really defines your table relationships for the Oracle7 database. You have created tables with the proper relationships in them by adding columns for foreign keys. The final step is to create the foreign key constraint to tell Oracle7 you have a definite connection between the tables. This section shows you how to make and destroy foreign keys using SQL*Plus.

In older versions of Oracle7, programmers did not implement this final step, which meant that all the rules that go with enforcing a foreign key had to be programmed in by overpaid programmers. Today, who needs 'em? Now, the Oracle7 brain does it all!

Adding a foreign key with SQL*Plus

Chapter 5 goes into great detail on how to relate tables using foreign keys. This section shows you how to relate tables using SQL*Plus. After the two tables are created, you add a foreign key to one of them using the generic version of the ALTER TABLE command:

```
alter table tablename
add constraint foreignkeyname
foreign key (column1, column2, ... )
references reftablename(column3, column4, ... )
```

Replace `tablename` with the actual table name. Replace `column1, column2`, and so on with the actual columns in the table that comprise the foreign key.

Replace `reftablename` with the table name that is the reference for the foreign key.

Replace `column3, column4`, and so on with the list of columns that comprise the primary key in the referenced table. The column list should be in the same order as the primary key to which the list refers.

Many times, only one column exists in each set of parentheses in the foreign key constraint because the primary key contains only one column.

You have returned to your natural state as a cyberpunk mermaid. Now, you want to add a foreign key constraint to define the connection between your SEAWEED_SAMPLE table and the TYPE_OF_SEAWEED table (you created these to document your fine selection of seaweed). Figure 16-6 shows the three tables and their relationships with one another. Two foreign key relationships exist here. One relationship is between SEAWEED_SAMPLE and TYPE_OF_SEAWEED. The other connects SEAWEED_SAMPLE with the CUSTOMER_ACCOUNT table. Your task involves defining these two foreign key constraints, so you write two SQL commands to run in SQL*Plus.

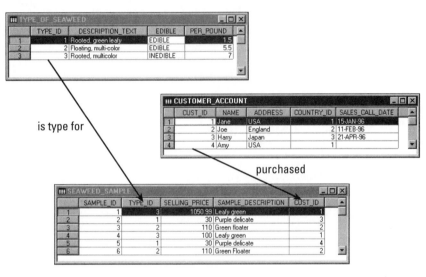

Figure 16-6:
Your swishy-tailed collection of seaweed, with the different types purchased and the customers who bought them.

The first constraint tells Oracle7 that every row in the SEAWEED_SAMPLE table has a TYPE_ID found in the TYPE_OF_SEAWEED table.

```
alter table SEAWEED_SAMPLE
add constraint FK_SEAWEED_SAMPLE_TYPE
foreign key (TYPE_ID)
references TYPE_OF_SEAWEED (TYPE_ID);
```

When you run this command, Oracle7 first checks the existing table rows for compliance with the rule. If any of the rows has a value in the TYPE_ID column that does not appear in the TYPE_OF_SEAWEED table, Oracle7 returns an error:

```
ERROR at line 1:
ORA-02294: cannot add referential constraints
(FK_SEAWEED_SAMPLE_TYPE) - parent keys not found.
```

If Oracle7 succeeds, you see this message:

```
Table altered.
```

The second foreign key constraint is that every CUST_ID in the SEAWEED_SAMPLE must have a corresponding row in the CUSTOMER_ACCOUNT table with the same value in the CUST_ID column.

```
alter table SEAWEED_SAMPLE
add constraint FK_SEAWEED_SAMPLE_CUST_ID
foreign key (CUST_ID)
references CUSTOMER_ACCOUNT (CUST_ID);
```

Once run, both the foreign keys are active and enforced on the SEAWEED_SAMPLE table. Good work, you smart little mermaid!

Here's one more example, in which the keys contain two columns. You have to switch hats now and become the ruler of the universe. The CITY table has a foreign key that is the two-column key of the COUNTRY table. Here's the code:

```
alter table CITY
add constraint FK_CITY_COUNTRY_CONTINENT
foreign key (COUNTRY_ID, CONTINENT)
references COUNTRY (COUNTRY_ID, CONTINENT);
```

As you can see, the foreign key lists two columns and so does the reference to the COUNTRY table. Both lists must be in identical order and in the same order as the primary key of the referenced table. I know you'll remember this information because the ruler of the universe is infallible and has the memory of an elephant.

Removing a foreign key with SQL*Plus

Guess what! You use that ALTER TABLE command again. All this talk about alters makes me feel like I'm in church! Here's the code to remove a foreign key:

```
alter table tablename
drop constraint foreign_key_name;
```

Replace tablename with the actual table name and then use the actual name of the foreign key where I type foreign_key_name.

Here's an example to remove the foreign key you just added for the customers in the SEAWEED_SAMPLE table:

```
alter table SEAWEED_SAMPLE
drop constraint FK_SEAWEED_SAMPLE_TYPE;
```

Naming a foreign key

Make sure that you follow the naming rules and suggestions that I list in Chapter 2. In addition to these guidelines, I suggest that you name your foreign keys like this:

`FK_table_column`

Replace *table* with the table name or a shortened version of the table name.

Replace *column* with the column in the foreign key. If more than one column exists in the foreign key, name all of the columns in shortened versions.

---

*Changing a foreign key with SQL*Plus*

A foreign key is much easier to change than a primary key. All you need to do is follow the preceding instructions to drop the foreign key and create a new one. Read on to find out how to add an index that helps Oracle7 use your foreign key constraints more quickly and efficiently. Or you can just lie down and take a nap. I'm going to do that right now.

Creating Your Own Indexes

Oracle7 has very few restrictions on what you can do when creating indexes. The main rules:

- ✔ You cannot make two indexes that include the same columns.
- ✔ You cannot index columns that have LONG datatype. These kinds of columns can contain a huge amount of data. Indexing these makes no sense anyway. Oracle7 made a logical choice on this one.

Always create an index on a foreign key. This will speed up your queries, because indexes are very efficiently stored and maintained for fast matching and lookups. Queries that join two tables always use the foreign key in the WHERE clause connecting to the primary key in the other table. Having an index on the foreign key allows Oracle7 to quickly match the two indexes — the foreign key index and the primary key index — before going after the data.

Indexes can also speed up response time on a popular online screen. For example, if you create a screen on which users search for phone numbers based on a person's last name, you can create an index for the LAST_NAME column.

The 20 percent rule

The fastest way to retrieve rows from a table is to access the row with the exact row ID. An index is the second-fastest way, but it decreases in performance as the proportion of rows retrieved increases. If you are retrieving approximately 20 percent of the rows in a table, using an index is just as fast. But beyond that, not using an index is faster.

Keep this in mind when you create indexes with which you want to help speed a query.

Queries vary in the rows they select from a table, but if you have one that is typical, you can determine the number of rows that are selected from the table. If this number is more than 20 percent of the total number of rows in the table, an index on the table may or may not improve the performance of the query. You may just want to try it both ways. If the number of rows is less than 20 percent, an index will almost certainly help performance.

Avoid adding an index on a column that includes many of the same values in many rows, except in the case of a foreign key. For example, a column called SEX has three possible values: MALE, FEMALE, and NULL. In a table with 10,000 rows, an index that narrows down the number of rows to 3,333 may not speed performance much.

Creating an Index Using the Navigator Index Dialog Box

When you want to create an index, you can use the PO7 Navigator Create Index dialog box to help you. You can easily remove and modify an index as well.

An index can be either *unique* or *non-unique*. A unique index validates every new or changed row in a table for a unique value in the column or set of columns in the index. A non-unique index does not validate the data. A non-unique index is added to speed up the query.

The only kind of index allowed by PO7 Navigator is a non-unique index. If you need to create a unique index, use the instructions on how to create an index using SQL*Plus.

Adding an index with PO7 Navigator

1. **Start up PO7 Navigator.**

2. **Click the table owner's database connection icon in the left window and connect to the database as the owner of the table you wish to work on.**

3. **Right-click the Index icon (Version 7.2) in the right window and select New from the sub-menu that pops up.**

   In Version 7.3, this step requires a few extra mouse moves. First, click the plus sign next to the database connection you clicked on in Step 2. This expands a list of icons below the database connection. Next, click the plus sign next to the Table icon. You see a list of tables in the left window. Scroll down and find the table you want to work with. Then click on the plus sign next to the table to which you wish to add the index. This shows you the Index icon. Right-click the Index icon and select New from the sub-menu.

   The Create Index dialog box appears, as shown in Figure 16-7.

Click OK to save it ⌐

Type name of index here

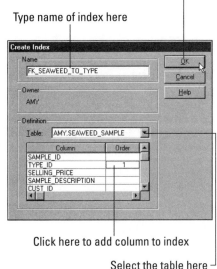

Figure 16-7:
Index
creation
made easy
with PO7
Navigator.

Click here to add column to index

Select the table here ⌐

4. **In the Create Index dialog box, type in the index name.**

   Refer to Chapter 2 for Oracle7 naming standards.

5. **Select the table.**

   Click on the arrow on the right side of the Table box to reveal a selection list of tables, and then click on the table name that needs the index. In Version 7.3, the table name has already been filled in, so you skip this step.

6. Add columns to your index.

After you select a table, you see all the table's columns listed in the box below the table name. Use the scroll bar to find the first column in your index. Place the mouse in this row under the Order column. Click once to add this column to your index. The first one you select becomes number one and should correspond to the first column in your index.

7. Double-click anywhere in the Order column to reset and start over if you make a mistake.

8. Repeat Steps 6 and 7 for each additional column of your index.

9. Click the OK button in the Create Index dialog box after you're done.

Oracle7 builds the index.

Removing an index with PO7 Navigator

1. Start up PO7 Navigator.

2. Click the table owner's database connection icon in the left window and then connect to the database as the owner of the table you wish to work on.

In Version 7.3, this step requires a few mouse moves. First, click on the plus sign next to the database connection you clicked on in Step 2. This expands a list of icons below the database connection. Next, click on the plus sign next to the Table icon. You see a list of tables in the left window. Scroll down and find the table you want to work with. Then click on the plus sign next to the table to which you wish to add the index. This shows you the Index icon. Right-click on the Index icon and select New from the sub-menu.

3. Double-click the Index icon in the right window.

4. Arrange index list in order (optional).

Click on the Name column or on the Owner column to arrange for the index list to order by Name or by Owner.

Skip this step in Version 7.3.

5. Right-click the index you wish to remove and select Delete from the pop-up sub-menu.

A dialog box appears as shown in Figure 16-8, making sure that you want to delete the index.

6. Click the Yes button in the dialog box.

Oracle7 removes the index.

Figure 16-8:
Click the
Yes button
to remove
the index.

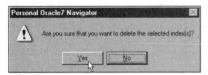

Changing an index with PO7 Navigator

To change an index you actually remove the index and then re-create it, so follow the steps in "Removing an index with PO7 Navigator" and then follow the steps in "Adding an Index with PO7 Navigator."

Viewing an index with PO7 Navigator

1. **Start up PO7 Navigator.**

2. **Click the table owner's database connection icon in the left window and then connect to the database as the owner of the table you wish to work on.**

3. **Double-click the Index icon in the right window.**

   In Version 7.3, this step requires a few mouse moves. First, click on the plus sign next to the database connection you clicked on in Step 2. This expands a list of icons below the database connection. Next, click on the plus sign next to the Table icon. You see a list of tables in the left window. Scroll down and find the table you want to work with. Then click on the plus sign next to the table to which you wish to add the index. This shows you the Index icon. Right-click on the Index icon and select New from the sub-menu.

4. **Arrange index list in order (optional).**

   Click on the Name column or on the Owner column to arrange for the index list to order by Name or by Owner.

   Skip this step in Version 7.3.

5. **Double-click the index you want to view.**

   The Index dialog box appears, as shown in Figure 16-9. This dialog box looks a lot like the Create Index dialog box but does not allow any changes.

Figure 16-9:
The Index
dialog box
appears.

Creating an Index Using SQL

No matter which platform you use for Oracle7, good old SQL*Plus is always there like a faithful dog, just waiting for you to throw him a bone. You can use SQL*Plus to add or remove an index, but you cannot change an index with SQL*Plus — you have to remove the old index and create a new one.

Index versus primary key constraints

You probably already know that you can create your own unique index for a table's primary key *if you do not define a primary key constraint*.

If you are working with a legacy system, you may face a situation where you have many of these indexes attached to the older tables. Why go through all the trouble of removing those indexes and adding the primary key constraints? Do you get royalties every time the primary key is used?

The best reason for replacing unique indexes with primary key constraints is because you

cannot create any foreign keys that refer to a table that has no primary key. You may start with the older tables and then build on new tables that fit in and enhance these older ones. Foreign keys define all the connections between the old and new tables. If you don't create a primary key constraint, you are handicapped. Ultimately, you will be unable to create the foreign key constraints that make your schema (set of database tables) have integrity with good values in all the foreign keys. You don't have to be a Boy Scout to know that good values and integrity are desirable traits.

Adding an index with SQL*Plus

The basic format for creating an index with SQL looks like this (the default is a non-unique index):

```
create index indexname on tablename
(column1, column2, etc.);
```

You can create a unique index with this code:

```
create index indexname on tablename
(column1, column2, etc.);
```

Replace *indexname* with a real index name. Replace *tablename* with the actual table name and replace *column1, column2* and so on with the actual column names included in the index.

Oracle's Brain on Index

Oracle7 uses indexes to get at your data faster. Oracle7 has a special part of its brain called the *Optimizer*. The Optimizer looks over any SQL command and decides the fastest and most efficient way to deliver the results.

The Optimizer has a set of rules it uses to determine the best way to go after your data. Its job is to scrutinize your WHERE clause like an IRS auditor pores over your books. The Optimizer weighs all the options, compares, contrasts, combines, unravels, and finally comes up with a plan. It uses this plan to execute the SQL command.

Under most circumstances, the Optimizer obtains great results. Indexes speed up your queries, right? Sure they do, *when the Optimizer decides to use them*.

Here's the catch: Sometimes, you inadvertently write something into your WHERE clause that makes the Optimizer say, "Okay, if you want that, I'll do it, but I'll have to do it the hard way — without the index." Rules are rules!

Just to prepare you and to keep the Optimizer on your side, here's a list of conditions in which the Optimizer cannot use an index, even when one is available.

Do you have an index?

Whenever a query is slow, make sure that the indexes you expect to exist actually exist. Chapter 22 has a query to list indexes.

All your indexes appear as rows in the USER_INDEXES table. You can quickly verify the existence of an index by looking at the USER_INDEXES table in SQL*Plus or PO7 Navigator.

After you verify that the indexes exist, your next step is to verify that the indexes are used in the query. The following sections explore the ways in which a WHERE clause can be your downfall. I present them with the ones that seem to occur the most frequently appearing first.

Indexing and the infamous null value

The null value is not indexed. Any row in which the indexed column contains a null value is not included in the index. Even in cases in which the index has multiple columns, the row is not included in the index if any of those columns contains a null value.

For example, I've built an index on the DEATH_DATE column of the FISH table in Figure 16-10 containing only two rows. The two rows that are indexed contain data. The two remaining rows have nulls in the DEATH_DATE column and therefore cannot be indexed.

These two rows get indexed

Figure 16-10:
Two of
these rows
are indexed
and two
are not.

NAME_OF_FISH	AQUARIUM_NAME	BIRTH_DATE	DEATH_DATE	COLORS	BREED	SEX	COMMENT_TEXT
1 Fish Two	Fishbowl	01-JAN-96	15-MAR-96	black and tan	guppy	Female	Eaten by Wesley
2 Fish Three	Fishbowl	01-JAN-96	08-APR-96	red and white	guppy	Male	Eaten by Wesley
3 Fish Four	Fishbowl	01-MAR-96		transparent	guppy		Died while I was on vacation, probal
4 Wesley	Fishbowl	01-JAN-96		gold	guppy	Male	

These two rows do not appear in the index

What does this mean to you? When you write a query that checks for nulls in a column, an index on the column does not increase your performance. See Chapter 18 for more discussion about when the Optimizer cannot use your carefully planned and beautifully laid out indexes.

Concatenated text-type columns

You have a query that finds anyone with the name JOHN SMITH. Your
PERSON table has the name split between two columns, so you combine the
two columns with the *concatenation* function, which adds a single space
between the columns, and then compare the combined columns to the
name. Here's the code:

```
select * from PERSON
where FIRST_NAME || ' ' || LAST_NAME = 'JOHN SMITH';
```

This code works very well, except that the Optimizer is unable to use the
index that you created on LAST_NAME. I did tell you about the index, didn't I?

Here is an alternative method of writing the query so that the index is used:

```
select * from PERSON
where FIRST_NAME = 'JOHN'
  and LAST_NAME = 'SMITH';
```

Wildcards can throw everything off

Looking at the same PERSON table with an index on LAST_NAME, you now
have to look for any person whose last name has SMITH in it. To find hy-
phenated last names like ADAM-SMITH, you use a wildcard (%). Your query
may look like this:

```
select * from PERSON
where LAST_NAME like '%SMITH';
```

In this case, because the wildcard appears at the beginning of the word
you're searching for, the Optimizer cannot use the index. It goes through the
table one row at a time. First, the Optimizer reads a row's LAST_NAME
column, checking for SMITH anywhere inside the column, and then it either
chooses or eliminates that row and proceeds to the next one that is physically adjacent to it.

Sometimes you cannot avoid this kind of a query. Just remember that the
wildcard can slow down the query.

When the wildcard appears elsewhere in the string, the Optimizer can use
the index. For example, the index applies in this query:

```
select * from PERSON
where LAST_NAME like 'J%';
```

Mixing and matching different datatypes

Sometimes, you write a query where a column value gets compared to a *literal,* or constant, value. For example, this query on your now world-famous seaweed collection looks for samples that are selling at more than $150.00.

```
select SAMPLE_ID
from SEAWEED_SAMPLE
where SELLING_PRICE > '150.00';
```

In this example, Oracle7 compares a number datatype column to a literal, which is a character datatype. In most cases, you convert the literal to a number and then do the comparison. Occasionally, however, Oracle7 decides to convert the column to a character datatype and then do the comparison. This method happens for several reasons that Oracle7 documentation goes to great lengths to explain. I won't bore you with it.

Implicit data conversion is when Oracle7 converts a column or a literal from one datatype to another out of necessity. *Explicit data conversion* is when you use a special data conversion function to do the conversion yourself. You decide how the data gets converted by writing in functions within your SQL code that do the conversion to the proper data type.

If, for any reason, Oracle7 decides to convert the `SELLING_PRICE` (in the example) to a character string instead of converting the literal 150.00 to a number, your performance time suffers. The Optimizer invokes one of its rules, *No functions allowed on the indexed columns,* and ignores the index. Make sure that you use explicit data conversion to aid the Optimizer in using indexes.

Here's the explicit data conversion added to the preceding query:

```
select SAMPLE_ID
from SEAWEED_SAMPLE
where SELLING_PRICE > TO_NUMBER('150.00');
```

Oracle7 needs no implicit data conversion, because both the column and the results of the function on the right have the same datatype.

The logically illogical order of data

Imagine that you store a calendar of events in your database table. As people call you about events, you enter them into the table called `CALENDAR_EVENT`. Oracle7 stores each event sequentially as you enter them.

One day you put in three events in February. Later you put in two events for January. You want to see them in chronological order, so you add an index in the EVENT_DATE column.

You write and run this SQL query that lists everything in your CALENDAR_EVENT table.

```
select * from CALENDAR_EVENT;
```

To your surprise, when you query the table, the events are coming out in the order you entered them and not in chronological order. Here are the results of the query:

```
EVENT_DATE EVENT_DESC
--------------------------------------------------------------
14-FEB-97  Valentine's Day Parade
01-FEB-97  Boss's Birthday Party
07-FEB-97  Bill and Kelly's Wedding
14-JAN-97  Martin Luther King, Jr.'s Day Art Show in the
           Capitol
01-JAN-97  New Year's Day picnic in the mall
```

What went wrong? You put an index on the right column, but Oracle7's Optimizer does not use it because it has no reference to the EVENT_DATE column in the WHERE clause. In fact, there is no WHERE clause at all. For chronological results, add an ORDER BY clause to your SQL query that tells Oracle7 to sort all the data by EVENT_DATE. The ORDER BY clause, like the WHERE clause, gets evaluated by the Optimizer. The Optimizer looks for indexed columns in the ORDER BY clause that it can use to speed up the query. Your fast-running, tuned, and in-order query looks like this:

```
select * from CALENDAR_EVENT
order by EVENT_DATE;
```

Oracle7 returns this response:

```
EVENT_DATE EVENT_DESC
--------------------------------------------------------------
01-JAN-97  New Year's Day picnic in the mall
14-JAN-97  Martin Luther King, Jr.'s Day Art Show in the
           Capitol
01-FEB-97  Boss's Birthday Party
07-FEB-97  Bill and Kelly's Wedding
14-FEB-97  Valentine's Day Parade
```

Adding an index to a table does not actually reorder the data in the tables. Oracle7 saves a lot of time by leaving the data alone and building an index containing only indexed columns and row IDs. The index is sorted for very fast retrieval. When the Optimizer finds a part of the WHERE clause or ORDER BY clause in a query that refers to an indexed column, the Optimizer uses the index for getting data more quickly. Oracle7 races through the data in the index because it is presorted and only a few columns long. After Oracle7 has found a row in the index, it reads that row's row ID and retrieves the entire row from the table. Retrieval of a row by its row ID is the fastest and most efficient method of all.

Indexes Can Be Too Much of a Good Thing

The price to pay for indexing columns is that indexing slows down the process of inserting, updating, and deleting rows. Under normal circumstances, you won't notice the performance change at all. If you use an on-line screen to update your table, the added overhead of an index or two does not make a noticeable difference.

You may notice the performance change if you load a table with a bunch — I'm talking thousands — of rows at once. I suggest trying to load the table with the indexes in place first and then deciding if the response time is bearable. If it is not, you can remove the indexes during data loading and then replace them afterwards.

Follow these steps for loading a bunch of data quickly:

1. **Remove all indexes from the table and keep the primary key constraint.**

2. **Load the data.**

3. **Re-create the indexes.**

Chapter 17

Correcting Flaws

· ·

In This Chapter

▶ Making changes to columns

▶ Restricting changes to column attributes

▶ Re-creating tables

▶ Saving data before a change

▶ Restoring data after a change

▶ Adding and rearranging columns

▶ Cleaning your closets

· ·

*V*ery often, tables get created as you develop your plans, which is called the *prototype* or *wing it!* method. You may want to read this chapter when, just as you finish making a table, you notice an error — such as a column with the wrong datatype. Another time you may scurry to this chapter in the book is when you have a table or schema (set of tables) that you want to upgrade with more tables and additions. Whatever the reason, now is the time to change things!

Changing Columns in a Table

You can attempt to make two kinds of changes to a table: the kinds you can make and the kinds you cannot make. Oracle7 has rules about what parts of a table you can change. So if you need to change a part of a table and Oracle7 says "Not!" you can get around the rule by dropping the table and then re-creating it. Table 17-1 shows the breakdown of table changes.

Table 17-1	Changing Table Structure				
Kind of Change	*Allowed?*	*Requires Table Re-creation*	*Can Use PO7 Navigator*	*Can Use SQL*Plus*	*Other Restrictions*
Datatype of column	Yes	No	Yes	Yes	Column must have no data
Column name	No	Yes	No	Yes	
Add a column	Yes	No	Yes	Yes	Add on end only
Reorder columns	No	Yes	No	Yes	
Length of column	Yes	No	Yes	Yes	Column must have no data
Remove a column	No	Yes	No	Yes	
Null to not null	Yes	No	Yes	Yes	Column must not have any nulls
Not null to null	Yes	No	Yes	Yes	

All the other changes listed in Table 17-1 are reviewed in this chapter. Enjoy! It's like they always say, "Nothing is constant in this world except change." Anyone who can accurately prove to me just who "they" are gets a free copy of my next book, *Godlike Alterations of the Time/Space Continuum For Dummies.*

The Requires Table Re-creation column in Table 17-1 shows which kinds of changes are easy to do and which require more time and steps. Changes that are allowed can be done using either PO7 Navigator or SQL*Plus in a single step. A few restrictions exist, which I list in the last column of the table. Check out the section on restrictions in this chapter for more details on what these restrictions involve.

Changes listed as *not allowed* require you to jump through hoops. First, you decide what to do with existing data. You then drop the table and then re-create it with the changes in place. Finally, you reload the data if needed. Look over the section on re-creating tables for more details on how this works.

You're about to read about how to change columns, both with the Personal Oracle7 Navigator (if you're lucky enough to have that) and with SQL*Plus (if you're not). But to make changes, you first need to understand the options available in Oracle7. If you need a refresher, check out Chapter 9.

Changing columns using PO7 Navigator

This section shows you how to make changes to your existing tables using that faithful tool, the Personal Oracle7 (PO7) Navigator. You can make these kinds of changes using PO7 Navigator:

- ✔ Modify a column's data type.
- ✔ Change a column's size and scale.
- ✔ Change a column to allow or disallow nulls.
- ✔ Add a new column at the end of the table.

If you are making a change that requires you to drop and re-create the table, you can do part of the change using PO7 Navigator and then complete the work using SQL*Plus. See "Re-creating a Table" later in this chapter for details about these kinds of changes.

Everything you change in the table structure is done in the Design Table dialog box. Follow these steps to get to the Design Table dialog box and start to make changes:

1. **Start up PO7 Navigator.**

2. **Click the table owner's database connection icon in the left window, and connect to the database as the owner of the table you wish to work on.**

3. **Double-click the Table icon to view a list of tables in the right window.**

4. **Find the table name in the right window and right-click it and then select Design (Properties in Oracle7.3) from the pop-up sub-menu.**

   The Design Table dialog box appears, as shown in Figure 17-1.

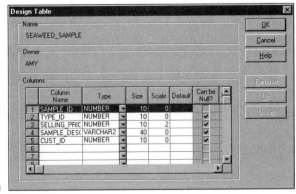

Figure 17-1:
Getting
ready to
modify a
table in PO7
Navigator.

In Oracle7.3, click the Design tab to see the Table Design portion of the dialog box.

5. **Make the changes by simply typing them in.**

For instance, to change a column length, type the length you want.

6. **Click the OK button after you're done.**

If you get an error message when you click the OK button, you probably tried to change a column in a way that has other restrictions, as noted in the last column of Table 17-1. For example, you may try to change the size of a column from 20 characters to 10 characters. If the table has data in the column you try to change, you get an error message. Read the error message carefully to determine how to make the change. If the change requires you to remove data from your column, refer to the upcoming "Column must be null" section for instructions on how to preserve your data while making the change.

Changing columns using SQL*Plus

Any change you can make with PO7 Navigator, you can do with SQL*Plus on any platform. You can change a column's attributes as well as add new columns with the `ALTER TABLE` command. The basic format of the command is

```
alter table tablename [add/modify]
(columnname datatype length null/not null)
```

You specify the `tablename`, `columnname`, `datatype`, and `length`. You also specify if the column is to be added (`add`) or changed (`modify`). Finally, specify whether the column allows nulls (`null`) or does not allow nulls (`not null`).

The `ALTER TABLE` command allows you to make many of the same changes you can make with PO7 Navigator. You can do these things:

✔ Modify a column's datatype.

Here's an example. You need your `CAR` table changed so that you have a date instead of a 4-digit number in the `YEAR_MADE` column. Enter the new datatype into the `ALTER TABLE` command as follows:

```
alter table CAR modify
(YEAR_MADE date );
```

Oracle7 replies:

```
Table altered.
```

✔ Change a column's size and scale.

Here's another example for you. You want to increase the ACTUAL_NAME column from 10 to 30 characters in length. The SQL code is

```
alter table SPY_MASTER modify
(ACTUAL_NAME varchar2(30) );
```

Oracle7 replies:

```
Table altered.
```

✔ Change a column to or from allowing nulls.

Perhaps you forgot to add the NOT NULL constraint onto your primary key column. Here's the command to do that for the SPY_MASTER table:

```
alter table SPY_MASTER modify
(CODE_NAME NOT NULL );
```

Oracle7 replies:

```
Table altered.
```

✔ Add a new column at the end of the table.

Now that you're used to this spy scenario, here's one last example: I want you to add a new column to the table called TRAVEL_RANGE, which will be the number of miles the spy can travel on a mission. The column is numeric, with a maximum of 9,999 miles. Got it? Here's the code — the SQL code, that is:

```
alter table SPY_MASTER add
(TRAVEL_RANGE number(4,0) );
```

Oracle7 replies:

```
Table altered.
```

Notice that in this last example, I use the ADD parameter instead of the MODIFY parameter. The ADD parameter works for adding a new column to the end of the table only. The MODIFY parameter works on existing columns.

Restrictions for Changing Column Attributes

Don't ask me why. Oh, go ahead and ask. Reply hazy, ask again later. Whatever the reason, Oracle7 has nit-picky rules about making changes to the column attributes. My own theory is that these rules came about because of the space-saving conventions that Oracle7 uses when it stores table definitions and data. Shuffling the order of columns around is more difficult when they are arranged in compact, abbreviated forms. Just a theory, really.

However, you can make some changes without a second thought. Oracle7 calls these *unrestricted changes*.

Changes that you can make with no restrictions include:

- ✔ Making a column longer
- ✔ Allowing nulls

You can go ahead and make these changes. See the following sections for instructions on how to make changes using PO7 Navigator and SQL*Plus. Other kinds of changes have restrictions on them. The first group are changes that can only be made to columns when every row in the column contains null values.

Column must be null

Changes that require every row in the table to have a null value include

- ✔ Making a column shorter
- ✔ Changing the data type

In these two cases, you eliminate the data in this column for all rows in your table. If you're using PO7 Navigator, you get an error message like the ones in Figure 17-2 or Figure 17-3, stating the problem. If you're using SQL*Plus, you get the same error messages, but they're not wrapped up and tied with a bow.

You may not need the data at all. In these cases, you can run a SQL*Plus command that removes the data very quickly.

Figure 17-2:
This error
message
can pop up
when you
change a
column's
datatype.

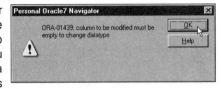

Figure 17-3
You might
get an error
when
making a
column size
smaller.

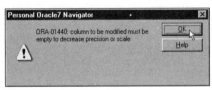

Before running the following SQL command, make sure that you do not need the data in the column you're updating. If you do need the data, see the following example to find out how to preserve it.

The general format to remove all data from a column is

```
update tablename set columnname = null;
```

Replace *tablename* and *columnname* with the actual table and column that you are working on.

For example, I can remove the data from the SEX column of the FISH table like this:

```
update FISH set SEX = null;
```

No WHERE clause exists, so every row in the table is updated. The WHERE clause restricts the rows that are affected by the UPDATE command. See "The Basic SQL Query" in Chapter 3 for more information about the WHERE clause. Oracle7 replies with the number of rows it changed:

```
4 rows updated.
```

Many times, you may want to keep the data. In these cases, you can use
SQL*Plus to save your data in a table you create just for that purpose, make
the change, and put the data back into the table.

You have a table for tracking your total sales each day called DAILY_SALES.
You've decided to shorten the maximum size of the SALES_AMOUNT from ten
digits to eight digits. You have good data in the table, so you definitely want
to save the data. Before you adjust the column size, you create a holding
table for the data using SQL*Plus. The holding table contains only two
columns, the primary key column and the column you will change:

```
create table HOLD_SALES as
select SALES_DATE, SALES_AMOUNT
from DAILY_SALES;
```

Oracle7 responds, after it creates the table:

```
Table created.
```

Next, you remove the data from the original table's SALES_AMOUNT column:

```
update DAILY_SALES set SALES_AMOUNT = null;
```

Oracle7 complies:

```
10 rows updated.
```

Now you can modify the column size using either SQL*Plus or PO7 Navigator (refer to the previous sections for instructions).

Finally, you copy the data back into the newly modified column:

```
update DAILY_SALES set SALES_AMOUNT =
(select  SALES_AMOUNT from HOLD_SALES
where SALES_DATE = DAILY_SALES.SALES_DATE);
```

Oracle7 matches up the SALES_DATE primary key columns and then copies
the data back into the correct row in the original table. When it's finished,
Oracle7 replies:

```
10 rows updated.
```

The last task to complete is minor but very important. You remove the
holding table you created. Here's the SQL command:

```
drop table HOLD_SALES;
```

Oracle7 replies:

```
Table dropped.
```

You have completed the task. Congratulations! Well done.

Before you go to all of this trouble, make sure that the data is worth saving. This project is like cleaning out your closet. As you remove all of the stuff from your closet, you notice how much of it you actually don't want or you can't squeeze into anyway. Don't waste time saving data that is old or incomplete or that you haven't fit into since high school. Send it off to the Salvation Army Thrift Store for someone else to enjoy.

Column must not have nulls

The second kind of restricted column change requires that every row have some data in the column to be changed. Only one change falls into this category: changing a column constraint from *null values allowed* to *null values not allowed.* Every row in the table must comply with this new constraint. In other words, all the rows need data in the column you change. If any of the column's rows include nulls, you get an error message like the one in Figure 17-4, which informs you that you cannot change the column.

What do you do if you have null values in this column? You decide what to put into each row that contains nulls and then update the rows with the value. In some cases, you can use the PO7 Navigator data spreadsheet to update the rows. In other cases, you may want to use SQL*Plus to run a SQL statement that plugs in a default value for every null value.

Figure 17-4:
Hmmmm!
Oracle7
is trying to
tell you
something.

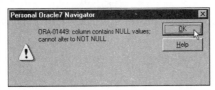

Re-creating a Table

You've probably noticed the long list of changes that are not allowed. Oracle7's great storage efficiency and retrieval speed have a cost: Changing certain parts of a table structure can be laborious. Here's what you do when you actually need to make these changes:

1. **Copy the table, including data, into a new table.**

   Skip this step if the table contains no data, or if you can throw out the data permanently.

2. **Remove the table.**

3. **Rebuild the table, incorporating the changes.**

4. **Copy the data from the copy of the original table into the rebuilt table.**

   Skip this step if you skipped Step 1.

How exactly do you do the above tasks? Glad you asked. The next two sections explain how, depending on whether you use PO7 Navigator or SQL*Plus.

PO7 Navigator steps for restructuring a table

So you have to restructure your table. You have determined that you must make a change to your table's structure that requires you to actually remove the entire table and then re-create it with a different structure. You need, for example, a column renamed. Or perhaps you want to change the order in which the columns appear in the table. Another reason to restructure your table is because you want to add a new column somewhere in the middle of the table. This section describes the steps for restructuring your table using PO7 Navigator.

One of the steps below removes a table from the database. When you remove a table, you also remove two other important database items.

✔ Any indexes you created on the table disappear and must be re-created.

✔ Any foreign keys in other tables that refer to this table's primary key also get removed.

1. **Start up PO7 Navigator.**

   See Chapter 1 for instructions.

2. **Click the table owner's database connection icon in the left window.**

   You connect to the database as the owner of the table you wish to work on.

3. **Double-click the Table icon.**

   This allows you to view a list of tables in the right window.

4. Find the table name in the right window and click it.

5. Copy the table by choosing Edit⇨Copy.

6. Paste the table by choosing Edit⇨Paste.

The Copy Table As window pops up, asking for a table name.

7. Type in a table name, click the Structure and Data button to include the data, and then click OK.

Version 7.3 sometimes pops up an additional question when you click OK, asking "The source table, *tablename,* has constraints. Do you want to copy its constraints?" Click the No button to copy the table with data without copying the constraints. The constraints are not needed because this table is really just a holding place for your data and will be removed soon.

Figure 17-5 shows that I pasted the FISH table into a new table I call HOLD_FISH.

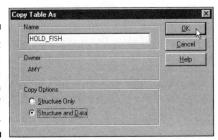

Figure 17-5:
Pasting a table into a new table using PO7 Navigator.

8. Re-create your table.

Right-click the Table icon and select New. Then create the table all over again, making the changes you need (adding new columns, renaming columns, and so on) as if you were creating a brand-new table. See Chapter 9 for steps on using PO7 Navigator to create a table.

9. Copy the old data back into your new table.

- Click the Toolbox icon in the left window of PO7 Navigator. This opens the Toolbox project. Navigator shows the contents of the Toolbox in the right window.

- Double-click the SQL*Plus icon in the right window. It's the one that has a yellow plus sign.

- Fill in your user name and password in the security screen that pops up.

- Copy the data into the new table.

The following insert command is a general guideline for the SQL*Plus command that you create. Your command will reflect the changes that you made in the columns, column names, and so on.

```
insert into newtablename (newcolumn, newcolumn, ...)
select (oldcolumn, oldcolumn, ...)
from copytable;
```

Oracle7 replies with a message informing you how many rows it created, such as:

```
3 rows created.
```

- Exit SQL*Plus.

- Click the *X* in the upper-right corner if you are in Windows 95. Exit your usual way on other platforms.

10. Re-create any Foreign Key references in other tables.

PO7 Navigator automatically removes foreign key constraints from other tables that refer to a table that is removed. After you re-create your table, you must also re-create all the foreign keys that refer to the re-created table. See Chapter 16 for instructions on creating foreign keys.

11. Re-create any additional indexes.

If your table had extra indexes you added to improve performance, you must now re-create those indexes. See Chapter 16 for instructions on creating an index.

12. Remove the old copy of the table.

- Right-click the table icon next to the table that you pasted as the copy of your old table. Select Delete from the sub-menu.

- PO7 Navigator pops up a warning window asking you if you really want to delete. Click Yes. PO7 Navigator removes the table from the database.

Finished! You have now restructured your table as you like it. This kind of change is difficult to do and takes careful attention to detail. Good job!

The next section goes through the same steps, except it shows you how to do it all using SQL*Plus commands instead of using PO7 Navigator.

Using SQL*Plus to restructure a table

You find yourself in the awkward position of needing to change your table's columns. Yes, you wish you had done this earlier, but now, after inserting 3,000 rows in the table, you have decided that you need a new column in the middle of the table, or you need to rename a column or make some other change that requires a complete rebuild of the table. This section shows how to accomplish this task (using SQL*Plus) without losing the data you worked so hard to create.

1. **Log on SQL*Plus as the table owner.**

   See Chapter 1 for a refresher if needed.

2. **Copy the table into a new table to save the data.**

   Here's the general SQL*Plus command:

   ```
   create table newtable as
   select * from oldtable;
   ```

   Replace *newtable* and *oldtable* with your table names. Run the command by pressing Enter. Oracle7 replies:

   ```
   Table created.
   ```

3. **Remove the table.**

   Type this SQL*Plus command and press Enter:

   ```
   drop table oldtable;
   ```

   When you remove a table, you lose all the indexes you created for the table, so you re-create these indexes along with the table.

   Oracle7 replies:

   ```
   Table dropped.
   ```

4. **Re-create the table.**

   Use the same table name as the table you just removed. Include all the new changes. The general SQL*Plus create table command looks like this:

   ```
   create table tablename
   (columnname datatype (size) null / not null,
   columnname datatype (size) null / not null, ...);
   ```

   See Chapter 9 for details on creating a table. After you run the command, Oracle7 replies:

   ```
   Table created.
   ```

5. **Copy the data into the table.**

   The SQL*Plus command is an insert command with a sub-query:

   ```
   insert into newtable (newcolumn, newcolumn, ...)
   select oldcolumn, oldcolumn, ...
   from oldtable;
   ```

   The actual command you use depends on what you changed. For example, if you added a new column, exclude the new column from the insert command, because there is no data in the old table that corresponds to the new column. After you run the insert command, Oracle7 tells you how many rows were created. For instance:

   ```
   3 rows created.
   ```

6. **Re-create any Foreign Key references in other tables.**

   After you re-create your table, you must also re-create all the foreign keys that refer to the re-created table. See Chapter 16 for instructions on creating foreign keys.

7. **Re-create any additional indexes.**

   If your table had extra indexes you added to improve performance, you must now re-create those indexes. See Chapter 16 for instructions on creating an index.

8. **Remove the old copy of the table.**

   Type in the following SQL*Plus command and press Enter:

   ```
   drop tablename;
   ```

   Oracle7 removes the table from the database and replies:

   ```
   Table dropped.
   ```

All done! You added a new column, rearranged the old columns and restored all the data. Stop. Place your No. 2 pencils on the table and turn to the next section. Do not begin until your proctor says "Begin."

Chapter 18

Utilizing Oracle7's Space-Saving Features

Sometimes you can operate an engine better if you know a little about how the engine works. This chapter describes how Oracle7 stores data on the physical disks in your computer. You discover how to review the amount of space each of your tables uses. You also find out why Oracle7 grabs a bit more space for small tables and why it is incredibly efficient at storing large tables. This chapter doesn't tell you why your brother ran away to Canada in the '70s or why life seems to have more questions than answers. But it does answer questions about Oracle7. Unscrewing the inscrutable, as it were.

Why should you learn about Oracle7's internal structure? Well, you could just skip over this entire chapter. (In fact, I thought about calling this chapter "Warning: Technoid Bologna Ahead," because it is full of technical details.) Place the book on the floor and, with a wiggly little hopping motion, step over it. Of course, you had better make sure that your office door is closed, otherwise your co-workers will wonder what you're up to. They may wonder anyway.

But if you do skip this chapter, you'll miss out on how to harness Oracle7's storage techniques to make your database run faster and consume less space. That's why you should read this chapter. See, one of life's questions answered already.

Oracle7 is a Blockhead, Charlie Brown

Any Oracle7 table, even one with no data, takes up 5K (kilobytes) of space. Why does an Oracle7 database require so much space right off the bat? Oracle7 ruthlessly grabs chunks of your hard drive for its own use and then maps the hard drive into Oracle7 *blocks* (refer to Chapter 5). These blocks are usually 2K in size, but like IQs, sometimes they are larger or smaller, depending on the hardware. Oracle7 always grabs whole Oracle7 blocks when creating a new table and follows the rule that only one table's data is allowed in a block. So even if your table is really small, Oracle7 grabs a whole block for it. Something similar happened to me with a playmate in kindergarten. I grabbed the blocks back, which led to a fight that I got blamed for starting. I feel the entire event left me with a sort of mental block.

Anyway, consider how a bricklayer works. Before the bricklayer begins working on her first wall, she has already reserved the space for it. The bricklayer works row by row, just as Oracle7 files your data row by row. This is shown in Figure 18-1. The bricklayer finishes with one wall and moves to another. She has already reserved space for this, just like Oracle7. After you've filled one block, Oracle7 grabs another whole block of space. And just as a partial brick wall pretty much precludes doing anything else in that space, Oracle7 holds an entire block of space, even though not all the rows are filled. When you delete rows from a block, the actual table size may not change.

Unchain my data

Every once in a while, a row begins in one block and overflows into the next block. When this overflow happens, Oracle7 links the blocks together, which is called *chaining*. Chaining slows down the database because Oracle7 doesn't know the chain exists until it retrieves the beginning part of the row. As Oracle7 moves along looking for a column, it finds the link to the chain to the next block, follows the chain, and finally retrieves the data. Chaining is similar to the sort of business networking that happens at multilevel

marketing conventions, and is almost impossible to eliminate, even if you slam the phone down. Chaining occurs more frequently in tables with long text entries, such as a table of book chapters.

You can eliminate chaining once it has occurred by restructuring the table using the EXP (export) and IMP (import) commands. Restructuring the table is not to be confused with Daisy Chaining, a practice of underground programmers in the late '60s.

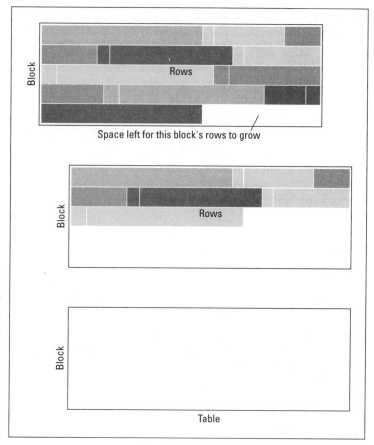

Block

Rows

Space left for this block's rows to grow

Block

Rows

Figure 18-1:
Oracle7,
like a brick-
layer,
works with
blocks in a
methodical
way.

Block

Table

Overhead Storage

My friend and I flew home from San Francisco recently. When the plane hit a bump in the atmospheric road, the overhead bin directly above my sleeping friend's head popped open. The bin's contents fell out and 20 people reached for their valuables, which covered my friend's head. It just goes to show you that as the overhead storage goes, so go the rows. Anyway, my friend is fine after only two months of psychotherapy for Post-Aeronautic Stress Disorder.

Oracle7's big job behind the scenes is to keep track of the data you send, which is where *overhead* comes in. Any time data is created, changed, added, deleted, or otherwise folded, spindled and mutilated, Oracle7 makes a note of it in its overhead storage bin. Figure 18-2 and Table 18-1 show that Oracle7 keeps many bins for various kinds of data.

Table 18-1	Oracle7's Overhead Storage Bins (A Partial List)
Category	*What It Stores*
Database	Location of all tablespaces (storage space)
Tablespace	Location and usage of all blocks in the tablespace
Table	Location of all blocks used by the table
Blocks	Starting point of each row in the block; running total of used and unused space
Row	Starting point of each column in the row
Column	Length of the column

Figure 18-2: All together now! Sing with me! Here an overhead, there an overhead, everywhere an overhead, overhead.

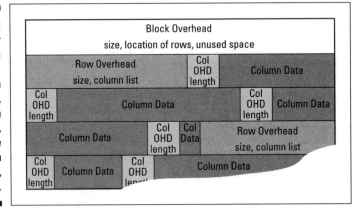

Oracle7 goes totally bananas on overhead. Oracle7, in its wisdom, knows that this kind of detailed storage scheme *actually saves space and works more efficiently* in the long run. The more data you store, the more you benefit from Oracle7's painstaking attention to overhead.

How Oracle 7 Saves Space

Oracle7 does not do table reservations for columns, even if you phone ahead. Oracle7 is a first-come, first-served kind of joint. If a column (diner) comes in without any data (money), the overhead for that column (chair) is taken away. The column (diner) is then ushered politely but firmly to the door (the virtual bum's rush). Only columns with actual data have space at the table, and only the exact space needed for the data is used in the columns.

Other databases reserve space for every column once you insert a row. The amount of space reserved is based on the definition of the column. A 200-character text column gets enough space for 200 characters. This happens regardless of whether the column is blank, has only three characters, or has 150 characters of data. For those three characters, other databases use a total of 600 characters of space. In contrast, Oracle7 uses no space at all for the blank column, five characters of space for the three-character column of data, and 152 characters for the 150-character column of data. So instead of using 600 characters of total space, Oracle7 uses only 157 characters. Figure 18-3 shows the difference between Oracle7 and the others.

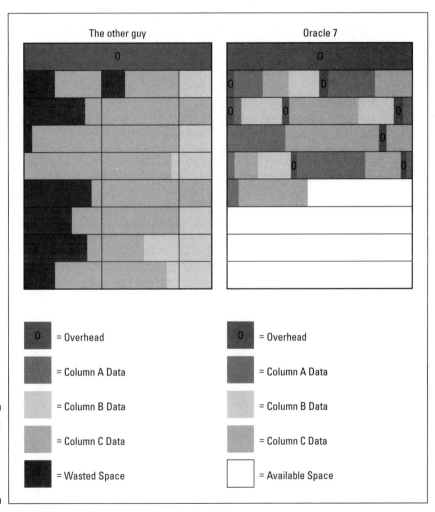

Figure 18-3:
Oracle7 is a space-saving demon.

So now that you understand the space-saving features of Oracle7, how do you put them to work? Read on. The next section shows you how to detect when Oracle7 has taken your table and spread it from one end of the disk drive to the other, and how to fix it.

Everything Was So Great — Until . . .

Picture yourself falling down the side of a mile-high skyscraper. It may seem like everything is fine until you get to that darned last little inch. You've had that beautiful *schema* (set of related tables) up and running in Oracle7 for weeks — maybe even months now! Then, seemingly overnight, you notice that performance has slowed to a crawl. Queries that used to finish in seconds now take agonizing minutes. You have not made any changes to your table structure. All your indexes are intact and being used. What has gone wrong? What has caused this dip in performance?

The physical layout of the table data may need attention. Over time, tables become *fragmented:* They spread out over a larger area on your hard drive. You add rows, change rows, delete rows, and tweak data in the columns. Gradually, Oracle7 finds more space to tack onto the table. Rows that overflow their initial space allocations spill over to more blocks on the hard drive. Rows deleted from the table leave gaps of unused and wasted space in some of the blocks.

The gaps and overflows cause Oracle7 to work a lot harder to retrieve your data. This is a lot like keeping a few playing cards in each room of the house and trying to achieve a winning hand in bridge, only to find you're not playing with a full deck. You must regroup your table back into a more compact and organized unit. Oracle7 refers to this process as *reorganizing* a table.

To *reorganize* means to rebuild the internal physical structure of a table by removing it and then re-creating it. You remove and restore data by using the EXP and IMP commands, which are discussed in greater detail in Chapter 14, but which I show you how to apply in "The SQL*Plus cure" in this chapter.

The SQL*Plus checkup

The first step in reorganizing is to find out which table needs to be reorganized. You can run the ANALYZE command in SQL*Plus on any tables you wish to check. This may take some time, especially if the tables are large.

If your table contains more than 10,000 rows, running these commands can take a long time — even hours. If you are working on a large database at work, you should definitely consult with the database administrator (DBA) before running ANALYZE on any table. Some companies have a policy to never run this command. Some companies have harsh policies regarding what they do to employees who run this command. Substantial penalties may apply.

The ANALYZE command actually does more than just collect statistics for you to use when evaluating your table's space consumption. These same statistics are also used by the Optimizer to make your queries and other SQL commands run more efficiently.

To find out what size your table is, follow these steps:

1. **Go to the SQL*Plus part of the Oracle7 interface.**

   If you don't remember how to get to the Oracle7 interface screen, refer to Chapter 1.

2. **Run the following command line, and substitute the name of your table for** *tablename*.

   ```
   analyze table tablename compute statistics;
   ```

   Oracle7 responds when the command is done:

   ```
   Table analyzed.
   ```

3. **Look at the results of the analysis. The results are put into the system table called** USER_TABLES.

4. **Query the** USER_TABLES **table, selecting only the rows for the table you are analyzing.**

   Here's an example of the SQL code to query the USER_TABLES table for the ARTIST table:

   ```
   select TABLE_NAME, NUM_ROWS, BLOCKS, EMPTY_BLOCKS
   from USER_TABLES
   where TABLE_NAME = 'ARTIST';
   ```

Oracle7 executes the query and displays the following results. The results are the statistics that the ANALYZE command generated and are not created by the query itself.

NUM_ROWS	BLOCKS	EMPTY_BLOCKS	AVG_ROW_LEN	CHAIN_CNT
10	9	0	737	0

These columns show you information about your table's blocks. Here's what the columns mean:

- ✔ NUM_ROWS: Total number of rows in the table.
- ✔ BLOCKS: Total number of blocks used by the table.
- ✔ EMPTY_BLOCKS: Total number of blocks that the table ties up but that are actually empty. A number other than zero here means that your table has had a lot of activity (a lot of inserts and deletes). Reorganize the table to reduce the amount of wasted space in these empty blocks.
- ✔ AVG_ROW_LENGTH: Average length, in bytes, of a row in the table. This can help you determine the number of blocks to allocate to the table. See the "Calculating table space" sidebar in this chapter for more information.
- ✔ CHAIN_CNT: Number of blocks that are chained. Any chaining at all degrades the retrieval speed for this table.

To reset the statistics to blank again, run the following command in SQL*Plus:

```
analyze table tablename delete statistics;
```

This is only necessary if your DBA has instructed you to reset the statistics. Ordinarily, you can skip this step.

When the EMPTY_BLOCKS or the CHAIN_CNT columns are greater than zero, your table is *fragmented*. You'd better fix it before you get a sliver in your finger. A fragmented table is one that contains one or both of these conditions:

- ✔ Gaps in the table's blocks that are empty and unusable. (EMPTY_BLOCKS is greater than zero.)
- ✔ Rows that span multiple blocks. (CHAIN_CNT is greater than zero.)

Both of these conditions make Oracle7 work much harder to get at the data in the table. How do you fix the situation? Glue won't work. You've got to do something more drastic. Time to *reorganize* your table.

*The SQL*Plus cure*

You discover that your table is a total mess, like my kitchen table is. You run the ANALYZE command in SQL and find that you have chaining or empty blocks. You decide to tidy up the place — to reorganize your table. Here's how:

1. Save your entire table's data.

Refer to "EXP and IMP commands" in Chapter 14 for complete step-by-step instructions on how to use the EXP command. Follow the instructions, keeping in mind that your goal is to export one table. Figure 18-4 shows the dialog that occurs when using EXP. Answer "Y" or "Yes" (as instructed in Chapter 14) when Oracle7 asks you whether to compress extents. Compressing the extents lets Oracle7 save your data without all the gaps and chaining that exists in the current table's physical structure.

Important to answer Y here

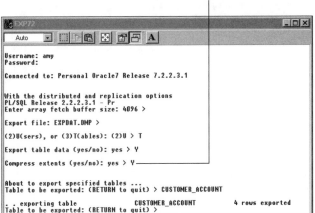

Figure 18-4:
Run the
EXP
command
to
reorganize
your table's
data.

2. Get ready to remove the table.

Verify that you have SQL commands to re-create any foreign key constraints *in other tables* that refer to this table's primary key. To accomplish this task, do these steps:

- Find the foreign keys that refer to this table's primary key. In SQL*Plus, run the following query, replacing *tablename* with the table you're working on.

```
select TABLE_NAME, CONSTRAINT_NAME
from USER_CONSTRAINTS
where CONSTRAINT_TYPE = 'R'
and R_CONSTRAINT_NAME in (select CONSTRAINT_NAME
  from USER_CONSTRAINTS
  where TABLE_NAME = 'tablename');
```

This shows you which foreign key constraints to remove.

- Write SQL code that creates the foreign key. Refer to Chapter 17 for plenty of examples.

Calculating table space

The statistics you gather when you run the ANALYZE command give you enough data to predict how much space your table will use in the future. Yes, even you can predict the future with this amazing technique.

Run ANALYZE and run the SQL query to see the statistics. The how-to steps are in this section of the book. Calculate the number of rows per block as follows:

RB = NUM_ROWS / BLOCKS

RB = Rows per Oracle7 block.

NUM_ROWS = NUM_ROWS column of USER_TABLES for your table.

BLOCKS = BLOCKS column of USER_TABLES for your table.

Estimate the number of rows your table will have a year (or five years) from now. Use that number in the equation below to calculate the total space your table needs.

TF = ER x RB

TF = Table space (in Oracle7 blocks) used in the future.

ER = Estimated total rows.

RB = Rows per block from the equation above.

The final step involves one more calculation to convert from Oracle7 blocks to kilobytes.

K = TF x KO

K = Space in kilobytes.

TF = Table space (in Oracle7 blocks) from equation above.

KO = Kilobytes per Oracle7 block.

Usually, Oracle7 blocks are 2 kilobytes. Some operating systems use a larger or smaller block size. Check with your DBA for this information. This knowledge is very useful for determining the space the whole schema requires. You simply repeat the process for each table. If you have real data to use in the tables, great! Your predictions will be so accurate that you will baffle and amaze your pets and maybe even your co-workers.

3. **Remove the primary key and all referenced foreign keys.**

See Chapter 17 on how to do this step by step. You can do this in PO7 Navigator or in SQL*Plus.

4. **Remove the table.**

Type the following code in SQL*Plus (substituting the name of the table you want to remove for *tablename*) and press Enter.

```
DROP table tablename;
```

Oracle7 replies:

```
Table dropped.
```

This removes all the indexes, grants, and foreign keys in the table.

5. Import the table.

Use the IMP command. Chapter 14 has complete step-by-step instructions on how to use IMP. Make sure, as noted in Chapter 14, that you answer "Yes" or "Y" when Oracle7 asks you whether to import the data. Figure 18-5 shows the import dialog for importing the CUSTOMER_ACCOUNT table. The area pointed to in the figure is one of the questions that Oracle7 asks you while doing the import. Answer Y to import all the table's rows back into the table.

Figure 18-5:
Run IMP to bring your table's data back into the database.

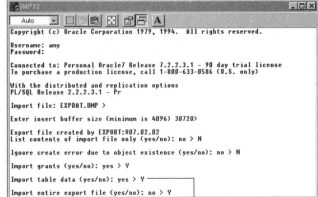

Important to answer Y here

6. Re-create the foreign key constraints that refer to this table on any tables that have foreign keys.

The foreign keys you need to re-create are those found in other tables, not those in the table you just rebuilt. If the table you rebuilt was used as a reference table in other tables' foreign keys, you must re-create those foreign keys.

You just completed the steps to repair your table. Now your table resides in a more compact area on your hard drive so that any query using the table can get at the data faster. These steps accomplished a lot all at once.

When you export a table, you export that table's primary and foreign key constraints, its indexes, its grants, and optionally, its data. When you import the table from that export file, these items are imported with the table.

Preventive Maintenance for Healthy Tables

What do you do when you have a kid with no cavities? Do you skip her six-month dentist visit? No way! The Oracle7 database needs the same kind of preventive maintenance. Put Oracle7 on a regular six-month checkup schedule and stick to it, even if everything is running smoothly. Every six months, run the ANALYZE command on all your tables and then review the results. Reorganize any table that has chaining or empty blocks, as described in this chapter.

As your Oracle7 database schema grows and matures, it needs regular checkups, like any child you create. Watch over its growth and buy new shoes and new hard drives when it outgrows its old ones. Be on the lookout for decreased performance of online screens or queries. Slowed performance signals you to run the ANALYZE command to review your tables and possibly reorganize them. It may be time to take your tables out for walks in the park and to play ball with them on weekends. Don't forget to tell them that you love them, even though they're not carbon-based life forms.

Part V
The Part Of Tens

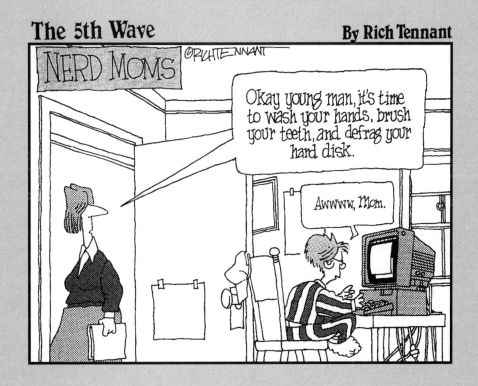

In this part...

*T*his is my favorite part. Here are five short and sweet chapters, each containing ten golden jewels for your treasure chest of Oracle7 know-how. You'll leave this section with a trick up your sleeve for every occasion. Have fun! I did!

Learn here my secrets for designing the best darned relational tables around. If you're going to do it, do it right! Get inside secrets on cracking the power and versatility of SQL*Plus. I have a chapter on fun tricks that make SQL*Plus really versatile and cool. On top of that, I've written a chapter full of SQL*Plus scripts that help you track down problems, document your tables, and figure out security problems.

Another subject covered here shows you around some of the additional tools you can buy that add power to your Oracle7 engine. These software tools connect your database to the World Wide Web, create data entry screens, add visual table design tools, and lots more. I include World Wide Web addresses for many of these tools so you can get free samples to download or get more information.

Chapter 19
Ten Tips for Good Design

• •

In This Chapter

▶ Naming tables with a flair

▶ Jumping to conclusions with prototypes

▶ Throwing caution to the wind

▶ The benefits of talking to other humans

▶ Key points about keys

▶ Clues about changes to keys

▶ Exploring derived data columns

▶ Perusing the security options

• •

1 want to share some useful ideas here that may lighten your load when you sit down to create an Oracle7 database schema of your own. These ideas save you time and make convincing your boss that you know what you're doing easier. If you tear out this part of the book, you will look even smarter.

Naming Tables and Columns Creatively and Clearly

What kind of silly person made up the rules about naming Oracle7 tables, columns, and so on? Probably Scott and his cat Tiger, who prowl the bowels of every Oracle7 database from here to Mars, had something to do with the rules. Refer to Chapter 9 to see the naming rules spelled out in detail. Once you know the rules, it is up to you to create names as you see fit.

The best way to annoy your own brain is to name tables and columns inconsistently. For example, imagine you have a real estate business. Figure 19-1 shows two of the tables you use. One of the tables, called HOME, has a column in which you enter a short description of the house. You call the column HOME_DESC. Another table, called LAND, has a column in which you enter a description of the land, which you call LAND_DESCR. You have abbreviated *description* two different ways: DESC and DESCR.

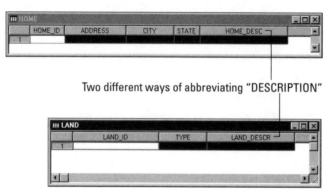

Figure 19-1:
The pitfall of naming columns inconsistently is that you must memorize everything.

Two different ways of abbreviating "DESCRIPTION"

A month later, you write a query using the LAND table and type in LAND_DESC by mistake. Because you were not consistent in how you abbreviated *description,* you need to look up the exact column name.

This problem is multiplied each time another table designer is added to your company's team of designers. Each person has a personal style for naming columns, tables, indexes, and so on. Pretty soon, you have to keep a list by your side that contains every table and every column, just to keep all of the names straight.

Make sure that you establish a naming standard to share with the group. Establish clear and concise naming standards for tables, columns, indexes, primary keys, foreign keys, synonyms, views, and roles, so that others can quickly understand your table design. Decide ahead of time what abbreviations and acronyms you plan to use and then be consistent. Don't hesitate to use force, threats, bribes, or name-calling to make your team members see things your way.

Get creative in your names, so they truly describe their real life counterparts. For example, your LAND table has a column called TYPE, as shown in Figure 19-2. What does that mean? Type of what? Land? Soil? Vegetation? Perhaps it means type of selling contract, or type of parcel.

Figure 19-2:
What type
of type is
this type?
Not my
type,
anyway.

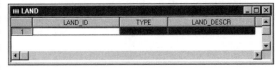

A table and its columns are a lot like a filing drawer. Have you ever tried valiantly to find a letter that you know you filed, but you can't recall which folder you filed it in? Perhaps you have asked your spouse to get a paper from your desk drawer or file drawer at home, but you had a hard time describing exactly where you wanted your spouse to look, even though you could clearly visualize the place in your mind. The more intuitively you name your tables and columns, the better.

Here's another example of how *not* to name columns. This problem crops up even in commercial databases I see, and appears when a table evolves over time to handle a more diverse amount of data than it was originally designed to hold. Often, one column has become obsolete and a new column is needed. Rather than creating a new column, the atrophied column is used for the new data. What you get is a single column with a mixture of data. For example, a column, named MANUFACTURER, initially only stored manufacturer names but now also stores distributor names. There's no way to tell whether you're looking at the name of a manufacturer or a distributor.

Look Before You Leap — Designing Before Building

I have found that a little planning goes a long way. Grasping the big picture of your database project may seem overwhelming. Even so, no matter how big the project appears, once you have the vision and can see it as a whole in your mind, you will be better equipped to create the end product. I don't mean that you have to know how you will build the database. You figure out the details as you go along. I mean that you picture in your mind how the final product will appear. What will it look like on the computer screen? Who will use it and how? How good will it feel to get it done right? Who is on your team helping you? Would you like French fries with that?

This may seem silly, but this is my own personal experience from years of designing and leading database projects: Fixing a vision of the end result in a tangible way (how it feels, looks, sounds) can smooth out your process tremendously. Vision is critical. Conveying your vision to others is also critical.

Go Ahead, Leap! — Building a Prototype

Building a *prototype* has become standard operating procedure these days for projects large and small. A prototype is a small, working model of the end product. It may be actually working on a small scale, or it may be a simulation. With an Oracle7 database, you can easily build the actual tables you plan to use. By only adding 10 or 20 rows to your tables, you can experiment with queries, relationships, reports, or online screens built with Oracle Forms or other software.

If you're on your own using Oracle7, not much stands in the way of your experimenting. In a larger organization, you may have some ground rules to follow. Plan out your prototype, and include critical portions of your project in the prototype:

- **Bottlenecks:** The parts that could slow you down, such as converting data from an old database.

- **Popular features:** Include the features that you know people are excited about. They've heard so much about Oracle7 and all of its cool special talents. One feature that a lot of projects include is a table or group of tables for creating mailing labels.

- **A little of everything:** Add a small portion of your whole plan. Incorporating small parts of your plan helps you refine it so that when you are ready to create the real thing, you have valuable experience under your belt.

Don't be afraid to throw out the entire prototype. The beauty of a prototype lies in its disposability. You put a small amount of time and effort into a prototype so that, if you go down the wrong road, you do not lose too much time or energy. You can create another prototype. You can create two more prototypes. Hopefully you are paid by the hour.

Share — Don't Re-invent the Wheel

Share information, share ideas, share your fears, and share your new red bike. Tell others you'll even share your *Oracle7 For Dummies* book with them, and then go buy several copies of the book to share. Remember that others have gone down the path you travel, unless you're really on the cutting edge. They are usually proud to share what they know with you. Don't be afraid to ask for help.

Contact with your co-workers can bring you a fresh perspective that helps speed up your design and development time.

A great resource is the International Oracle Users Group. The International Oracle Users Group — Americas (IOUG-A) is an independent, not-for-profit organization of Oracle products and services users. The group's goal is to help you, the Oracle7 user, learn how to create great databases using Oracle7. The IOUG-A publishes a newsletter and holds meetings all across the country. A European branch of the group also exists. Appendix B has information about the IOUG-A and other resources.

Primary Keys Are Your Friends

Primary keys form a core for your tables. Foreign keys contain primary keys from other tables. Primary keys are one of the few pieces of data that must be carried in multiple tables. You can retrieve all other data in a row from a table when you know the primary key.

The size and intelligence of primary keys help you streamline tables. The primary key should be small and stupid (not intelligent), which sounds really strange, especially to my single friends. "Small and stupid?" they ask. "That was my last date!" Let me explain why primary keys should be small and stupid.

Small keys take up less room

Any column that holds a four-digit number takes up less space than a column that holds 20 characters. This very obvious fact is magnified when the column is a primary key. Primary keys are almost always copied into other tables as foreign keys. The more rows you have in the second table, the one with the foreign key, the more space you use. Saving 16 characters in several thousand rows may seem insignificant at first, but it does make a difference.

Non-intelligent keys are easy to maintain

An *intelligent key* (as opposed to a non-intelligent key) is a column or set of columns that is used as the primary key for a table while at the same time used to store meaningful data.

A *non-intelligent key* is a column or set of columns whose sole purpose for existing is to be the primary key for the table. The advantage of using a non-intelligent key as the primary key in your table lies in its stability. No matter what happens to the data in that row, the data in the primary key remains the same. This advantage is magnified as soon as you take the primary key and duplicate it in the foreign key of another table.

There are two important arguments against using an intelligent key as the primary key for your table:

✔ The data you place in this type of key can and does change over time. Any foreign key that uses this primary key must also be changed to match. This can change a simple single row update into a cascading update involving a number of rows in many tables.

✔ If you define a primary key constraint (and you should) on your primary key column(s), Oracle7's rules don't allow an update to the primary key column(s). An intelligent key tends to need updates, so you are out of luck. You must go through some major hoop-jumping to get that key updated.

What is an intelligent key anyway? An *intelligent key* is a primary key that has meaning for the row of data.

For example, you, as self-proclaimed ruler of the universe, have a table called HUMAN that tracks this tiny corner of your domain. The table helps you locate your subjects and call them on your cellular phone. The primary key, HUMAN_ID, is a unique identifier you created for your subjects. It is an intelligent key because it contains information about the person, rather than being a simple sequential number. HUMAN_ID has two parts (although it is all stored in the one column) — a code number that identifies the town a person lives in, and a sequential number assigned when you hand out his or her ID card. The sequential number is not unique by itself, but is unique within the town.

Figure 19-3 shows the table with example rows. The figure also shows how two other tables, CONTACT_LIST and PROPERTY_LIST, connect with the HUMAN table. These tables have foreign keys that reference the HUMAN table's primary key. Now you have an intelligent key replicated as a foreign key in two tables. This all seems fine until something happens that causes you to reconsider your choice of the intelligent key. Read on (the suspense thickens).

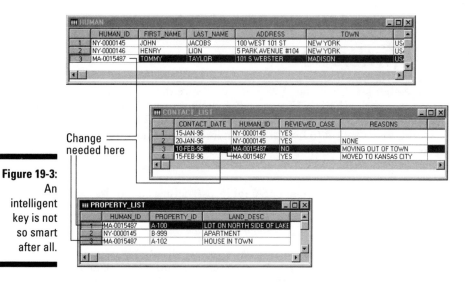

Change needed here

Figure 19-3:
An intelligent key is not so smart after all.

One day, a subject moves to another town. You forgot to impose a law preventing this sort of nonconformist act. Now the primary key (a.k.a. the intelligent key) contains the wrong town code, so you need to change the key in order to keep the data in your table accurate. You assign the person a brand-new HUMAN_ID with the correct town code and a new sequential number. You print a new ID card for your loyal but mobile subject and then go about modifying your data. First, you update the HUMAN table with the change in the primary key column for this person. Next, you change all the rows of data in the CONTACT_LIST and PROPERTY_LIST tables that are connected to this person so that they reflect the new correction in the primary key. Finally, just to be sure that you remember what you did, you create a new table called ID_HISTORY that tracks the changes in the HUMAN_ID as people move from town to town. What a lot of work!

The problem with intelligent keys crops up when all or part of the information in the key changes. Updating a primary key causes a ripple effect that requires more work, time, and effort to maintain. There must be a better way! There is: non-intelligent keys. Non-intelligent keys are much easier to manage.

Imagine the same scenario, but this time you generate a unique sequential number for every subject as you sign them up. The number you assign to a person has no significance to that subject. If he or she moves to a new town, the primary key (a.k.a. non-intelligent key) stays the same. If the subject gets married and changes his or her name, the key stays the same. If the subject gets a promotion for all that incredible work designing databases, the key stays the same. This means that none of the related tables, like CONTACT_LIST and PROPERTY_LIST, need to be changed either.

Presto and voilà! Small and non-intelligent makes a great combination for primary keys.

Use Caution When Modifying Table Definitions

Remember last Christmas Eve when you were determined to peek at your presents under the tree? You sneaked down the stairs and cleverly pried open the corner of wrapping paper on the big present. Having seen the big secret, you went off to bed feeling smug. The next morning, however, the excitement of the day seemed spoiled. The climax of opening that big box had lost its thrill. You can never undo the knowledge once you have it.

Similarly, changes you make to a table's structure cannot be easily undone. Changing a column name requires a whole series of tedious and time-consuming steps.

When you make changes to a table structure that require the table to be removed and re-created, you need to remove and re-create all foreign keys in every table that relates to the table you change. You may need to run a report first to be sure that you catch all of the foreign keys.

Handling Derived Data

Derived data is any data that exists as an extrapolation from other data. Derived data is contained in a column like any other data. The difference is simply that the source of the data in the column is some kind of manipulation of the data in other columns. For instance, if you add the subtotal and the tax, you *derive* the total sale. The easiest way for me to explain derived data is to show you an example.

You track sales totals for the day in your table, DAILY_SALES. You create a new table called MONTHLY_SALES so that you can compare monthly totals quickly. The two tables are shown in Figure 19-4.

The SALES_AMOUNT column in the MONTHLY_SALES table is derived data. You calculate the number in this column from the SALES_AMOUNT column in DAILY_SALES. Here's the SQL code that calculates SALES_AMOUNT for the month of February 1996 and places the amount into the MONTHLY_SALES table.

```
update  MONTHLY_SALES set SALES_AMOUNT =
    (select sum(SALES_AMOUNT)
     from DAILY_SALES
     where SALES_DATE between '01-FEB-96' and '28-FEB-96')
where SALES_MONTH = '01-FEB-96';
```

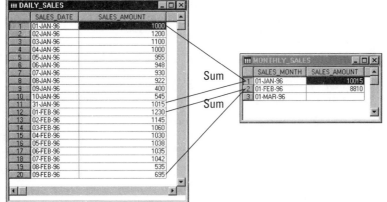

Figure 19-4:
Derived
data can
derive you
crazy.

This example illustrates data that you derive by summarizing data in many rows of a table. Derived data can also be calculated within a row, such as a person's age, which you calculate from a birth date. Another form of derived data results from comparing data in two columns. An example might be a column that indicates when a bank account is below its established minimum balance. In all these cases, the value that you store in a column of derived data can always be re-created by redoing the calculation or comparison.

Derived data has a tendency to be quickly outdated. In the previous example, the monthly total for the current month changes daily. Should you recalculate the monthly total every day? Once a week? Only at the end of the month? You decide and then delegate the task, because it's a pain in the you-know-where.

I recommend that you avoid storing derived data unless you find it necessary to improve performance. You can always use SQL code to calculate the total sales for a month. You don't need to store the results in a table to have them readily available. You could create a view that does the calculation, or do the calculation whenever you print a report.

Practical Ways to Approach Roles for Security

A million opinions exist on how to handle security for databases. I have the million-and-first opinion. My practical method was developed on the job over the years. I offer it for your consideration. Hopefully, it will help you to sort out a good strategy to use for your unique situation. Security concerns vary greatly depending on these factors:

✔ **The number of people involved who use your database:** The more people that use it, the more likely it is that someone will try accessing data they're not authorized to access.

✔ **The kind of people allowed in your database:** If you let every Tom, Dick, and Harry who's surfing the Net drop in for a visit to your database, you'll definitely want to protect your data. If, on the other hand, your database is for employees only, your security risk is a lot smaller.

✔ **The kind of data in your database:** Data that must be kept private needs tight security. Bank and government information may need this kind of high security.

Low security

If you run Personal Oracle7 on your PC or Mac, you need not worry about security. The roles that the PO7 Navigator automatically sets up for you are adequate.

Medium security

This approach works very well for the average internal corporate database, and even works if the public has limited access to the database. The following breakdown of roles makes a practical, easy-to-manage security plan.

✔ **Shared Read-Only role:** This role can see all tables but not modify any data. Every Oracle7 user ID is assigned this role when it is created. In some cases, a simple Oracle7 name, like READONLY, with an easy-to-remember password, like PASSME, is set up for everyone who does not have his or her own private Oracle7 user ID.

✔ **General roles:** These roles correspond with a broad area of the database, such as an entire schema. For example, a schema and a set of online data entry screens are created to support the Personnel department. A general role called PERSONNEL has update privileges on all the tables in the schema. Each person in the Accounting department gets assigned to this role. Another department, such as the Sales department, might have its own schema and its own role.

High security

I describe some forms of high security here, but it is not, by any means, the limit of high security. This just gives you an idea of how you can use the same basic techniques and achieve a higher level of security.

✔ **Theme-based roles:** These roles mirror job responsibilities in the real world. The roles have authority to change tables according to the duties of the people in each role. For example, one role might be called ACTUARY. A person given this role can review insurance claims and assign risk factors to the claimants. The ACTUARY role has update authority on tables that relate to these tasks.

✔ **Unique IDs for everyone:** Another feature for high security involves assigning a unique Oracle7 user ID for every person, which allows for better auditing. This goes hand-in-hand with the theme-based roles. You assign each user ID the appropriate role or roles for the user's job.

When you assign unique Oracle7 user IDs, your database administrator (DBA) is handed a lot of work. It becomes a security issue if the DBA cannot add or revoke roles quickly enough. I recommend creating SQL routines that can help automate adding and revoking roles in an accurate and timely manner.

Be Smart about Test Data

Test data is a set of fake rows of data. The purpose of test data is to verify the schema that you have designed and any queries, screens, or other fancy finagling you intend to use with your data. Most people skip using test data because it's boring and can seem like a waste of time: First you have to create all the test data yourself, and then you have to use it for a while. The final step is to get rid of the test data so that it does not get confused with real data.

Why would anyone ever want to use test data? Some very good reasons to take the time and care to create and use test data exist. Test data lets you create a controlled environment for experimenting and exercising your queries and SQL commands. The benefits of using test data:

✔ You control the data and therefore can predict and verify the results of queries and other SQL commands.

✔ You work with a smaller set of data compared to real-life data. Test data is usually limited to a small number of rows (10 or 20 is usually enough) in each table.

✔ You don't have to worry about destroying actual data when trying out new SQL commands, screens, or other changes.

If you choose to create and use test data, remember these pointers about Oracle7:

- ✔ Oracle7's `ROLLBACK` command in SQL*Plus can speed up testing because it gives you a fast way to restore data back to its original state. The `ROLLBACK` command undoes inserts, updates, and deletes to all tables back to the last time you used the `COMMIT` command or when you logged on.

- ✔ Another fast way to get back to your starting point with test data is to use `EXP` and `IMP`. After you create the test data, use `EXP` to make a copy of all the tables. After you run SQL commands or use online screens to experiment with changes to the data, you may want to restore everything to its original state. Use `IMP` to bring back all your original data. Refer to Chapter 5 for a description of the `EXP` and `IMP` commands.

Talk to Non-Techie-Type Humans

Ricky Ricardo, talking about a neighbor's dog, says, "Oh, she doesn't mind sleeping in the yard. She's used to it."

Lucy, talking about the neighbor's wife, says, "Well, if that's the way he treats her, I don't blame her for going home to Mother!"

A misunderstanding like this one can sometimes creep into an otherwise solid design. For example, I worked with a project where the word *grantee* was misinterpreted for months. The project was halfway completed, after hundreds of hours of work, before an outsider made an offhand comment about the grantee — which made it clear that I had incorrectly designed part of the system.

Make sure that you take your design for a walk to meet the neighborhood. Sometimes getting feedback from another person helps you improve your design and saves you a lot of time and trouble down the road. Other times, you wind up scooping up a lot of you-know-what.

Chapter 20

Ten Cool SQL*Plus Tricks

. . . .

In This Chapter

▶ Having fun with a snazzy trick using the current date

▶ Applying cool functions to columns

▶ Discovering rarely discussed settings for SQL*Plus

▶ Examining unheard of asexual fish stories

▶ Making math easier

. . . .

*S*till looking for more from Oracle7? This chapter has sections on some of the functions and settings that people commonly use and misunderstand.

Putting a Date into a Title

The TTITLE command works great for those little extras. Wonder why there's an extra *T* in the command name? Because TTITLE stands for *top title.* SQL*Plus also has a BTITLE command for *bottom title* to round things out.

You have a burning desire to see today's date on the top left corner of every report you create using SQL*Plus. For starters, you modify a small report in the CAR table.

Today's date and the current time is always stored in the pseudocolumn SYSDATE. (A *pseudocolumn* is sort of a ghost column that is available to use as if it were a real column, except that you cannot update or insert into the column. See Chapter 11 for a sidebar that tells more about pseudocolumns.) Use SYSDATE in your title and you get the current date. If you wish, you can add both date and time. The following steps take you through the process of adding the date and the time to your report.

1. With SQL*Plus open, start with a query.

For example, a query on a SQL*Plus table to show all the cars in the table, ordered by year and make, might look like this:

```
select YEAR_MADE, MAKE_OF_CAR,
STYLE, MODEL_NAME, ID_NUMBER
from CAR
order by YEAR_MADE, MAKE_OF_CAR;
```

2. Save the query to a file.

The filename in this example is CAR.SQL. You can use any valid file name and include the full pathname, if needed.

```
save CAR.SQL
```

3. Add the pseudocolumn SYSDATE **to the query.**

Edit your file to place SYSDATE in front of the whole query. Begin with

```
edit CAR.SQL
```

Oracle7 responds by starting up a text editor, where you work on the contents of the file. Modify the query by adding SYSDATE to the beginning of the query. Add an alias (in this example use TODAYS_DATE) to the column so that the column command you add next does not interfere with other queries that may use SYSDATE. Add the TO_CHAR function to SYSDATE to format the date and time. I've chosen the format that includes the month, day, year, hour, and minute, followed by AM or PM. (See the "Formatting Dates" section in this chapter for more information on the TO_CHAR function.)

```
select TO_CHAR (SYSDATE, 'MM/DD/YY HH:MI') TODAYS_DATE,
        YEAR_MADE, MAKE_OF_CAR
STYLE, MODEL_NAME, ID_NUMBER
from CAR
order by YEAR_MADE, MAKE_OF_CAR
```

4. Add a COLUMN **command before the query:**

```
column TODAYS_DATE new_value TODAYS_DATE noprint
```

This command tells Oracle7 several things about the TODAYS_DATE column:

The NEW_VALUE command tells Oracle7 to update the column before printing it on your report. Otherwise, Oracle7 does not know it is a column and treats it as a *literal* (a word or phrase used exactly as it is typed). Without NEW_VALUE, Oracle7 prints the word TODAYS_DATE instead of the value of the date that you want.

The NOPRINT command tells Oracle7 not to print or display the TODAYS_DATE column at all as part of the query results. Without this command, 15-JUN-97, or whatever today's date is, prints on every line of your report. So far, you have added a column and made it invisible. Magic!

5. **Add a title.**

In our example, use the column TODAYS_DATE in the TTITLE command.

```
ttitle left TODAYS_DATE center 'The Car Report' skip 2
```

This example tells Oracle7 to place TODAYS_DATE on the left side of the top line. The TTITLE command says that the words *The Car Report* are centered on the page and on the top line of the report. The skip 2 portion of the command tells Oracle7 to go down two lines before displaying the rest of the report.

When you are finished editing, save the file if Oracle7 prompts you to save, and then close the file. You automatically return to SQL*Plus. The completed file — called CAR.SQL — contains the following set of SQL*Plus commands and the query.

```
ttitle left TODAYS_DATE center 'The Car Report' skip 2
column TODAYS_DATE new_value TODAYS_DATE noprint
select
TO_CHAR (SYSDATE, 'MM/DD/YY HH:MI') TODAYS_DATE,
        YEAR_MADE, MAKE_OF_CAR,
STYLE, MODEL_NAME, ID_NUMBER
from CAR
order by YEAR_MADE, MAKE_OF_CAR
```

6. **Run the report using the START command.**

In our example, you'd enter

```
start CAR.SQL
```

Oracle7 retrieves the CAR.SQL file, reads every line, and then executes the file a command at a time as if it were an actor reading a script. (That's why a file like this that contains more than just a single SQL or SQL*Plus command is known as a *script*.) The report looks like Figure 20-1, in PO7 Navigator's SQL*Plus window.

This script is found on the CD-ROM that was attached to the back of this book. See Appendix B for details about the contents of the CD-ROM.

```
± Oracle SQL*Plus                                            _ □ ×
File  Edit  Search  Options  Help
SQL> edit CAR.SQL
SQL> start CAR.SQL

01/05/97 08:49 AM                              The Car Report

YEAR_MADE MAKE_O STYLE       MODEL_NAME ID_NUMBER
--------- ------ ----------  ---------- ----------------
     1982 BUICK  4-DOOR      CENTURY    1158A-JJJJ8669
     1989 DODGE  MINIVAN     CARAVAN    331111-NUY911
     1993 ISUZU  5-DOOR      TROOPER    23977-AA97-A876
     1994 FORD   2-DOOR      MUSTANG    11990-ABC-HH889
     1996 JEEP   5-DOOR      CHEROKEE   2211198-AAI8776
SQL>
```

Figure 20-1:
A fabulous
example of
a magic,
invisible
pseudo-
column.

Formatting Dates

Imagine what the world would be like if you had not started to date. Just kidding. I like you, really! The TO_DATE function converts an Oracle7 date to an interesting date format. Oracle7 stores dates in the database as compact numbers and then converts the number to a default date format, where dd equals the day of month, mon equals three letters of the month, and yy equals the last two digits of the year:

```
dd-mon-yy
```

For example, my birthday, July 5, 1986, give or take a decade, is 05-JUL-86 in Oracle7 date format. Once again, Oracle7 has baffled the masses, in the United States at least, by doing something weird — which is why the TO_CHAR function exists.

Oracle7 decided when users complained about the strange date format to cover all the bases right away. Voila! A function that was so flexible it would shut everyone up. Well, I have one last complaint: The TO_CHAR is complicated! Actually, it's not that complicated.

Your FISH table has a BIRTH_DATE column that you want in your next feat of SQL*Plus magic. You want the so-called normal United States non-military date format of *mm/dd/yy* in your query. Using the TO_CHAR function on the BIRTH_DATE column handles this. The SQL*Plus query looks like this:

```
select  NAME_OF_FISH ,
        to_char(BIRTH_DATE,'mm/dd/yy')
from FISH;
```

Figure 20-2 shows the report. Unfortunately, side effects of using the TO_CHAR function are the incredibly long width of the resulting column and the really ugly column heading.

What is a function?

A *function* changes the looks or the contents of a column. Special functions exist for dates, numbers, character datatypes, and groups. Functions perform a much needed service.

Once you understand their syntax, you will love functions to pieces and use them every chance you get.

Figure 20-2:
The TO_CHAR function sometimes creates ugly column headings.

```
★ Oracle SQL*Plus                                    _ □ ✕
File  Edit  Search  Options  Help

NAME_OF_FI TO_CHAR(BIRTH_DATE,'MM/DD/YY')
---------- --------------------------------------------
Fish Two   01/01/96
Fish Three 01/01/96
Fish Four  03/01/96
Wesley     01/01/96

SQL> |
```

Figure 20-2 has the right date style but the wrong size. You want to curb both the very long size and the nasty column heading at once. To do so you add a column command to adjust the size of the column, and an alias in the query. In this example, add alias B_DATE to BIRTH_DATE with the TO_CHAR function wrapped around it. Add a COLUMN command formatting the new B_DATE to a width of ten characters. The column command and the script look like this:

```
column B_DATE format a10
select  NAME_OF_FISH ,
        to_char(BIRTH_DATE,'mm/dd/yy') B_DATE
from FISH
```

Figure 20-3 shows the resulting report. As you can see, the width on the date column looks much better. The heading is BIRTH_DATE, which is not beautiful but passable.

Table 20-1 shows a quick list of most of the abbreviations used in the TO_CHAR function.

Figure 20-3:
The date
column is
no longer
hogging
space.

Table 20-1	Date Conversion Abbreviations for the TO_CHAR Function
Abbreviation	**Meaning**
mm	Month (01 through 12)
Month	Month spelled out and capitalized
MON	First three letters of month in capital letters
yy	Year (00 through 99)
yyyy	Year (including century, such as 1999)
mi	Minute (00 through 59)
hh	Hour (01 through 12)
hh24	Hour (01 through 24)
ss	Second (00 through 59)

Make sure that you watch out for the small but critical difference between mm, the month abbreviation, and mi, the minute abbreviation.

The WHENEVER *Setting*

The WHENEVER setting helps you put on the brakes once something goes wrong and is especially helpful when you have a series of SQL commands in a row that depend on each other.

You create a SQL*Plus script (a set of SQL*Plus commands) in a single file that gathers statistics about the past month's sales. The routine creates tables used to gather, update, summarize, and report data. Then it updates all your accounting tables. If the SQL code to create the tables fails, all your subsequent steps are no good. You certainly don't want to update the accounting tables with bad data. Your best bet is to stop the script if you find any errors and then review the error, make corrections, and start over.

The WHENEVER setting has several parameters. The most straightforward variation looks like this:

```
whenever sqlerror exit rollback
```

Place the WHENEVER setting before your SQL command. You need no semicolon after the command. The WHENEVER setting changes your SQL*Plus environment and remains in effect until you exit SQL*Plus. You can add the ROLLBACK parameter to the setting, as seen previously, or you can leave it out. Actually, you can combine the ROLLBACK parameter with any of the variations on the WHENEVER setting.

```
whenever sqlerror exit rollback

create table NEW_SUMMARY
   (ANNUAL_SALES_TOTAL number(10,2),
   AVERAGE_PER_MONTH_SALES    number(10,2));

insert into NEW_SUMMARY
 select sum(SALES_AMOUNT), avg(SALES_AMOUNT)
 from MONTHLY_SALES;
```

In this example, the second SQL command, the one that begins with INSERT INTO, does not execute if the first SQL command, the CREATE TABLE command, fails. Instead, your SQL*Plus session ends.

Another parameter you can add returns a status code to the operating system. The format looks like this:

```
whenever sqlerror exit sql.sqlcode
```

The SQL.SQLCODE is a special variable created in SQL*Plus that holds the error message number. Programmers use the variable so that they can write fancy programs in C or COBOL or some other programming language that grab the error message number and display it in an error log report, so don't worry about it.

Another option returns any number that you want. For example, you have a program script that calls SQL*Plus to run SQL commands. After completing this, the script carries out other tasks. You want the script to check and make sure the SQL commands completed successfully. If they haven't, you want the script to issue a big error message and fax it to you. Use the WHENEVER setting and then check for a *return code* — the status of the most recent operation — in your programming script. In this example, the return code is the number 4.

```
whenever sqlerror exit 4
```

The EMBEDDED *Setting*

Imagine you created a great report using SQL*Plus for your small business. Now you want a nice summary report to appear right below it. By default, SQL*Plus starts a new page for every new report. You don't see this until you print the reports out.

Change the EMBEDDED setting to start the next query on the same page as the first one. Like other settings, you change the EMBEDDED setting during your SQL*Plus session and it stays that way until you leave SQL*Plus or you change the setting again. To turn on the setting, type this code:

```
set embedded on
```

Now, when you run your script, all the commands get displayed first, followed by the report itself.

To turn off the setting, type:

```
set embedded off
```

PO7 Navigator has a handy menu and settings window to adjust the settings of the EMBEDDED setting, and other settings. Here's how to change the EMBEDDED setting:

1. **Start up the PO7 Navigator.**

   Refer to Chapter 1 if you forgot how.

2. **Click the Toolset Project to the left.**

3. **Double-click Plus32.exe (SQL*Plus) to the right.**

   In Oracle 7.3, double-click Plus 33W.

4. **Log in with your user name and password.**

5. **Select Options⇨Set Options (Environment in Oracle 7.3) from the menu at the top of the dialog box, as shown in Figure 20-4.**

Figure 20-4:
PO7
Navigator's
Options
menu.

```
Oracle SQL*Plus                                                    _ □ ×
File  Edit  Search  Options  Help
Name              Screen Buffer...      Null?     Type
----------        Set Options...        --------  ----
SAMPLE_ID                               NOT NULL  NUMBER(10)
TYPE_ID                                 NOT NULL  NUMBER(10)
SELLING_PRICE                                     NUMBER(10,2)
SAMPLE_DESCRIPTION                                VARCHAR2(40)
CUST_ID                                           NUMBER(10)
SQL> |
```

The Set Options dialog box appears with all the settings that are available to you, as shown in Figure 20-5.

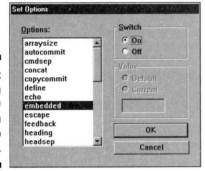

Figure 20-5:
When
EMBEDDED
is on, you
have no
breaks.

6. **Click embedded in the Set Options dialog box and the buttons show you if** EMBEDDED **is on or off.**

   In Figure 20-5, EMBEDDED is on.

   Click the On button to set EMBEDDED on. In Oracle 7.3, click the Current button first and then clisk On.

7. **Run the script to create the report.**

The RECSEP *and* RECSEPCHAR *Settings*

The RECSEP setting has a default setting that seems confusing at first. RECSEP means *record separator*. The RECSEP setting tells SQL*Plus what to do between two rows on your report.

The default is *wrapped,* which tells SQL*Plus to add a line between two rows only when the first row has a column that wrapped to a second line. Figure 20-6 shows a script that shows off the RECSEP setting.

Other setting possibilities are:

```
set recsep off
```

Set RECSEP off when you never want a line between two rows in your report.

```
set recsep each
```

┌Blank line between two rows.

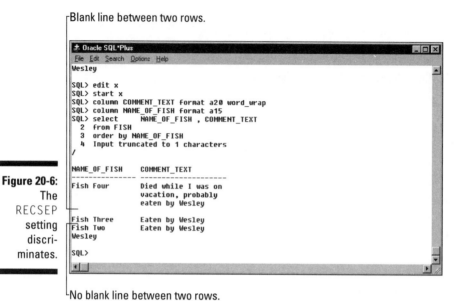

Figure 20-6:
The
RECSEP
setting
discri-
minates.

└No blank line between two rows.

Set RECSEP to each when you want a line between every row in your report.

RECSEPCHAR goes hand in hand with RECSEP. RECSEPCHAR is a record separator in a chair. Actually, the RECSEPCHAR setting tells SQL*Plus what characters to use to fill in the line that separates the rows. The default character is a *blank,* which gives a blank line, as you see in Figure 20-6. You can make this a different character. For example, if you can figure out how, use Dumbo the elephant. Of course, then you might have lawyers for the Walt Disney company showing up on your doorstep. You can also change the character to a dashed line, by typing:

```
set recsepchar -
```

The DECODE *Function*

The DECODE function is used inside a query. Apply DECODE to any character datatype column. DECODE works as a filter and a transformer. For example, your FISH table has a column for SEX. This column contains either *Male, Female,* or *null* in every row. You want to run a query that translates the column into French and shows *Homme, Femme,* or *?* instead of the actual value of the SEX column. DECODE can help. Here's the query:

```
select NAME_OF_FISH, SEX, decode(SEX,'Female','Femme',
                                     'Male','Homme',
                                     '?')
from FISH;
```

The report looks like Figure 20-7.

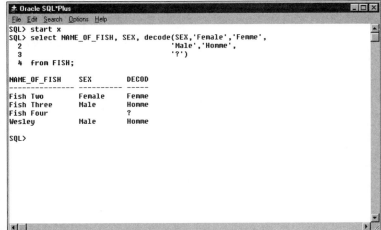

Figure 20-7:
The
DECODE
function
has lots of
potential.

You can use the DECODE function anywhere you use a column. DECODE is a very powerful tool worth keeping in your toolbox.

The preceding example is found on the CD-ROM in the back of the book. Appendix B has information on how to use the CD.

The INSTR *Function*

INSTR, short for INSTRING, is a function that you apply to a column that is a character datatype. (A column's *datatype* defines the type of information that can be stored in the column, such as dates, numbers, or characters. See Chapter 9 for a discussion of datatypes.) INSTR hunts down a phrase or letter and tells you exactly where it starts.

For example, the letter *a* is in the second position in my name, Carol. If the column does not contain the phrase or letter, `INSTR` returns zero. Here's an example:

```
select NAME_OF_FISH, instr(COMMENT_TEXT,'b'), COMMENT_TEXT
from FISH;
```

In this example, you look for the letter *b* in the `COMMENT_TEXT` column. The report, shown in Figure 20-8, show that two of the rows have a letter *b* in the seventh position and one has the letter *b* in position 34.

This example of `INSTR` is in a file on the CD-ROM in the back of the book. Appendix B has information on how to use the CD-ROM.

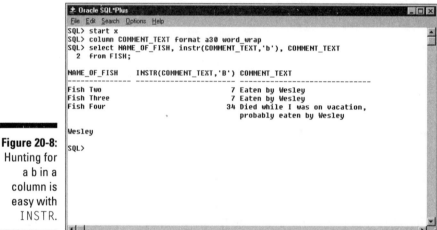

Figure 20-8: Hunting for a b in a column is easy with `INSTR`.

The SUBSTR *Function*

`SUBSTR`, which you can also call `SUBSTRING`, cuts off a portion of a column's data. You tell SQL*Plus what character position to start at and how far to go using `SUBSTR`. An example looks like this:

```
substr(COMMENT_TEXT,1,15)
```

`SUBSTR` grabs the first 15 characters, starting at position 1, of the column `COMMENT_TEXT`. If you leave off the last parameter, the length, SQL*Plus assumes that you want the remaining data.

Here's a nifty example that combines two functions, INSTR and SUBSTR. You want to grab the first word in the COMMENT_TEXT column and use it in your report. Use INSTR to find a blank character inside the COMMENT_TEXT column, and then use SUBSTR to cut off the column at that point. The INSTR function acts as a parameter, the starting point, for the SUBSTR function.

```
select NAME_OF_FISH,
substr(COMMENT_TEXT,1,instr(COMMENT_TEXT,' ')) ONE_WORD,
    COMMENT_TEXT
from FISH;
```

In this example, I add the complete COMMENT_TEXT so that you can verify the results easily. Figure 20-9 shows what it looks like when the report runs.

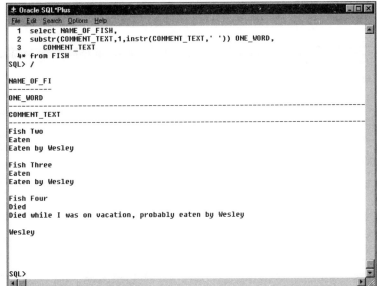

Figure 20-9:
You can easily remove extraneous, overweight data using SUBSTR.

You can run this example yourself using one of the files on the CD-ROM in the back of the book. Appendix B has information on how to use it.

The CONCATENATE *Symbol*

Do not confuse this function with the DISCOMBOBULATE function, which appears in a later book called *Discombobulation For Dummies*. The CONCATENATE symbol combines two columns. You can also use it to combine a column and a literal phrase. For example, if you want to throw the words *The Honorable* in front of your fish's names, you use the CONCATENATE symbol:

```
select 'The Honorable ' || NAME_OF_FISH
from FISH;
```

Figure 20-10 shows the report. One small detail: I add a blank space at the end of the phrase because SQL*Plus does not add space between the two columns or phrases being combined.

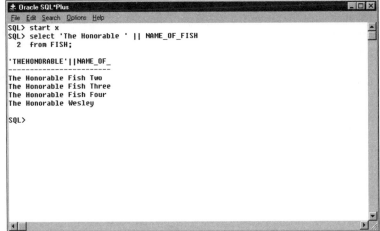

Figure 20-10:
The
honorable
fish are
honored.

This example is one of the files on the CD-ROM in the back of the book. Appendix B has information on what's on the CD-ROM.

The CONCATENATE symbol consists of two vertical bars on nearly all platforms. On rare occasions, the CONCATENATE symbol gets mistranslated when you port between some platforms. To accomodate this problem, Oracle7 provides a function called CONCAT, which can be used as a substitute.

The NVL *Function*

The NVL function lets you substitute a phrase, number, or date for a null value in a row's column. Here's an easy example:

```
select NAME_OF_FISH, nvl(SEX,'Unknown') SEX
from FISH;
```

In this example, when a fish has a null value in its SEX column, the word *Unknown* appears in its place, which does not change the underlying data. The NVL function only changes the report. Figure 20-11 shows the report.

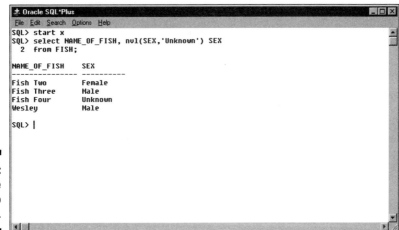

Figure 20-11:
One of the fish has no known sex.

Try out the NVL function by running this example yourself using one of the files on the CD-ROM in the back of the book. Appendix B has information on how to use the CD-ROM.

NVL helps when you are calculating numbers and you need to replace nulls. Nulls, as you may have seen, gum up calculations. Any math done on a null results in a null. Change null values to zeros using the NVL function, to smooth out this problem.

Chapter 21

Ten Common Problems and How to Fix Them

In This Chapter

▶ Figuring out why Oracle7 can't see your table

▶ Changing a password

▶ Playing Password when the database administrator isn't looking

▶ Adding permission for updates

▶ Getting SQL that works in different databases

▶ Using only certain rows for testing queries

So you spent time properly preparing your Oracle7 database, diagramming everything, getting all the relationships worked out, and fine-tuning your columns and rows and tables, and now you've got problems? I can't imagine! Well, actually I can. That's why I included this list of my "been there, done that" solutions to ten nagging situations every Oracle7 user puzzles over at one time or another.

What Do You Mean, My Table Doesn't Exist?!

One error message causes more confusion than any other message Oracle7 sends — the `table or view does not exist` error, which tends to cause panic in users. They run around shouting, "I did too create that table!" Managers start questioning the sanity of their workers. Users start doubting the managers. Doubt ripples through the office like a black cloud. Never fear, *Oracle7 For Dummies* is here! Read on to discover that you are not insane, and you have not lost your memory.

Solution 1: That table does too exist!

You have created a beautiful *schema* (group of related tables) with a dozen tables and some online forms. Now you want others to be able to use them. Because the users already have Oracle7 user IDs, they log on and use your forms. The first time they try anything, Oracle7 coughs up this error message:

```
ORA-00942: table or view does not exist
```

There are several reasons why a user could get this error, but Oracle7 does not offer any clues as to where to start looking for the answer.

By far the most common reason for the `table or view does not exist` error is when you do not grant table privileges to the user. You may suggest the user wear a jacket and tie next time.

To verify that the table grants are missing, run the appropriate SQL*Plus script from Chapter 22.

Grant the appropriate privileges to the Oracle7 user ID that received the error message. Refer to Chapter 10 for specific instructions about granting privileges to tables. For example, to grant `INSERT`, `UPDATE`, `DELETE`, and `SELECT` privileges on the `ARTIST` table to user ID `GEORGE`, type:

```
grant select, insert, update, delete on ARTIST to GEORGE;
```

Oracle7 replies:

```
Grant succeeded.
```

Solution 2: Really! That table does too exist!

Your schema works fine for you, but other Oracle7 users cannot use your tables when they use your schema. In fact, they receive this error message:

```
ORA-00942: table or view does not exist
```

The prior section covers the most common problem that causes this error. You rule out the first problem by verifying that the Oracle7 users do indeed have the appropriate privileges granted to them on the appropriate tables. What next?

Refer to Chapter 10 to discover how synonyms are set up. The proper way to use synonyms is to leave the owner out of all your table references. Your schema can use synonyms with a query like this:

```
select * from ARTIST;
```

Synonyms don't get used when you include the owner in your table references, like this:

```
select * from CAROL.ARTIST;
```

Assuming that you set up synonyms and have no owners in your table references, a good place to look for errors is in the synonyms themselves.

Synonyms can wreak havoc on your schema, a fact you may not notice when you run your forms or queries. You, as owner of the table, are by default using the tables themselves and not the synonyms. Once a different user begins using your forms and queries, Oracle7 looks for a synonym with the same name as the table.

The most common problems with synonyms are:

- **Misspelled synonym name:** The synonym name does not have to be identical to the underlying table name. Making the names identical is a common practice, however, and makes testing and deploying your schema easier. A misspelled synonym name means that Oracle7 cannot find a synonym with the name it's looking for, so it sends its favorite error: `table or view does not exist`.

- **Missing underlying table:** A synonym stands on its own and does not disappear when the table it points to is dropped. As you verify that you spelled your synonym correctly, also verify that the underlying table actually exists.

Solution 3: That $@!#!! table does too exist!

Last but not least, the `table or view does not exist` error occasionally crops up for another reason: Conflicting synonyms, scenario in which several synonyms have identical names. This scenario can occur when one user has set up his or her own private synonyms and the DBA has set up public synonyms. In these cases, Oracle7 looks at the private synonym. The following list shows the most common problems occurring with private synonyms and how to correct the problem. (For more information about synonyms, see Chapter 11.)

- **Synonym is misspelled:** Re-create the synonym with correct spelling.
- **Underlying table does not exist:** Create the table, or re-create the synonym to reference the correct table.
- **User does not have privileges granted on underlying table:** Issue grants to the user.
- **Underlying table is different from the public synonym's underlying table:** Re-create the private synonym to agree with the public synonym.

I Can't Log onto Oracle7

If you can't log into Oracle7 you may not have an Oracle7 user ID. Then again, you may have merely forgotten your password. In either case, Oracle7 issues the same error:

```
ORA-01017: invalid username/password; logon denied
```

Creating a new user ID requires two commands. First, establish the user and give the user a password:

```
create user username identified by password;
```

Oracle7 replies:

```
User created.
```

Next, assign the CONNECT role to the user. This role allows the user to log into Oracle. If other roles are also needed, you can assign those as well:

```
grant CONNECT to username
```

Oracle7 replies:

```
Grant succeeded
```

When you need to change a password, you as the DBA can assign a new password to a user. The user can also change only his or her password. The command is:

```
alter user username identified by newpassword;
```

Oracle7 replies:

```
User altered.
```

See Chapter 9 for step-by-step instructions on how to change your password in PO7 Navigator.

I Can Look at the Data, But I Can't Update the Table

Generally speaking, this problem only occurs when you attempt to update tables that do not belong to you. Missing table privileges happens to be the most common cause. If you don't eat your meat, you can't have any pudding.

Whenever a user ID besides the table owner wants to make changes to the table data, Oracle7 requires that the user ID have a corresponding privilege. To update a row, the user ID must have the UPDATE privilege granted to it. To delete a row, the user ID must have the DELETE privilege granted to it. To insert a new row, the user ID must have the insert privilege granted to it. If the user ID has not earned these privileges with good behavior, it goes to bed without any supper.

Log into SQL*Plus as the owner of the table and issue the needed grant commands. See Chapter 10 for more about grants.

This SQL Code Works in Oracle7 But Not in Access

Access, a desktop relational database by Microsoft, has recently become popular. Some people now have both Oracle7 and Access on hand. Access can run SQL code, just like Oracle7. So some people now have SQL code they created for Oracle7 that they try running in Access. Sometimes it works fine, but other times the code runs only in Oracle7 and not Access.

SQL has an official standard form that Oracle7 meets completely. The problem lies in the extras that Oracle7 has embellished onto its own version of SQL. These extras are of great value and enhance the power of SQL, but they only work with Oracle7. Here's a partial list of Oracle7 enhancements that are not part of the SQL standard:

- ✔ Insert command using sub-queries
- ✔ Alter table
- ✔ Drop table
- ✔ Analyze
- ✔ Column aliases in the select command
- ✔ Update command with a sub-query that refers to the table being updated
- ✔ All the functions except MAX, MIN, AVG, and SUM are additions to the SQL Standard; these include TO_CHAR, DECODE, SUBSTR, and TO_DATE
- ✔ Pseudocolumns
- ✔ Names can be 30 characters long rather than the standard 18 characters

The *Oracle SQL Language User's Guide* has all the details on these enhancements. Most likely, one of these has caused the translation problem. Of course, each database software has its own method for the implementation of standards. The other database may also have enhancements or may not comply with the standard in every area. You need to carefully read the fine print.

How Can I Tell Blanks From Nulls?

Imagine for a moment that you have a desire to seek out all the humans with nine-digit ZIP codes. You include the dash in the ZIP code column, so the total length of the ZIP code in the ZIP_CODE column is ten. In your Oracle7 database, you create a query like this:

```
select FIRST_NAME, LAST_NAME, ZIP_CODE
from HUMAN
where length(ZIP_CODE) = 10;
```

Oracle7 shows you the results, as in Figure 21-1; but wait a darn minute! The second ZIP code is only five digits. The fourth row has a completely blank ZIP code. Why did Oracle7 return these rows?

The reason Oracle7 assumes that a five-digit ZIP code has ten characters has to do with the datatype. The ZIP_CODE column is the datatype CHAR with a length of ten characters. (See Chapter 9 for a great description of Oracle7 datatypes.) The CHAR datatype includes blanks padded to the end of the

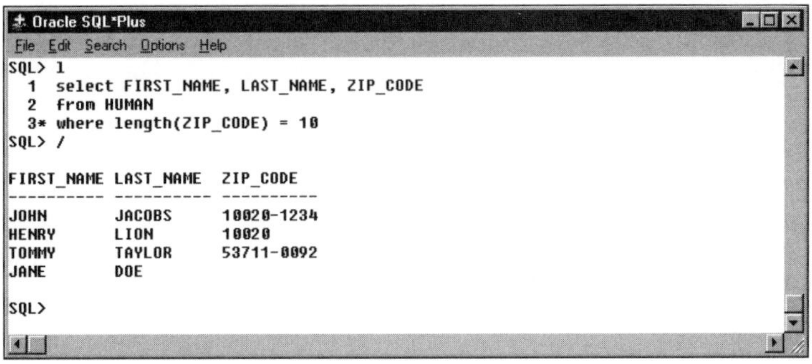

Figure 21-1:
It appears
that Oracle7
made a
mistake on
this query.

column, so a five-digit ZIP code is padded with five more blanks on the end —
and is actually ten characters long. In fact, every row has ten characters in
the ZIP_CODE column, except for a row where the ZIP_CODE column contains nulls. In this case, the length is zero.

The unusual case, which can get really confusing, is when a CHAR datatype
column contains all blanks. In the preceding example, the last row returned
in the query has blanks rather than nulls in the ZIP code. The following SQL
query shows how to locate rows where the ZIP_CODE column has blanks
instead of nulls:

```
select HUMAN_ID, FIRST_NAME, LAST_NAME, ZIP_CODE from HUMAN
where ZIP_CODE=RPAD('', 10);
```

Oracle7 replies with the results, as in Figure 21-2. I include the HUMAN_ID in
this query so that you can identify the offending rows by their primary key.

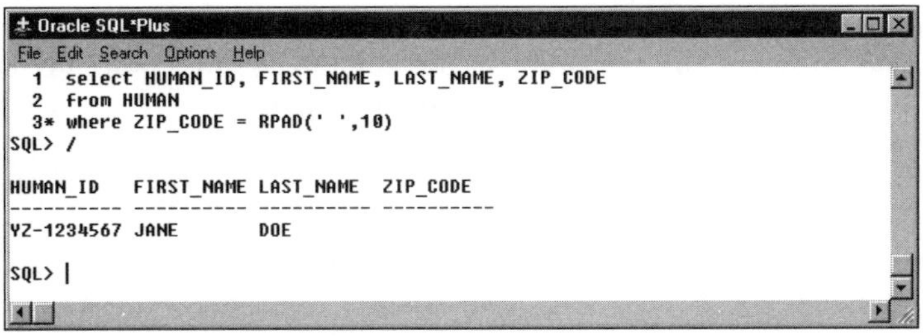

Figure 21-2:
Seeking out
the rows
with blank
ZIP codes.

Use this same query, adjusted a little, to change the ZIP_CODE from blanks:

```
update HUMAN set ZIP_CODE = null
where ZIP_CODE = RPAD(' ',10);
```

Oracle7 replies:

```
1 row updated.
```

ON THE CD

These two examples of SQL code are on the CD-ROM. See Appendix B for the details.

I recommend using VARCHAR2 (the datatype for variable-length character data) for all your character data to avoid this problem.

I Forgot to Put In a Primary Key

Use the ALTER TABLE command to add a primary key to an existing table. For example, if the HUMAN table needed a primary key, the HUMAN_ID, the SQL code would look like this:

```
alter table HUMAN add primary key (HUMAN_ID);
```

Oracle7 replies:

```
Table altered.
```

I Want to Test a Query

Selecting a portion of your table can be useful as you experiment with reports or queries. You can test your query while you limit the number of rows you choose. After you finish developing, you can modify the query slightly to select all the rows. Use the ROWNUM pseudocolumn to specify the maximum rows you want returned in your query.

A simple example of this selects the first three rows of the RECIPE table:

```
select * from RECIPE
where ROWNUM < 4;
```

Figure 21-3 shows the results of the query.

Figure 21-3:
A query can
be limited
to returning
only the
first few
rows.

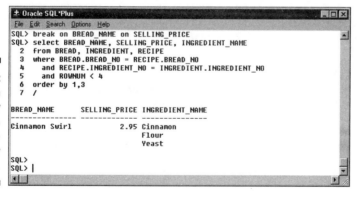

A more complex example shows a join between the BREAD and RECIPE
tables so that you have a report of all the ingredients in each bread you
make. The ROWNUM again is set so that you return only the first three rows.

```
break on BREAD_NAME on SELLING_PRICE
select BREAD_NAME, SELLING_PRICE, INGREDIENT_NAME
from BREAD, INGREDIENT, RECIPE
where BREAD.BREAD_NO = RECIPE.BREAD_NO
  and RECIPE.INGREDIENT_NO = INGREDIENT.INGREDIENT_NO
  and ROWNUM < 4
order by 1,3;
```

Oracle7 returns the first three rows again, as shown in Figure 21-4.

Figure 21-4:
You can
limit a query
to return
only the
first few
rows.

This fun example is on the CD-ROM. See Appendix B for detailed instructions.

In the preceding example, Oracle7 returns the first three rows of the final
report rather than the first three rows it finds in the database. SQL*Plus
executes the query as if it were going to return all the rows and then cuts
off the results at the specified number of rows.

Sometimes Oracle7 actually does execute the full query and then returns the subset of rows. You don't save a lot of time in these cases, and this method is probably not beneficial. Usually, Oracle7 must first execute the entire query on all the rows when you specify an ORDER BY clause that is on an unindexed column. Chapter 16 has more on indexes.

Oracle7 can also return the subset of rows without actually performing the full query. You reap the most benefits from this kind of query because you get fast response time even when your tables have loads of data. Generally, Oracle7 can cut short the execution when your query has either no ORDER BY clause or an ORDER BY clause on indexed rows. Oracle7 also stops its processing faster when your query has no grouping or grouping only in indexed columns. Oracle7 can stop processing quicker because it can use an existing index to return the rows and make sure that all the rows are in the correct order without first retrieving and sorting the rows.

I Want to Display the Date Without Changing My Query

I describe a way of adding the current date into a report in Chapter 22. Here's another way you can display the date if you don't want to revise the existing query: Add a query for the current date and then use the results in the title. Here are the steps to display the data without changing the report query. You can try this yourself, using the example table CAR (on the CD-ROM). Appendix B has instructions on how to install the example tables into your Oracle7 database.

1. **Begin with a query.**

   For example, you create a report on cars, sorted by the year and make of the car. The query looks like this:

   ```
   select YEAR_MADE, MAKE_OF_CAR,
   STYLE, MODEL_NAME, ID_NUMBER
   from CAR
   order by YEAR_MADE, MAKE_OF_CAR;
   ```

2. **Add a new query above the report query that gets the pseudocolumn** SYSDATE **and is assigned an alias.**

   In this example, put the following query above the CAR query and assign it the alias TODAYS_DATE:

   ```
   select SYSDATE TODAYS_DATE from DUAL;
   ```

3. **Add a** COLUMN **command that allows you to use the alias column in the title of your report but hides it on the main report.**

   The NEW_VALUE parameter tells SQL*Plus to update the value of the column before putting the column's value into the title. This is needed because the value of TODAYS_DATE is not actually found until after the TTITLE command has been executed. Once the query runs (immediately after the TTITLE command), SQL*Plus plugs the value of TODAYS_DATE into the title.

   You can hide the alias column by using the NOPRINT command. In our example, here's what you have:

   ```
   column TODAYS_DATE new_value TODAYS_DATE noprint
   ```

4. **Add the** TTITLE **line just above the original query.**

   The full example script looks like this:

   ```
   column TODAYS_DATE new_value TODAYS_DATE noprint
   select SYSDATE TODAYS_DATE from DUAL;
   ttitle left TODAYS_DATE center 'The Car Report' skip 2
   select YEAR_MADE, MAKE_OF_CAR,
   STYLE, MODEL_NAME, ID_NUMBER
   from CAR
   order by YEAR_MADE, MAKE_OF_CAR;
   ```

   The results of the query show the date in the report, as you want. See Figure 21-5.

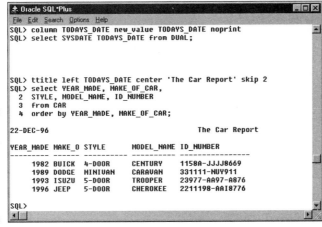

Figure 21-5: Another way to display the date in your title.

Chapter 22

Ten Handy SQL Scripts

*O*kay, folks, here's what you've been waiting for: ten SQL scripts to make your scripting life more interesting. But wait; that's not all. The SQL scripts in this chapter also appear on the CD-ROM attached to the back of this book. See Appendix B for details on how to find and use the scripts on the CD-ROM.

Finding the Duplicate Rows

When creating a table, you usually are wise to plan on having a column or set of columns that are designated as the primary key. A *primary key* contains data that uniquely identifies each row in your table. By definition, no two rows can contain identical data in the column (or columns) you designate as your primary key.

Sometimes you add the primary key constraint itself later on in the development process. In these cases, Oracle7 looks at each row to verify that they all have unique data in the primary key column(s). If by chance your data is out of whack (that is, you have two or more rows with the same primary key), you must correct the situation before you can create that primary key constraint.

You plan to add a primary key later, after you create a table and add a bunch of data. To add the primary key you go to SQL*Plus or the Personal Oracle7 (PO7) Navigator and add the primary key constraint (refer to Chapter 5 for information on how to add a primary key). Occasionally, your data contains duplicate keys. Oracle7 checks for this and issues an error message like this one:

```
ORA-02299: cannot add or enable constraint (AMY.PK_BREAD)-
duplicate keys found
```

Your mission is to find all the rows that have the same primary key and determine the problem. Here's the general format:

```
select KEYCOLUMN , COUNT(*)
from TABLENAME
group by KEYCOLUMN
having COUNT(*) > 1
order by KEYCOLUMN;
```

For the BREAD table, you use this query:

```
select BREAD_NO , COUNT(*)
from BREAD
group by BREAD_NO
having COUNT(*) > 1
order by BREAD_NO;
```

Figure 22-1 shows the results.

Figure 22-1:
A list of
keys and
the number
of rows
with the
same key.

```
± Oracle SQL*Plus                                          _ □ X
File  Edit  Search  Options  Help
  1    select BREAD_NO , COUNT(*)
  2    from BREAD
  3    group by BREAD_NO
  4    having COUNT(*) > 1
  5*   order by BREAD_NO
SQL> /

BREAD_NO  COUNT(*)
--------- ---------
       2         2

SQL>
```

You can view all the data for rows that have duplicate keys using this query:

```
select *
from TABLENAME
```

```
where KEYCOLUMN in
   (select KEYCOLUMN
   from TABLENAME
   group by KEYCOLUMN
   having COUNT(*) > 1);
```

For the BREAD table, the SQL code looks like this:

```
select *
from BREAD
where BREAD_NO in
   (select BREAD_NO
   from BREAD
   group by BREAD_NO
   having COUNT(*) > 1);
```

Figure 22-2 shows the results of this example. You can see by looking at the data returned from the preceding query that the two rows are identical. See the next section for the SQL code to remove only one of the rows.

Figure 22-2:
A list of
keys and
the number
of rows
with the
same key.

```
± Oracle SQL*Plus                                         _ □ ×
File  Edit  Search  Options  Help
   1   select *
   2   from BREAD
   3   where BREAD_NO in
   4      (select BREAD_NO
   5      from BREAD
   6      group by BREAD_NO
   7*     having COUNT(*) > 1)
SQL> /

BREAD_NO  BREAD_NAME       SELLING_PRICE
--------- ---------------  -------------
       2  Nutty Banana            3.25
       2  Nutty Banana            3.25

SQL>
```

Removing One of Those Duplicate Rows

How can you delete a row when every column in the row is a duplicate of another row? What will the guys in the Department of Redundancy Department say about this? Writing an ordinary WHERE clause always selects both rows. Say you know the value of the key column and wish to delete one of the two rows with the same value in the key column. You don't care which one is deleted, because they are identical. Here's a general example of the SQL code to do it:

```
delete from TABLENAME
where KEYCOLUMN = 'keyvalue'
and ROWNUM = 1;
```

If the key consists of multiple columns, the general form looks like this:

```
delete from TABLENAME
where COLUMN1 = 'keyvalue1'
and COLUMN2 = 'keyvalue2'
and ...
and ROWNUM = 1;
```

For the BREAD table example from the first section, here is the SQL code to eliminate one of the two rows that contain the value 2 in the BREAD_NO column:

```
delete from BREAD
where BREAD_NO = 2
and ROWNUM = 1;
```

Oracle7 replies:

```
1 row deleted.
```

Sniffing Out Broken Relationships

Most relationships wither away from sheer neglect. Perhaps you didn't tell your lover "I love you" often enough. Sniff, sniff. Perhaps you never got around to implementing the foreign key constraints in the database. Now your tables have plenty of new data added and you want to verify that the foreign key relationships are valid. You also want to find any records in which problems lie. You must find any rows that contain invalid foreign key values.

In general terms, the SQL query finds all rows in a table that have an invalid value in the foreign key column. Here's the generic SQL code:

```
select KEY_COLUMN, FK_COLUMN
from FK_TABLENAME
where not exists (SELECT 'X' from PK_TABLENAME
where FK_TABLENAME.FK_COLUMN = PK_TABLENAME.PK_COLUMN);
```

In the preceding example, the column and table names mean:

- ✔ *KEY_COLUMN:* The primary key column of the table that you're validating (the one with the foreign key).

- ✔ *FK_COLUMN:* The foreign key column that you are validating.

- ✔ *FK_TABLENAME:* The name of the table that you are validating.

- ✔ *PK_TABLENAME:* The name of the table that is the parent of the foreign key you're checking.

- ✔ *PK_COLUMN:* The primary key that matches the foreign key in the *FK_TABLENAME* table.

If your foreign key contains two columns, here is the general pattern. This same pattern also applies for foreign keys with three or more columns.

```
select KEY_COLUMN1, KEY_COLUMN2, FK_COLUMN1, FK_COLUMN2
from FK_TABLENAME
where not exists (SELECT 'X' from PK_TABLENAME
where FK_TABLENAME.FK_COLUMN1 = PK_TABLENAME.PK_COLUMN1
   and FK_TABLENAME.FK_COLUMN2 = PK_TABLENAME.PK_COLUMN2);
```

You want to check the CAR table to be sure that every row has a valid value in the STYLE column. Every value in the STYLE column must match a value in the STYLE column of the STYLE table. Here is the code:

```
select ID_NUMBER, STYLE
from CAR
where not exists (SELECT 'X' from STYLE
where CAR.STYLE = STYLE.STYLE);
```

Figure 22-3 shows the results of the query.

Figure 22-3:
One row in the CAR table has an invalid STYLE.

```
± Oracle SQL*Plus                                    _ □ ×
File  Edit  Search  Options  Help
    1   select ID_NUMBER, STYLE
    2   from CAR
    3   where not exists (SELECT 'X' from STYLE
    4*  where CAR.STYLE = STYLE.STYLE)
SQL> /

ID_NUMBER           STYLE
----------------    ----------
11990-ABC-HH889     2-DOOR

SQL>
```

Mend Broken Relationships

You can make two choices to correct your data when a foreign key is invalid:

✔ Change the data in the foreign key.

✔ Add a new row in the referenced table.

Here's the SQL code for the first case, which changes the data in the foreign key. This UPDATE command changes all the mismatched foreign key data into one valid value. You type this into the command in place of 'valid FK value'.

```
update FK_TABLENAME set FK_COLUMN = 'valid FK value'
where not exists (SELECT 'X' from PK_TABLENAME
where FK_TABLENAME.FK_COLUMN = PK_TABLENAME.PK_COLUMN);
```

You may instead want to update the foreign key to be a null value. In this case, you use NULL after the equal sign. See the following example to find out how to use NULL.

You want to modify the CAR table rows that have an invalid STYLE by changing the invalid STYLE with a null value. The SQL UPDATE command is:

```
update CAR set STYLE = NULL
where not exists (SELECT 'X' from STYLE
where CAR.STYLE = STYLE.STYLE);
```

Oracle7 replies:

```
1 row updated.
```

The second choice is to add a new row into the referenced table. You do this with the INSERT command, which inserts a row into the referenced parent table. Refer to Chapter 4 for step-by-step instructions on inserting rows into tables using SQL*Plus or PO7 Navigator.

Checking Your Access to Any Table

Try to remember when you were a teenager. Privileges could be confusing. Now that you are an adult, how can you tell what you can and cannot do? In Oracle7 look at the data in one of the data dictionary views, that's how. All the information is in those views. You can only see the privileges that were given to you or that you gave to someone else. The whole thing gets complicated when you use *roles* because the privileges are granted to the role and not directly to the user ID. The following query finds both kinds of privileges — privileges granted to your user ID and privileges granted to any role you belong to. See Chapter 10 for more about roles.

```
select TABLE_NAME, SELECT_PRIV,
INSERT_PRIV, DELETE_PRIV,
UPDATE_PRIV
from ALL_TAB_GRANTS_RECD
where GRANTEE = USER
or GRANTEE IN (select GRANTED_ROLE from USER_ROLE_PRIVS
where USERNAME = USER)
order by TABLE_NAME;
```

You don't replace any of the column names in the query, but you log in using the user ID you wish to check. The SQL*Plus query above does not work to check someone else's privileges. Figure 22-4 shows the results and how to interpret them once you have set up privileges for other users on a table.

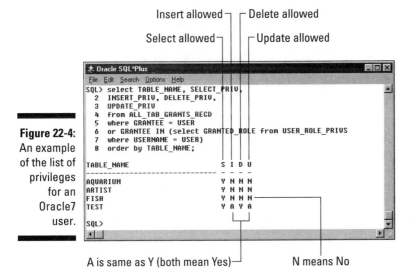

Figure 22-4: An example of the list of privileges for an Oracle7 user.

Listing All the Tables

You may find having a current list of tables on hand to be handy, especially when you are in the middle of developing a schema that contains more than ten tables. Here's the long SQL code:

```
set echo on
/*
     Produces an alphabetical listing of tables
     with a comment describing the purpose of the table.

   Prompts for a table prefix.
   If left blank, all tables are listed.
*/
set echo off
set termout  on
set verify off
set feedback off
set pagesize 66
set linesize 80
set newpage  0
set space    1
set arraysize 5
/* ++++++++++++++++++++++++++++++++++++++++ */
column tab_COMMENTS    format a45 word wrap
column TABLE_NAME   format a30
/* ++++++++++++++++++++++++++++++++++++++++ */
column TODAY       noprint  new_value  date_var
column USER_NAME   noprint  new_value  user_var
/* ++++++++++++++++++++++++++++++++++++++++ */
ttitle left 'Date: ' date_var -
  center 'Table Listing (' user_var ')   TABLES' -
  right  'Page ' format 99  SQL.PNO -
  skip 2 ;
/* ++++++++++++++++++++++++++++++++++++++++ */
spool LISTTABS.LIS
/* ++++++++++++++++++++++++++++++++++++++++ */
     select   to_char(SYSDATE,'mm/dd/yy') TODAY,
              user                 USER_NAME,
              A.TABLE_NAME,
              A.COMMENTS TAB_COMMENTS
     from   USER_TAB_COMMENTS A
     where  A.TABLE_NAME like '&tables_prefix%'
       order by A.TABLE_NAME;
/* ++++++++++++++++++++++++++++++++++++++++ */
spool off
set termout on
```

Everything that appears between a beginning comment marker, /*, and an ending comment marker, */, is for documentation only and is ignored by SQL*Plus. Figure 22-5 shows an example of the results of this SQL*Plus script.

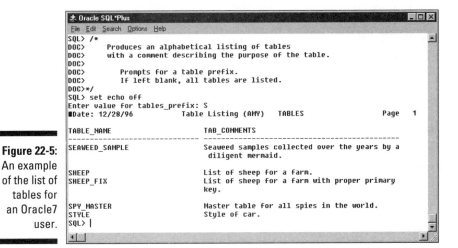

Figure 22-5: An example of the list of tables for an Oracle7 user.

You can enter the comments that appear by using the SQL*Plus command:

```
comment on table TABLENAME is
'put comment here';
```

Listing All the Columns

This SQL query is a great one to add to your collection! I use this query all the time to keep track of my tables. You can design the query to list all tables for one user, to list only one table, or to list all tables that begin with a certain letter or phrase. Here's the code:

```
/*     Produces a listing of table(s) and associated
        columns (fields).

    You will be prompted to enter a table prefix.
    Leave it blank for all tables.
*/
set termout  on
set feedback OFF
```

(continued)

(continued)

```
set verify off
set pagesize 59
set linesize 132
set newpage  0
set space    1
set recsep off
set arraysize 5
/* +++++++++++++++ */
column COL_COMMENT format a40  word_wrap
column COLUMN_NAME format a30
column DATA_SCALE  format 9     heading  'DEC'
column DATA_TYPE   format a8    heading  'TYPE'
column LENGTH      format 9999  heading  'LENGTH'
column NULLABLE    format a5    heading  'NULL?'
/* +++++++++++++++ */
column TABLE_NAME  format a30 HEADING 'Table Name '
column TODAY       noprint   new_value   date_var
column USER        noprint   new_value   user_var
/* +++++++++++++++ */
break on TABLE_NAME SKIP 3
/* +++++++++++++++ */
ttitle left 'Date: ' date_var -
center 'Tables and their Columns (' user_var ') TABLES' -
  right  'Page ' format 99  SQL.PNO -
  skip 2
/* +++++++++++++++ */
spool LISTCOLS.LIS
select '&&TABLE_NAME',
             to_char(SYSDATE,'mm/dd/yy') TODAY,
             USER
from DUAL
/
select  C.TABLE_NAME TABLE_NAME,
             C.COLUMN_NAME,
             C.DATA_TYPE,
             NVL(C.DATA_PRECISION,C.DATA_LENGTH) LENGTH,
             C.DATA_SCALE,
             C.NULLABLE,
             U.COMMENTS COL_COMMENT
     from   USER_TAB_COMMENTS   A,
            USER_COL_COMMENTS   U,
            USER_TAB_COLUMNS    C
```

```
where     C.COLUMN_NAME = U.COLUMN_NAME
    and     A.TABLE_NAME  = U.TABLE_NAME
    and     A.TABLE_NAME  = C.TABLE_NAME
    and     C.TABLE_NAME  like '&&TABLE_NAME%'
    order by C.TABLE_NAME,
             C.COLUMN_ID;
spool off
set termout on
```

Figure 22-6 shows a sample of the output that you might get from running this script in SQL*Plus.

Remember, all the SQL*Plus scripts in this chapter are on the CD-ROM at the back of the book. See Appendix B for details on what the CD-ROM contains and how to use the contents.

You can enter the comments that show up by using the SQL*Plus command:

```
comment on column TABLENAME.COLUMNNAME is
  'put comment here';
```

For example, here's the SQL*Plus code for adding a comment to the SHEEP_NAME column of the SHEEP table:

```
comment on column SHEEP.SHEEP_NAME is
'This is the primary key of the SHEEP table.';
```

```
                                    ─Page Break─
Date: 12/28/96                 Tables and their Columns (AMY)  TEST TABLES

Table Name               COLUMN_NAME              TYPE     LENGTH DEC NULL? COL_COMMENT
-----------              -----------              ----     ------ --- ----- -----------
SEAWEED_SAMPLE           SAMPLE_ID                NUMBER      10  0  N
                         TYPE_ID                  NUMBER      10  0  N
                         SELLING_PRICE            NUMBER      10  2  Y
                         SAMPLE_DESCRIPTION       VARCHAR2    40     Y
                         CUST_ID                  NUMBER      10  0  Y

SHEEP                    SHEEP_NAME               VARCHAR2    10     N    This is the primary key
                         WOOL_COLOR               VARCHAR2    10     Y    Color of the sheep wool
                         NUMBER_OF_BAGS           NUMBER       3  0  Y    Number of bags of wool
                         OWNER_OF_BAGS            VARCHAR2    30     Y    Owners of bags of wool

SHEEP_FIX               SHEEP_NAME               VARCHAR2    10     Y
                         COLOR                    VARCHAR2    10     Y
                         NUMBER_OF_BAGS           NUMBER       4  0  Y

SPY_MASTER              CODE_NAME                VARCHAR2    10     Y
                         CURRENT_MISSION          VARCHAR2   255     Y
                         COUNTRY                  VARCHAR2    10     Y

Page 2   Sec 1      2/3   At     Ln     Col     8:52 PM  REC MRK EXT OVR WPH
```

Figure 22-6:
An example of the list of tables and columns for your Oracle7 user ID.

Listing All the Indexes

Here is yet another script that can be very useful when you document your schema. The script also helps you verify that you did indeed create all the indexes you wanted. The SQL*Plus script spools out a file that you can print out.

```
/*      Produces a listing of table(s) and associated indexes
        including the columns in the indexes.

*/
set termout  on
set feedback OFF
set verify off
set pagesize 66
set linesize 80
set newpage  0
set space     1
set recsep off
set arraysize 5
/* +++++++++++++++ */
column COLUMN_NAME format a20
column TABLE_NAME  format a20 HEADING 'Table Name' wrap
column index_name format a20 HEADING 'Index Name' wrap
column TODAY        noprint   new_value    date_var
column USER         noprint   new_value    user_var
/* +++++++++++++++ */
ttitle left 'Date: ' date_var -
  center 'Tables and their Indexes (' user_var ')  TABLES'
    -
  right  'Page ' format 99  SQL.PNO -
  skip 2
/* +++++++++++++++ */
select to_char(SYSDATE,'mm/dd/yy') TODAY, USER
from DUAL
/
break on table_name skip 3 on index_name on uniqueness
spool LISTIDXS.LIS
select ui.table_name, ui.index_name, ui.uniqueness,
          uic.column_name
from user_ind_columns uic,
     user_indexes ui
where ui.index_name = uic.index_name
```

```
order by 1,2,uic.column_position;
spool off
set termout on
```

Figure 22-7 shows the resulting report. The script sorts the report by table and index. The columns in each index are listed in the order in which they appear in the index.

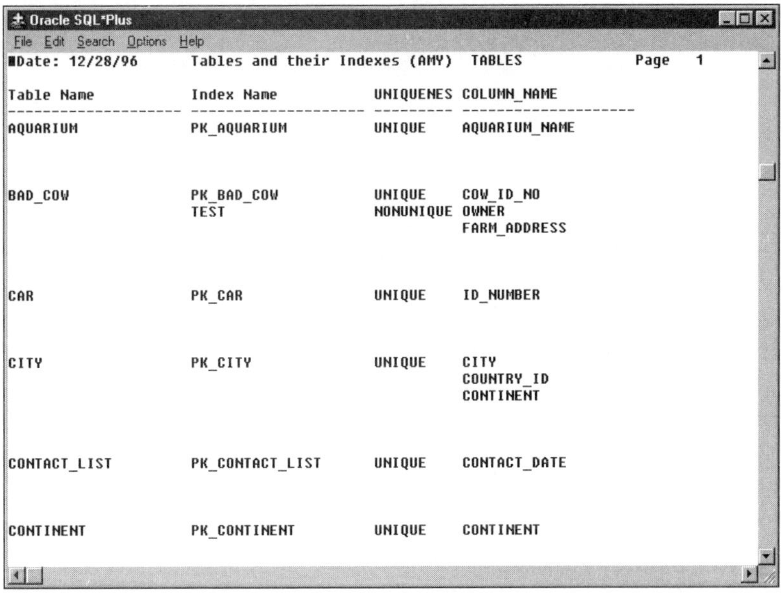

Figure 22-7: An example of the list of tables and their indexes for one Oracle7 user ID.

Generating a Spiffy Select Statement

This sample SQL script shows you the power of SQL*Plus. I created this script to generate another query. This example may inspire you to imagine the other kinds of SQL commands that you can create. I have used this technique to generate CREATE TABLE commands, GRANT commands, and REVOKE commands, to name a few. Here is the script:

```
/*  THIS SPOOLS OUT A SELECT STATEMENT
    WITH ALL THE COLUMNS IN IT.
    YOU PROVIDE THE TABLE NAME (IN CAPS)
    when prompted for a tablename.
*/
```

(continued)

(continued)

```
select '&&TABLENAME' from DUAL;
set echo off
set feedback off
set verify off
set recsep off
set pagesize 0
set linesize 70
set heading off
set termout off
set embedded on
/* ++++++++++++++++++ */
COLUMN NL NEW_LINE
COLUMN NL1 NEW_LINE
spool SELECT.SQL
prompt select
select '     '||COLUMN_NAME ||',' NL
from USER_TAB_COLUMNS
where COLUMN_ID < (select max(COLUMN_ID)
                   from USER_TAB_COLUMNS
                   where TABLE_NAME = upper('&&TABLENAME'))
  and TABLE_NAME = UPPER('&&TABLENAME')
order by COLUMN_ID
/
select '     ' || COLUMN_NAME ,
' from '||TABLE_NAME||';' NL
from USER_TAB_COLUMNS
where COLUMN_ID = (select max(COLUMN_ID)
                   from USER_TAB_COLUMNS
                   where TABLE_NAME = UPPER('&&TABLENAME'))
  and TABLE_NAME = UPPER('&&TABLENAME')
/
spool off
set termout on
set feedback on
set verify on
set pagesize 24
set heading on
undefine TABLENAME
set echo on
set embedded off
```

Figure 22-8 shows a very simple example in which I use this script to create a select statement for the SHEEP table. The exact SQL script works to create a SELECT command for any table. The number of columns the table has does not matter. This script saves time when a table with more than six columns is the issue.

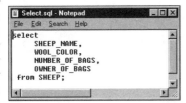

Figure 22-8:
Here is a
query
created by
another
query.

Prying the SQL Statement Out of a View

You may have trouble seeing the complete text of a view you created when you look in the USER VIEWS table. Oracle7 stores the text in a column of the LONG datatype. SQL*Plus has a default setting that truncates a LONG datatype after the first 200 characters. Many times, you do not see the complete text of the query that built your view. The following SQL*Plus script remedies this problem by resetting the default for LONG datatypes to 1,000 characters and spooling out the results in a readable format. Here's the script. By the way, this script spools the results into a file named VIEW.SQL so you can use it later.

```
/*   THIS SPOOLS OUT THE QUERY YOU RAN TO CREATE A VIEW.
     Type in the name of the view when prompted.
     Change the next line to increase the number of
     characters pulled if the query is truncated.
*/
set long 1000
select '&&VIEWNAME' from DUAL;
set echo off
set feedback off
set verify off
set recsep off
set pagesize 0
set linesize 70
set heading off
set termout off
```

(continued)

(continued)

```
set embedded on
ttitle off
/* ++++++++++++++++++ */
COLUMN VIEW_TEXT format A60 word_wrap
spool VIEW.SQL
select TEXT VIEW_TEXT
from USER_VIEWS
where VIEW_NAME = upper('&&VIEWNAME');
spool off
set termout on
set feedback on
set verify on
set pagesize 24
set heading on
undefine VIEWNAME
set echo on
```

Figure 22-9 shows the results for the `CUSTOMER_VIEW` view. There may be a few views where the query is longer than 1,000 characters. In this case, you can edit the line in the preceding script to handle 2,000 characters, or any other number of characters. The line to change is the sixth line in the script:

```
set long 1000
```

Change the line to extract twice as much by making it:

```
set long 2000
```

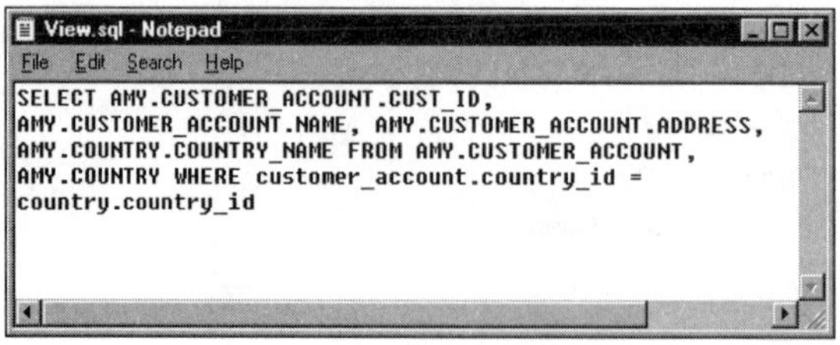
View.sql - Notepad
File Edit Search Help
SELECT AMY.CUSTOMER_ACCOUNT.CUST_ID,
AMY.CUSTOMER_ACCOUNT.NAME, AMY.CUSTOMER_ACCOUNT.ADDRESS,
AMY.COUNTRY.COUNTRY_NAME FROM AMY.CUSTOMER_ACCOUNT,
AMY.COUNTRY WHERE customer_account.country_id =
country.country_id

Figure 22-9: A view spooled into a readable format.

Now you have a serious arsenal of SQL scripts at your disposal. Have fun with them. Try out variations on the theme. When you are familiar with all the things these scripts do, you can use them in your own creations.

Chapter 23

Ten Other Tools That Go with Oracle7

In This Chapter

▶ Discovering cool tools

▶ Discovering tools to connect your database to the Internet

▶ Surveying screen designers

*Y*our computer desktop may clutter up with tools, documents, and paper-weights, just like my husband's workbench. I'm glad the author of this book doesn't experience similar mundane problems. Oracle7 has jumped on the bandwagon with its set of desktop goodies.

These tools are additions to the basic Oracle7 package, and almost all cost money. Certain tools are available for a free 30-, 60-, or 90-day trial. Oracle produces some of the tools, and others are produced by independent vendors. This chapter gives you a feel for the kind of products available to enhance the basic Oracle7 package.

PowerObjects

Oracle PowerObjects gives you a visual way to manage your database that is more sophisticated than the Personal Oracle7 Navigator (PO7 Navigator). You can build data entry forms quickly without any programming, and PowerObjects uses an icon system like the Windows one you're used to, including drag-and-drop capabilities. PowerObjects handles edits, validation of relationships, and complex *master-detail forms* with ease. An example of a master-detail form is an online form for entering customer information in the top part and line items of an order in the bottom part. Behind the scenes, there are two related tables in which to store the top and the bottom parts of this kind of screen. PowerObjects handles the connections for you — like a miniature version of Developer/2000 (described later in this chapter) at a tenth of the cost.

PowerBrowser

Another new and fascinating Windows tool is the Oracle PowerBrowser, an interesting combination of Web browser and database connector. This tool is available free from Oracle's on-line Web site at:

```
http://www.oracle.com/products/free_software/
```

Oracle PowerBrowser is a rather specialized tool that you can use to create database screens on the Web. It is not, however, really geared for the Internet; it's a desktop system for a small number of people sharing a small network, like a local area network (LAN) in an office. PowerBrowser includes:

✔ A Web browser, sort of like Netscape Navigator.

✔ A Web-database development tool for creating screens to search and update tables. You have to know Visual Basic to use this tool.

✔ A database engine for a mini-database called Blaze.

✔ A Web server, which means that users on your network can look at Web pages that you have created and stored in a directory on your PC.

WebServer

Because the Internet is of such great interest to everyone involved in computers these days, I want you to be aware of WebServer. You can purchase WebServer from Oracle using the company's online service, Oracle Store, if you are interested. The Web address is:

```
http://www.oracle.com/OracleStore/oawa/doc.show
```

Oracle's WebServer supports a Web site connecting to a database and is really great stuff for online catalogs and order forms. You can create a questionnaire, have people fill it out electronically on the Internet, and then enter the information directly into your database — a statistician's dream come true.

Other WebServer applications include:

✔ **ConText Option:** Context indexing, rather than plain word indexing. When you set up a profile of topics, ConText searches for Internet news articles, stock prices, even files in the company's internal database, and then sends them to you in an ongoing stream of information.

✔ **Video Server:** A plug-in that plays full-motion video, using Netscape Navigator and other browsers.

✔ **Web Request Broker:** Creates dynamic *HTML documents* on the fly at high speed, and plugs right into the server, so no middlemen exist. Web Request Broker is a direct conduit from the Internet to the database. HTML documents are commonly called Web pages. These documents are created for display through a Web browser. They consist of regular text and special HTML tags that determine the size of the font, color of the background, and lots of other formatting details.

The 2000 Series Packages

Oracle does not include these tools with Oracle7, and they are rather expensive. Oracle apparently has a thing for the year 2000 because they offer three products with 2000 in the name: Designer/2000, Developer/2000, and Discoverer/2000, which are like the executive toys you see on your boss' desktop.

✔ **Discoverer/2000:** This package helps you get something useful out of a database. You don't need to know SQL to create a report with Discoverer/2000. You can easily wind up with the shoe sizes of every left-handed citizen of the combined Americas in an easy-to-read report form. This may be a great way to impress your teacher!

✔ **Developer/2000:** This designer package has a lot of very useful tools. The online screen designer, Oracle Forms 4.5, is awesome. The *WYSIWYG* (what you see is what you get) report writer has many drag-and-drop tools. Developer/2000 even has a smart little tool called Enterprise Manager for handling the database administrator job. Enterprise Manager helps you constantly monitor the databases.

✔ **Designer/2000:** This package has one extra component that lets you do preliminary diagramming of your database and then generate the SQL code from the diagrams. It also generates screens and Web pages. Designer/2000 is a Computer Aided Systems Engineering (CASE) tool for the Oracle7 database. You can use it for other relational databases as well. This tool is nice but time-consuming to learn. You might have to read the manual or take a course or two. Otherwise it could wind up an expensive virtual paperweight on your desktop.

The newest release of Designer/2000 has special tools for creating applications for the World Wide Web. You can design your database and then tell the Designer what kind of module to run. The Designer then generates HTML and Java to run on the Web. Imagine that you're the sole proprietor of a coffee store that prepares mail-order gift baskets.

Designer/2000 can help you create a Web site so your customers can order gift baskets over the Internet. Olives are optional at this point, and please! Go easy on the vermouth.

Oracle Media Objects

Are you excited by live video, animation, or audio? Using the Oracle Media Objects design tool, you can design a kiosk or a Web site with cool audio and video delivered from the database. I'm not going to attempt a crash course on how to design a kiosk or a Web site in this paragraph. I will, however, give you the ...*For Dummies* flyby version:

1. You dream up some really cool idea that you want to put on interactive television, either using a kiosk with a computer in it or using the World Wide Web.

2. You build your idea in Media Objects by writing a *script* and a set of *cue cards*. Each cue card is like a multimedia window that can contain pictures, video clips, sound recordings, plain text, and control buttons in whatever combination you like. The *script* tells Media Objects in what order to present the cue cards. The script can include SQL commands that look up data in your Oracle7 database, which means that you can dynamically control the actions and the path between all your cue cards from the database.

3. You publish your finished Media Objects application — the cue cards, the script, the database — by putting it all into a computer that has a touch screen and is built into a kiosk in a mall.

4. As an alternative, you publish your application by making it a feature in some *virtual mall* on the World Wide Web where people from around the world can visit. A *virtual mall* is simply another Web site, usually with lots of things for sale.

NetDynamics

NetDynamics is a top software tool for launching a fully functional database application on the World Wide Web. NetDynamics uses Java to create dynamic Web pages. I've used this tool myself with Oracle7, and it delivers what is promised. NetDynamics is a bit complex to learn because it has a lot of capabilities. It runs with an Oracle7 database, plus several others, and works with Web servers on UNIX and Windows NT. This tool is not a toy. Read all about it at:

```
http://www.netdynamics.com/
```

WebBase

This fun product uses wizards to generate dynamic Web pages using your database tables. You can create Web pages that search your database directly on the World Wide Web. The WebBase Web site has a demonstration that puts an *X* on a street map of your town and fairly accurately locates your house. Fun stuff! To find out more information, point your browser at:

```
http://www.webbase.com/
```

WebBase offers a free 30-day trial. This software works with Microsoft Access, Oracle7, and other databases. You need to use a Windows NT Web server to complete the picture and get your database running on the Web. You may want to read up on this one, because I think it's the wave of the future.

ODBC Drivers

Several different software developers offer ODBC drivers for Oracle7. An ODBC driver is a software package that accepts database requests such as queries, update commands, and so on, in a standard format and transmits them to the Oracle7 database. The ODBC driver then retrieves the responses from Oracle7 and sends them back to the requester.

ODBC stands for *Open Database Connectivity,* a standard that is gaining acceptance around the world. Oracle7 accepts ODBC formats. Why does that matter? Any software company to write software that can communicate with Oracle7 because Oracle7 accepts this public and standardized format called ODBC. Before the ODBC standard was adopted by Oracle, and by virtually all other relational database vendors, only Oracle could write software that talked to the Oracle database engine. The format that Oracle used was a trade secret. The ODBC standard has thrown open the floodgates and made it possible to have a front end — the pretty Windows application part — that you can use with many relational databases.

e.g.
Ms Access

The ODBC driver is the pipeline between these new software products and Oracle7. A relational database requires a specialized translator to convert ODBC standards into Oracle7 standards. In Oracle's case, the ODBC driver connects to SQL*Net, which in turn speaks to the Oracle7 database.

Oracle offers its ODBC driver free on the Internet. You can download a free trial version from their Web site:

```
http://www.oracle.com
```

Intersolv also sells an ODBC driver. You can visit Intersolv on the Web at:

```
http://www.intersolv.com
```

Openlink also sells a generic version that runs on many platforms in conjunction with many databases. You can visit Openlink at:

```
http://www.openlinksw.com/index.htm
```

SQL*Net

You need SQL*Net to access your Oracle7 database from anywhere besides your own computer. If you are running Oracle7 on your desktop, you don't need SQL*Net. Otherwise, if you are running Oracle7 with multiple users across a network of any kind, you need SQL*Net to connect to the database. Chapter 13 has a good description of how SQL*Net connects your database to multiple computers.

SQL*Net is an Oracle product that comes free with your database. You need it to connect your Oracle7 database with many of the tools that I describe in this chapter, including WebBase, PowerBuilder, NetDynamics, and Designer/ 2000 (except when Designer/2000 and Oracle7 are installed on the same computer).

SQL*Net's sole purpose is to act as a communication bridge between Oracle7 and any network software that transmits data, commands, queries, and other database-related information from other software. Even Oracle's additional software needs SQL*Net to complete the circuit.

PowerBuilder

This software package has become a household word for relational database techies. PowerBuilder uses *object-oriented methods* to create online data entry screens. An object-oriented method means that each part of your data-entry screen becomes a separate entity that you can use as a building block in one or more data-entry screens. Using this method makes creating new data-entry screens faster because you build on what you have already created. There are libraries of ready-made objects that you can copy and use in your own creations available from PowerBuilder at:

```
http://www.powersoft.com
```

PowerBuilder connects to all the major relational databases, including Oracle7 and Sybase, and runs on UNIX, Mac, and Windows 95 platforms.

The PowerBuilder software tool set is offered by Powersoft. The company has recently enhanced PowerBuilder for use on the Web. It now allows you to develop a single application and convert it to dynamic HTML without making any programming changes.

The package ranges in cost from $99 (on sale for desktop Mac version) to $2,999 (for the enterprise model on UNIX).

The company offers extensive (expensive?!) training, consulting, and documentation to complement the software.

Part VI

Appendixes

AT 11:18 ON APRIL 25TH IN THE YEAR 2003, PC SOFTWARE AND HARDWARE REACHED A PERFECT APPLICATION-TO-MEMORY SYNCHRONICITY.

What the heck...?

In this part...

No book, not even this fantastic book in your hands, can cover everything! I've gathered together a list of resources that may be of interest to you, since you have this cool database called Oracle7. So, if you're still yearning for more learning — have a look!

Of course, you do need to have Oracle7 installed somewhere in order to use it! On the CD-ROM just inside the back cover I have included a trial version of Personal Oracle7 for Windows 95, Windows NT, and Power Mac. I've also provided all the tables I used in the examples and figures in the book so you can go on and try them out yourself. SQL*Plus scripts from some of the chapters, including Chapter 22, give you a jump start on writing your own queries.

Appendix A
Resources Guide

∙ ∙

*T*he World Wide Web has much to offer the database aficionado. This appendix explores a few of the hundreds of Web sites that pertain to database products or Web design, or that use databases.

Each section shows a Web address, in code text style, followed by my short description of the site's contents.

Web Database Products

WebLogic

```
http://www.weblogic.com/
```

Major source of Java-related tools and information.

WebBase

```
http://www.webbase.com/
```

An easy-to-use Web-to-database connection. The site uses WebBase to show you a map of your own location. Fun to do.

NetDynamics

```
http://www.netdynamics.com/
```

NetDynamics has a Java-based tool with complete Wizard-driven design tools for even complex Web-database applications. NetDynamics works on a variety of platforms and with a variety of databases, including Oracle7.

WebContact

```
http://www.avitek.com/demos/contact/demo.html
```

Avitek produces WebContact, a program that uses a Java applet to make Web-based databases more attractive and fun.

WebSeQueL

```
http://www.infospace-inc.com
```

Another applet-style database graphical user interface (GUI) is a product called WebSeQueL.

Web Designer Aids

Carol McCullough's Web resource page

```
http:www.maui.net/~mcculc/resource.htm
```

Your esteemed author holds forth on her own home page, which includes all the juiciest tips and tidbits about creating Web pages, from her tour of the trenches.

HTML language textbook

```
http://werbach.com/barebones/
```

Here's your source to acquire the Bare Bones Guide to the HTML programming language, in a vast array of different languages.

Web Sites That Use Databases On-Line

Shop texas style

```
http://www.texnet.com
```

A real estate shopping database, on-line in Texas.

Job search

```
http://www.isgjobs.com/
```

Informatics Search Group. Wanna job? Get a job here in computing.

Fun with Access

```
http://www.shenwebworks.com/
```

This is the Shenandoah Valley WebWorks Web site. An example of a shopping list service, including one called "Ain't Nothin' but a Found Dog" (I'm not kidding). This site uses a Microsoft Access database on the Web.

Shopping doggie

```
http://www.shopfido.com/
```

Fido, the shopping doggie, wants to fetch products for you.This is one of the most complex and sophisticated uses of a database on the Web that I've seen.

Web-Related Products

Microsoft Server

```
http://www.microsoft.com/InfoServ/
```

Here's the home page for Microsoft Information Server, which includes downloadable freeware for NT servers.

AOL Web Page Maker

```
http://www.gnnhost.com/index.htm
```

This is America Online's bid for your business as a novice Web designer. Create your own home page! Amaze your friends!

HTML editor

```
http://www.sausage.com/
```

Here's the Sausage Software home page. You'll find Hot Dog and other Web development goodies.

Web browser comparisons

```
http://www.colosys.net/~rscott/barb.htm
```

This Web site compares Microsoft's Internet Explorer and Netscape Navigator, the two most popular Web browsers today.

Adobe Acrobat

```
http://www.asymetrix.com/cstools/infomodeler/
```

Download a demo copy of Acrobat Reader, a tool for publishing word processing-style documents on the Web.

Database Software and Aids

International Oracle Users Group – Americas

```
http://www.ioug.org/
```

Get great support from the International Oracle Users Group – Americas. Oracle has become the second-largest software company in the world, with millions of users world wide. The IOUG-A's User's Week conferences are so popular that last fall's conference drew 11,000 people. The IOUG-A's Web site home page is shown in Figure A-1.

Figure A-1:
IOUG-A's
cool Web
site has
listings of
the latest
conferences.

SQL language textbook

```
http://waltz.ncsl.nist.gov/~len/sql_info.html
```

Herein lies an exhaustively complete textbook treatise on the SQL Database
language.

Oracle free trial software

```
http://www.oracle.com/products/trial/
```

Here are other Oracle products you can download, try, and buy on-line.

Sybase

```
http://www.sybase.com/products/internet/websql/
```

This is your source for shareware, add-ons, and information on Sybase, a
popular database.

Oracle books

```
http://www.bf.rmit.edu.au/Oracle/docs.html#TinaLondon
```

Here you find more textbook-style writing about SQL and other Oracle7 related information.

Database software by Anyware

```
http://www.applix.com
```

This is the home page for Applix, a software company that handles Anyware, among other goodies.

DB2 database

```
http://as400.rochester.ibm.com/QDLS/400home/
```

This is a connecting page to the IBM home page. This connecting page features the AS/400 computer and lots of nifty, abstruse flow charts about IBM's DB2 Database.

Appendix B

About the CD

● ●

This CD-ROM contains trial versions of Personal Oracle7 for PCs with Windows 95 and Windows NT, and Power Macintosh-type computers. Also included is a sample database that includes examples from the book.

System Requirements

There are three versions of Personal Oracle7. The system requirements for each are shown here.

Do not use disk compression applications such as DiskDoubler or SpaceSaver; they can cause irreparable damage to the Oracle7 database.

Windows 95

- An IBM-compatible 80486 or Pentium processor.
- Windows 95.
- A CD-ROM drive.
- A minimum of 16 megabytes (MB) of RAM.
- Approximately 60MB of hard disk space.
- The database must be installed on a non-compressed disk drive.

Windows NT

- An IBM-compatible 80486 or Pentium processor.
- Microsoft Windows NT, version 3.51 or later.
- A CD-ROM drive.
- A minimum of 16MB RAM, with 24-32MB recommended.
- Approximately 60MB of hard disk space.
- The database must be installed on a non-compressed disk drive.

Power Macintosh computer

- A minimum of 16MB of RAM (with virtual memory on); Oracle recommends you use 32MB of RAM.
- At least 50MB of free hard disk space.
- Macintosh Operating System version 7.5.1 or higher.

Trial Software

The CD-ROM contains trial software. I've included a short description of each item here along with short instructions on how to install each one.

If you are currently running Oracle version 7.2 and you have data you want to preserve, run a full database export (EXP utility) before you begin installation. Install the new database software, including a fresh database, and then import (IMP utility) your old data into the new database.

Personal Oracle 7 for Windows 95

PO7 for Windows 95 contains a fully functioning database. It includes SQL*Plus and Personal Oracle7 Navigator (also called Oracle Navigator). You can create users, tables, indexes, queries, and reports using this software. It does not include any tools for creating data entry screens. However, you can use SQL*Plus and Navigator to add, modify, and remove data in tables.

The following steps are for installation of the full system, called the Application Developer (Complete) system, with no replication. There are two other options: Custom and Runtime (database only). You can also choose to install any of these with replication.

1. **Close all open applications.**
2. **Click Start⇨Run from the bottom bar of the Windows 95 screen.**

   The Run dialog box appears.
3. **Type in** D:\PO7\WIN95\setup.exe **and click OK.**

   Replace D with the correct letter if your CD-ROM drive is not drive D. This starts the Oracle Installer and installation begins.
4. **Read the licensing screens (if they appear) and then click OK.**

5. **When the installer asks you, select a language that will be used during the installation and to display error messages when using Oracle7, and then click OK.**

   The Welcome Screen appears.

6. **Click OK.**

   The Oracle Installation Settings dialog box appears.

7. **Enter your information in the Oracle Installation Settings dialog box.**

   Type in your company (or personal) name. Accept the default or type in your own choice for the location of the Oracle home directory. Limit your directory name to a maximum of eight characters. Click OK. A dialog box appears with three installation choices.

8. **Select Application Developer (Complete) and click OK.**

   The Oracle7 Documentation dialog box appears.

9. **Select to locate your documentation files on the hard drive.**

10. **Select the Standard database and click OK.**

    The installation begins, showing the status of the file being copied and a percentage status bar. A confirmation message appears once installation is complete.

11. **Click OK.**

    You are returned to the Windows 95 screen. Two program groups are created during installation: Personal Oracle7 for Windows 95 and Oracle for Windows 95.

To start the Navigator:

1. **Click the Start button and select Programs.**

2. **Select Programs⇨Personal Oracle7 for Windows 95 and click on Oracle Navigator.**

   The Oracle Navigator screen appears. You are now ready to begin using Personal Oracle7 for Windows 95.

Before you exit Windows 95, *be sure to shut down the database.* Shut down the database using the Stop Database item located in the Personal Oracle7 for Windows 95 program menu.

Personal Oracle7 for Windows NT

PO7 for Windows 95 [NT] contains a fully functioning database. It includes SQL*Plus and Personal Oracle7 Navigator (also called Oracle Navigator).

You can create users, tables, indexes, queries, and reports using this software. It does not include any tools for creating data entry screens. However, you can use SQL*Plus and Navigator to add, modify, and remove data in tables.

The following steps are for installation of the full system, called the Application Developer (Complete) system, with no replication. There are two other options: Custom and Runtime (database only), with or without replication.

1. **Close all open applications.**

2. **Open the File Manager.**

3. **Double-click on the D drive icon (or the icon of whatever drive is assigned to your CD-ROM drive).**

4. **Double-click on the PO7 folder.**

5. **Double-click on the NT folder.**

6. **Double-click on the setup.exe file.**

    This starts the Oracle Installer. The License dialog box appears.

7. **Click OK.**

    The Oracle Installation Settings dialog box appears.

8. **Enter your company (or personal) name; accept the default or type in a different Oracle home directory path; then click OK.**

    The directory name can be no more than eight characters long. After you click OK, the Installation Options dialog box appears.

9. **Select Application Developer and click OK.**

    The Starter Database Installation Options dialog box appears.

10. **Select the Standard starter database and click OK.**

    A dialog box appears and requests character set confirmation.

11. **Make your character set selection in the dialog box.**

    Click Yes if you want the character set provided. If you click No, a list of character sets appears. Select the appropriate character set and click OK. Confirm your selection by clicking Yes. The installation begins.

    During installation, you see a progress bar with percentage completed and messages flashing the file names. You can click Cancel to stop the installation at any time.

12. **When the installation is complete, a confirmation message appears; click OK.**

    You are returned to the Windows NT desktop. Two program groups are created during installation: Personal Oracle7 for Windows NT and Oracle for Windows NT.

To start the database and the Navigator:

1. **From the Program Manager, double-click the Personal Oracle7 for Windows NT program group.**

2. **Double-click the Start Database icon.**

   When the database has been started, the following message appears: "Oracle7 database started successfully." Click OK.

3. **In the Personal Oracle7 for Windows NT program group, double-click the Personal Oracle7 Navigator icon.**

   The Personal Oracle7 Navigator screen appears.

Before you exit Windows NT, *be sure to shut down the database* using the Stop Database item located in the Personal Oracle7 for Windows 95 program menu.

Personal Oracle7 for Power Mac

PO7 for Power Mac contains a fully functioning database. It includes SQL*Plus and Personal Oracle7 Navigator (also called Oracle Navigator). You can create users, tables, indexes, queries, and reports using this software. It does not include any tools for creating data entry screens. However, you can use SQL*Plus and the Navigator to add, modify, and remove data in tables.

The following steps are for installation of the full system, called the Complete (with all documentation) system. There are two other options: Complete (no documentation) and Custom.

1. **Open the following folders to locate the "Oracle Installer":**
   CD⇨Personal Oracle7⇨Components⇨Installer.

2. **Double-click the Oracle Installer icon.**

3. **Navigate to the folder where you wish to install Oracle products or create a new folder (if necessary).**

   You can get help during the installation by clicking the Help button in the Installer window.

4. **Click the Choose... button to choose the folder where you want to install Oracle products.**

5. **Type your company name in the Customer Name dialog box and click OK.**

6. **Choose the Complete (all documentation) Installation Option.**

   The Installation status window appears, indicating installation progress. When the installation finishes, the Installation Complete dialog box appears.

7. **Click OK.**

Adobe Acrobat Reader

When you have completed installing Oracle7, install Adobe Acrobat Reader, which you need for reading your documentation.

1. **Double-click the AcroRead.mac icon.**

   The Acrobat Reader Installer starts.

2. **Follow the Acrobat Reader Installer instructions to continue the reader installation.**

To display documentation, simply double-click the PDF file icons to start Acrobat Reader and use the documentation in portable document format (PDF).

Sample Database

I have included an export of all the tables that are used in the examples in this book. After you install the trial PO7 database, you can install the sample tables by following these instructions (instructions are for Windows 95):

1. **Create a new Oracle user ID named AMY with password AMY123.**

   See Chapter 8 for instructions on how to create a user.

2. **Assign the CONNECT and RESOURCE roles to AMY.**

   See Chapter 10 for instructions.

3 **Start a DOS window by selecting Start⇨Programs⇨MS-DOS Prompt from your Windows 95 taskbar.**

4. **Change directory to the CD-ROM directory by typing the line below and pressing Enter:**

   ```
   cd D:\tables
   ```

5. **Import the tables into the database by typing the line below and pressing Enter:**

   ```
   imp SYSTEM/MANAGER parfile=parfile.txt
   ```

Note: If you have changed the password for the SYSTEM user ID, replace MANAGER with the new password.

Oracle lists the tables that it is importing and tells you when the job is done.

Right at the end you get a warning message that is about six lines long and begins:

```
IMP-00041: Warning: object created with compilation
           warnings
```

The object in question (a view called TEST) must have slinked into my export file with a false passport! This view is not used in the book and you can ignore the warning message.

6. Close the DOS Window by typing the line below and pressing Enter:

```
       exit
```

You now have a user in your database named AMY with a password of AMY123 that owns a set of tables with all the columns and data that you see in the examples used throughout the book.

The tables that you have just created are the ones that I have after doing all the samples in the book. Therefore, some of the examples that actually create things, like new tables or indexes, may not work because they already exist in your set of sample tables.

Example SQL*Plus Scripts

Several of the chapters contain SQL*Plus scripts that you can run yourself once you install the trial Personal Oracle7 database and import the sample database.

Table B-1 shows all the scripts that are on the CD-ROM.

Table B-1	Sample SQL*Plus Scripts	
Directory	*File*	*Description*
scripts/Chap13	comma.sql	Spools a comma-delimited file of data.
scripts/Chap20	concat.sql	Sample of concatenation function to join columns together.

(continued)

Table B-1 *(continued)*

Directory	File	Description
scripts/Chap20	decode.sql	Sample of decode function to add logic to select.
scripts/Chap20	date.sql	Sample of formatting a date using to_char function.
scripts/Chap20	nvl.sql	Sample of nvl function to replace null value.
scripts/Chap20	ttitle.sql	Sample of ttitle command to create a title
scripts/Chap21	blanks.sql	Sample of pad for CHAR datatype in where clause.
scripts/Chap21	car.sql	Sample of adding date into a title.
scripts/Chap21	char.sql	Sample select with CHAR datatype that does not appear to work.
scripts/Chap21	rownum.sql	Sample of rownum psuedocolumn to limit rows selected.
scripts/Chap22	dupkeys.sql	Finds duplicate key values in a table.
scripts/Chap22	duprows.sql	Lists all data in rows with duplicate key values in a table.
scripts/Chap22	listcol.sql	Produces a listing of table(s) and associated columns.
scripts/Chap22	listidx.sql	Produces a listing of tables and associated indexes.
scripts/Chap22	listtab.sql	Produces a listing of tables with comments.
scripts/Chap22	mksel.sql	Produces a select statement of all columns in specified table.
scripts/Chap22	mkview.sql	Produces a listing of the query used to create specified view.
scripts/Chap22	privs.sql	Produces a listing of user's table privileges.

Glossary

● ●

alias: A nickname or alternative name for a table or column that is used in SQL.

attribute: A feature or characteristic. For example, the data type and size of a column are two of the column's attributes.

block: A unit of storage for data and other information in the database.

Cartesian join: An unconditional join between two tables resulting in a match between every row in one table and every row in another table.

column: A component of a database table. A column contains the definition of what kinds of data are to be collected and stored in the rows of the table.

comma-delimited file: A format for extracting data out of a database and placing it into a plain text file. Each line in the file contains one row and each column is separated from the following column by a comma.

commit: To permanently save all changes since the last commit was done to the database.

constraint: A rule applied to a table or a column that restricts the data that is allowed in any row in the table. For example, a primary key constraint defines the primary key for a table. All rows must have unique values in the columns included in the primary key constraint.

correlated sub-query: A sub-query that has references to the outer query.

DBA: The database administrator.

database engine: The set of programs that run the database, keeping track of all the information, monitoring usage, checking security, checking for errors, and so on.

datatype: Defines the type of information that can be stored, such as dates, numbers, or characters.

derived data: Data that can be calculated, summarized, or otherwise extracted entirely from other data in the database.

entity: A table or group of tables. Used interchangeably with *table* in this book.

Entity Relationship Diagram: A style of drawing a relational database model that uses boxes, text, lines, and a few simple symbols to represent the entities and relationships in the model.

explicit data conversion: The user controls conversion of a column or expression from one data type into another. This controls the data conversion in a predictable manner. See also *implicit data conversion*.

export: Oracle7 utility to pull data out of the database into a file. The file is in a special format for use only with the Oracle7 import utility. Also used to refer to the act of using the export utility.

expression: A column, a literal, or a column with some function applied to it, such as addition. In SQL queries, expressions can be used almost anywhere a column can be used.

field: See *column.*

foreign key: The primary key of a reference table that is stored inside another table. The foreign key connects the two tables. It allows access to all the information stored in both tables without repeating data from either table, other than the key column.

fragmented table: A table that contains wasted space in the form of empty blocks and chained blocks.

GRANT: SQL command for adding security privileges on a table, view, or synonym.

hierarchy: A relationship of tables where there is a parent table that has a child table and that child table has its own child table and so on.

HTML: Hyper Text Markup Language. The primary language used to create Web pages. HTML consists of normal text and special codes, called tags, which tell a Web browser how to display the text. Tags determine the size of the font, color of the background, and other formatting details.

implicit data conversion: Oracle7 converts a column or expression from one datatype into another using its own internal logic. This is unpredictable and subject to change with new releases. See also *explicit data conversion.*

import: Oracle7 utility to bring data into the database from a file. The file must be in a special format created by using the export utility. Also used to refer to the act of using the import utility.

incremental space: In a table definition, this specifies the amount of space reserved if the table runs out of room and needs more space. This is repeated again if the table again needs more space, until the table hits the maximum space limitation.

initial space: In a table definition, this sets the starting size of the table.

INSERT: A command to add a new row into a table.

intelligent key: An intelligent key is a primary key that has meaning for the row of data.

interactive: Any process where the computer asks for information from the user and then acts on it.

Internet: A global, public network of computers linked together with telephone lines and network software. See also *World Wide Web.*

intranet: A network of computers connected via phone or cable lines that is inside one organization for internal use only.

join: A type of query in which two or more tables are connected, or joined, together.

key: A column or set of columns in a table that identifies a unique row of data. See also: *primary key* and *foreign key.*

legacy system: A set of tables (schema) that have been brought into your Oracle7 system from an older source, such as Oracle6, or another database system.

literal: A word or phrase, number, or letter that is used at its face value (exactly as it is written) in a query or in a SQL*Plus command. A literal is always surrounded by single quotes.

local database: A database that resides on the computer the user is logged into.

logical operator: A connection between two columns or expressions in a where clause. Examples are: = (equal), <> (not equal), like, between, < (less than), > (greater than).

Non-intelligent key: A key that is unique and does not change, even when information in the row changes. A sequential ID number is an example of a non-intelligent key.

objects: Things in a database or groups of things that stand on their own. For example, a table is an object but a row is not an object.

optimizer: An internal part of the Oracle7 database engine that determines the fastest access path for any given SQL command.

overhead: Information about tables, columns, rows, indexes, and other structures in the database.

owner: The user who creates a table.

primary key: A column or set of columns in one table that uniquely identifies each row in the table. Every row in a table has a value in the primary key that is different from that of every other row in that table.

private synonym: A synonym that can only be used by the synonym creator, unless the creator grants privileges to others.

project: In Personal Oracle7 Navigator, a collection of tables, views, users, or other items grouped together. Projects can be exported and imported.

pseudocolumn: A column defined by Oracle7 that you can use in a query. For example, USER is a pseudocolumn that always contains the Oracle7 user ID of the current user.

public synonym: A synonym created by a database administrator (DBA) that can be used by anyone.

query: A question posed in SQL to look at data in the database.

record: See *row*.

relational database: A collection of tables connected together in a series of relationships so that they model some small part of the real world.

remote database: A database that does not reside on the computer the user is logged into.

reorganize: To rebuild the internal physical structure of a table by dropping it and recreating it. Data must be removed and restored using export and import.

REVOKE: A SQL command for removing security privileges.

Role: A set of privileges that can be assigned to or removed from a user.

ROLLBACK: A command that removes all changes since the last commit was done.

row: A component of a database table. It contains the actual data, compartmentalized in columns.

row ID: A pseudocolumn that contains the exact physical address of a row. Retrieving a table row using its row ID is the fastest method available.

schema: Everything created by a single user ID in Oracle7 (tables, grants, roles, indexes, and relationships).

script: A file that contains more than just a single SQL or SQL*Plus command.

synonym: An alternate name for a table or view. Synonyms can be private (for use only by its creator) or public (for use by any user).

table: A set of related columns and rows in a relational database.

third normal form: A set of rules specifying how tables and columns in a relational database relate to one another.

tree diagram: See *Entity Relationship Diagram.*

user: A unique login name in Oracle7. All users have a password. A user's capabilities inside the database are determined by the user's role assignments.

user ID: See *user*.

view: A query that is named in the database so that it can be used as if it were a table. Views can be used anywhere tables can be used, except there are some restrictions on adding, removing, or changing rows from views that join tables.

Web page: A screen of data, graphics, music, etc., that appears on the World Wide Web (Internet) or on an intranet. This is a general term referring to any document on the Web. It may be an order entry form, a database report, a video, a text document, or any number of other possibilities. The length of one page is totally flexible and the document contains HTML tags.

World Wide Web: A portion of the Internet dedicated to documents in the HTML format. The Web, as it is often known, is a versatile, colorful, and highly interactive area.

Index

requirement that after using the program for the period of time specified in its text, the user must pay a registration fee or discontinue use. By opening the Software packet(s), you will be agreeing to abide by the licenses and restrictions for these individual programs. None of the material on this disk(s) or listed in this Book may ever be distributed, in original or modified form, for commercial purposes.

5. <u>Limited Warranty</u>.

   (a) IDGB warrants that the Software and disk(s)/CD-ROM are free from defects in materials and workmanship under normal use for a period of sixty (60) days from the date of purchase of this Book. If IDGB receives notification within the warranty period of defects in materials or workmanship, IDGB will replace the defective disk(s)/CD-ROM.

   (b) **IDGB AND THE AUTHOR OF THE BOOK DISCLAIM ALL OTHER WARRANTIES, EXPRESS OR IMPLIED, INCLUDING WITHOUT LIMITATION IMPLIED WARRANTIES OF MERCHANTABILITY AND FITNESS FOR A PARTICULAR PURPOSE, WITH RESPECT TO THE SOFTWARE, THE PROGRAMS, THE SOURCE CODE CONTAINED THEREIN, AND/OR THE TECHNIQUES DESCRIBED IN THIS BOOK. IDGB DOES NOT WARRANT THAT THE FUNCTIONS CONTAINED IN THE SOFTWARE WILL MEET YOUR REQUIREMENTS OR THAT THE OPERATION OF THE SOFTWARE WILL BE ERROR FREE.**

   (c) This limited warranty gives you specific legal rights, and you may have other rights which vary from jurisdiction to jurisdiction.

6. <u>Remedies</u>.

   (a) IDGB's entire liability and your exclusive remedy for defects in materials and workmanship shall be limited to replacement of the Software, which may be returned to IDGB with a copy of your receipt at the following address: Disk Fulfillment Department, Attn: Oracle7 For Dummies, IDG Books Worldwide, Inc., 7260 Shadeland Station, Ste. 100, Indianapolis, IN 46256, or call 1-800-762-2974. Please allow 3–4 weeks for delivery. This Limited Warranty is void if failure of the Software has resulted from accident, abuse, or misapplication. Any replacement Software will be warranted for the remainder of the original warranty period or thirty (30) days, whichever is longer.

   (b) In no event shall IDGB or the author be liable for any damages whatsoever (including without limitation damages for loss of business profits, business interruption, loss of business information, or any other pecuniary loss) arising from the use of or inability to use the Book or the Software, even if IDGB has been advised of the possibility of such damages.

   (c) Because some jurisdictions do not allow the exclusion or limitation of liability for consequential or incidental damages, the above limitation or exclusion may not apply to you.

7. **U.S. Government Restricted Rights.** Use, duplication, or disclosure of the Software by the U.S. Government is subject to restrictions stated in paragraph (c) (1) (ii) of the Rights in Technical Data and Computer Software clause of DFARS 252.227-7013, and in subparagraphs (a) through (d) of the Commercial Computer — Restricted Rights clause at FAR 52.227-19, and in similar clauses in the NASA FAR supplement, when applicable.

8. **General.** This Agreement constitutes the entire understanding of the parties and revokes and supersedes all prior agreements, oral or written, between them and may not be modified or amended except in a writing signed by both parties hereto which specifically refers to this Agreement. This Agreement shall take precedence over any other documents that may be in conflict herewith. If any one or more provisions contained in this Agreement are held by any court or tribunal to be invalid, illegal, or otherwise unenforceable, each and every other provision shall remain in full force and effect.

Installation Instructions

• •

See Appendix B, "About the CD," which begins on page 333, for information about how to install the programs on the CD-ROM that accompanies this book.

IDG BOOKS WORLDWIDE REGISTRATION CARD

RETURN THIS REGISTRATION CARD FOR FREE CATALOG

Title of this book: ORACLE® 7 For Dummies®

My overall rating of this book: ❑ Very good [1] ❑ Good [2] ❑ Satisfactory [3] ❑ Fair [4] ❑ Poor [5]

How I first heard about this book:

❑ Found in bookstore; name: [6]

❑ Advertisement: [8]

❑ Word of mouth; heard about book from friend, co-worker, etc.: [10]

❑ Book review: [7]

❑ Catalog: [9]

❑ Other: [11]

What I liked most about this book:

What I would change, add, delete, etc., in future editions of this book:

Other comments:

Number of computer books I purchase in a year: ❑ 1 [12] ❑ 2-5 [13] ❑ 6-10 [14] ❑ More than 10 [15]

I would characterize my computer skills as: ❑ Beginner [16] ❑ Intermediate [17] ❑ Advanced [18] ❑ Professional [19]

I use ❑ DOS [20] ❑ Windows [21] ❑ OS/2 [22] ❑ Unix [23] ❑ Macintosh [24] ❑ Other: [25]_____
(please specify)

I would be interested in new books on the following subjects:
(please check all that apply, and use the spaces provided to identify specific software)

❑ Word processing: [26]

❑ Data bases: [28]

❑ File Utilities: [30]

❑ Networking: [32]

❑ Other: [34]

❑ Spreadsheets: [27]

❑ Desktop publishing: [29]

❑ Money management: [31]

❑ Programming languages: [33]

I use a PC at (please check all that apply): ❑ home [35] ❑ work [36] ❑ school [37] ❑ other: [38] _____

The disks I prefer to use are ❑ 5.25 [39] ❑ 3.5 [40] ❑ other: [41]_____

I have a CD ROM: ❑ yes [42] ❑ no [43]

I plan to buy or upgrade computer hardware this year: ❑ yes [44] ❑ no [45]

I plan to buy or upgrade computer software this year: ❑ yes [46] ❑ no [47]

Name: _____ Business title: [48] _____ Type of Business: [49] _____

Address (❑ home [50] ❑ work [51]/Company name: _____)

Street/Suite# _____

City [52]/State [53]/Zipcode [54]: _____ Country [55] _____

❑ **I liked this book!** You may quote me by name in future
IDG Books Worldwide promotional materials.

My daytime phone number is _____

IDG BOOKS

THE WORLD OF
COMPUTER
KNOWLEDGE

❑ YES!

Please keep me informed about IDG's World of Computer Knowledge.
Send me the latest IDG Books catalog.

COMPUTER
BOOK SERIES
FROM IDG

NO POSTAGE
NECESSARY
IF MAILED
IN THE
UNITED STATES

BUSINESS REPLY MAIL
FIRST CLASS MAIL   PERMIT NO. 2605   FOSTER CITY, CALIFORNIA

IDG Books Worldwide
919 E Hillsdale Blvd, STE 400
Foster City, CA 94404-9691